WE CARRY THEIR BONES

WILLIAM MORROW
An Imprint of HarperCollins*Publishers*

HarperCollins books may be purchased for educational, business, or sales promotional use. For information, please email the Special Markets Department at SPsales@harpercollins.com.

FIRST EDITION

Designed by Elina Cohen

Photograph credits for insert: page 1 (top): Image obtained from the Florida State Archives, Florida School for Boys Photographs, Box 1 FF10; pages 1 (bottom), 2 (top and middle), 3 (middle and bottom), 4 (bottom), 5, 6 (top and bottom), 7 (bottom), and 8: Photographs by Erin Kimmerle; pages 2 (bottom), 3 (top), 4 (middle), 6 (middle), 7 (top and middle): Photographs by Katy Hennig; page 4 (top): Photograph by Liotta Noche Dowdy

Library of Congress Cataloging-in-Publication Data has been applied for.

ISBN 978-0-06-303024-4

22 23 24 25 26 LSC 10 9 8 7 6 5 4 3 2 1

This book is for my children,
Sean and Reid

Know you what it is to be a child?

It is to be something very different from the man of today. It is to have a spirit yet streaming from the waters of baptism; it is to believe in love, to believe in loveliness, to believe in belief; it is to be so little that the elves can reach to whisper in your ear; it is to turn pumpkins into coaches, and mice into horses, lowness into loftiness, and nothing into everything, for each child has its fairy godmother in its soul; it is to live in a nutshell and to count yourself the king of infinite space; it is

To see a world in a grain of sand,
And a Heaven in a wild flower,
Hold infinity in the palm of your hand,
And eternity in an hour;

it is to know not as yet that you are under sentence of life, nor petition that it be commuted into death.

—FRANCIS THOMPSON

CONTENTS

The Florida State Reform School opened January 1, 1900, and closed in 2011, under the name Arthur G. Dozier School for Boys. From its inception, it was supposed to be a school, not a prison. Although all children committed were supposed to have been convicted of a crime and sentenced by a judge, the laws were later amended to include non-criminal offenses such as truancy and incorrigibility, leading it to become the largest reform school in the country and obscuring the line between "student" and "inmate." Until 1968, the reform school segregated into two completely separate campuses, or "departments," for white and "colored" persons. "Colored" meant anyone deemed non-white.

Throughout this book, the terms "white" and "colored" are used when necessary, according to the historical records and documentation. Attendance ledgers showed that for many boys who had mixed ancestry or Latino backgrounds, administrators were uncertain where to place them and, at times, transferred boys between the two departments. This occurred because race is a social construction with no biological association that uniquely identifies one race at the exclusion of all others. The classification system used during the Jim Crow era affected the availability of written records, documentation, and associated burial information. Vital records such as birth and death certificates were less commonly given to people of color.

Chapter 1

OPENING THE EARTH

Before the lawsuits and protests, before the ground-penetrating radar and DNA testing, before we were stalked and before the citizens of Jackson County tried to have me arrested, before we ever stuck a shovel in the red dirt of North Florida to exhume bodies, I stood in the women's restroom as the news media gathered in the large room outside and began setting up their cameras and checking their microphones and waiting for me to step before them and tell them what I had learned about the dead boys.

I did not want to do this.

I had spoken at a single press conference prior, years before, near a crime scene where I had been helping the local sheriff excavate the remains of a woman missing for ten years. The sheriff's office wanted me to give the press briefing, to deflect questions about the open homicide investigation toward the science of forensic anthropology. To tell the public what we were doing without saying anything about what we were doing. I can steel myself against unimaginable horrors, given my job, but reporters mean putting it all out there. I prefer to fly under the radar.

I'm a forensic anthropologist, a scientist, an academic. I'm not a showman. I strive for accuracy, and sometimes forensic science takes a lot of explaining. I don't *think* in sound bites. A peer-reviewed and long-winded scientific explanation is not what the television news reporters want, though. They want short, chippy, quotable sentences with strong verbs and hard nouns. They want the coach jogging off the field at halftime, summarizing the play so far and the strategy for the second half.

Here, now, I struggled with how to reduce a year of scientific investigation into a few punchy paragraphs to lead the nightly newscasts. They wanted me to address the mounting controversy around the clandestine cemetery on the property of the Dozier School for Boys, Florida's oldest state-run reform school, in the rural panhandle town of Marianna, where we had been searching for the truth. That meant I'd spend the next day answering tough questions and trying to soothe hurt feelings. Not from reporters, though. From politicians, Marianna residents, university administrators, fellow academics, and lawyers. Facing the press, as scary as it was, would be the easy part.

I looked at myself in the mirror.

I paced.

I twirled my fingers on both hands two at a time in small circles, an old high school theater trick to help me focus. Thumbs first. Then forefingers. Then the middles, rings, pinkies.

Over and over.

Ten times each.

I thought about how clean and gorgeous this bathroom was, with its granite walls extended to the ceilings. The bathroom cost more than our forensic anthropology lab's entire operating budget, and its beauty stood in such contrast to how I spent most of the past year, covered in mud and dirt.

The door swung open, and Lara Wade, the University of South Florida's director of media relations, entered. She asked me if I was hiding and laughed. I just smiled and then reached out and put the palms of my hands on the granite wall. It felt so cold.

This was her idea, putting us in front of the television cameras. I'd invited two fellow faculty members to join our team, and they

were gathering outside as well: Dr. Antoinette Jackson, a cultural anthropologist, and Dr. Christian Wells, an archaeologist. What was
supposed to be two weeks of fieldwork for us and a few students had
turned into a year of probing and research involving a growing group
of experts across disciplines.

Lara knew the value. This would be a big boost in earned media
exposure for my department and the university. She knew how important it was to keep the ball rolling. If we wanted to help the families, we had to be out front.

Lara had a calming effect; I trusted her. She started running
through the details and rattling off a list of all the dignitaries gathered
outside. She knew every reporter by name.

Then she stopped and looked at me in the mirror.

"You have five minutes," she said. "You got this."

I thought about what brought me to this moment, the rising tension from multiple sides. It all started simply enough: a friend had
introduced me to a local reporter who'd been working on a series of
stories about the reform school's dark history, about brutal beatings
and sadistic guards and mysterious deaths.

The stories raised questions about a purported cemetery on the
school's property, and the reporter had hit a dead end. He had found
the families of boys who died in custody and were buried at the school,
families that had never found peace, for they'd never been given the
opportunity to properly mourn. No one could point to the location
of the graves where their brothers and uncles were buried. No state
official had stepped up to find those burials.

This was my life's work. Not a lot of people have this particular
skill set, to find and identify the dead. It was easy enough to secure
permission to go take a look around. Back then, in early 2012, that
was essentially the scope of the project. To learn what I could about
the deaths at a reform school that had been in operation for more than
a hundred years on the edge of a warm and friendly Southern town.
How hard could it be?

The Florida Department of Environmental Protection controlled half of the fourteen-hundred-acre reform school property, the half that had been the "colored side" until racial integration in the late 1960s. That's where the old burial ground was located. The DEP gave us permission to document and research the historic site.

Across the street was off-limits. On the side of the school known as Department No. 1 for white boys, the south side, the property was controlled by the Department of Juvenile Justice, a troubled state agency that had faced a number of scandals since its formation in the mid-1990s as a step away from a social services model of juvenile rehabilitation. That side of campus, surrounded by tall fences topped with razor wire, had been a functioning residential juvenile prison until it closed in the summer of 2011, another result of the newspaper stories.

We weren't confident that the little cemetery on what had been the "colored side" of campus—a burial ground that locals and school records called Boot Hill—was the only burial yard, so we wanted to search the entire sprawling grounds. Officials from the Department of Juvenile Justice would not let us enter their side of the property. Even though the buildings were empty and abandoned, they maintained a tight vigilance, under lock and key.

We kept asking for permission, and the department kept denying. They said no, formally, in August 2012, citing the "pending sale of the property and other liability concerns."

Pending sale? Now that the school was shuttered, local economic development officials wanted to put the land, with its estimated value of over $10 million, on the market. It was prime real estate for a warehouse or major distribution center, with easy access to Interstate 10 and just sixty-five miles west of Tallahassee. The state was preparing to sell about 220 acres of the boys' school land, and the offers were already rolling in.

A sale would end our quest for the truth about the burials. If the property fell into private hands, some business could pave a parking lot on top of the graves of little boys, and we felt powerless to stop it.

Then I met a man named Glen Varnadoe.

Glen believed his uncle, Thomas, was buried somewhere on the school property. He told me his father, Hubert, and uncle had been sent to what was at the time called the Florida Industrial School for Boys in 1934 for trespassing. Family lore had it that his uncle died at the school under mysterious circumstances, and when his father came home, he never again spoke of what had happened there. From then on, he was deathly afraid of authority.

"They were poor," Glen told me, explaining that his grandparents could do nothing when the state came to take the boys away. "But we ain't poor anymore, and, by God, they are not selling that land with my uncle still buried on it." Glen spent forty years as an executive with a chemical company in Polk County, in Central Florida. He was well-off, and well-spoken, and he had the phone numbers of state lawmakers who knew how to get things done.

GLEN HIRED A tenacious Tampa lawyer, and they filed an injunction to stop the sale of the land. I met Glen on the Dozier campus a short time later to show him our findings. Glen had been there before, sometime in the 1980s or early '90s, on a random stop as he was passing through. He knew the story about his uncle, and he visited the campus to see his uncle's grave. When he arrived, nobody could tell him with confidence where young Thomas Varnadoe was buried. Glen remembered that a man showed him two separate graveyards far enough apart that they had to drive from one to the other.

"He took me to a second place and said . . . 'Your uncle could be buried here,'" Glen told a National Public Radio reporter.

I wanted to see if a trip to the school conjured any recollections for Glen, if he could remember both locations where the school official had pointed, but so much had changed that he had trouble orienting himself. The trees were taller, and there were pine forests where there should've been fields.

That October, as we waited for the court to make a ruling on Glen's injunction, the newspapers reported that the Department of Juvenile Justice was reconsidering their position and would possibly allow us and the families onto what was once the "white side" in order to search for graves. Then we got word that Glen's injunction worked: the state couldn't sell any part of the property until we made certain there were no burials.

Until then, I had not issued so much as a press release nor made any public statements about the research. I tried to go unnoticed as I wrote the report of our findings. Tensions were mounting. Neither local politicians nor state officials wanted the sale delayed. They were aggravated by the injunction. We soon discovered that the school was something of a source of pride for the Marianna locals, who had staffed it for more than a century, who knew the men being accused of horrendous beatings, who talked about us like unwelcomed outsiders.

That fall, someone tipped off a CNN reporter named Ed Lavandera and he met me on campus for an interview. When his report aired, it was the first time that a national audience heard what we were learning.

"A mystery haunts the grounds of this now-defunct reform school for boys in the Florida panhandle town of Marianna, involving teenage boys sent here decades ago, some never seen again," he said in a voice-over while images played of the decrepit buildings on campus and rolls of razor wire atop the fences. "Former students now in their twilight years have come forward with horrific stories of punishing abuse doled out by school leaders and of friends who vanished . . . They accuse leaders of beatings, sexual abuse, and even murder."

He pointed out that state authorities said they knew how all of the boys died: "Some killed in a fire, others in a flu epidemic, nothing criminal."

Over the past ten months, what our research was showing didn't fit the state's narrative. Reports from the Florida Department of Law Enforcement (FDLE) stated all the deaths and burials were accounted for and nothing suspicious or criminal had occurred.

We found others were buried at the school—possibly nineteen more boys than officially reported—with the possibility of a second cemetery.

There was more. As we dug into the dorm fire, we learned that the boys were chained and locked in rooms, unable to escape. The flu epidemic that wreaked havoc worldwide in 1918 left a gruesome scar in Florida when the state physician reported that Black boys at the school had been abandoned and found days later without food or clothing. The dead were stacking up.

"Not all the burials are accounted for."

I was reading aloud what I had written the night before, sitting at the kitchen table after I put my two sons to bed—notes scribbled on a clean stack of printed-out pages. I checked on them again and again as I wrote. At three and seven, they still looked like babies when they slept. I could not imagine them in a place like this reform school. I wondered about the mothers of the boys at the school. How desperate they must have felt.

The Florida Department of Law Enforcement had investigated the burials at the school, and after combing through school records and interviewing a slew of locals, they determined there were thirty-one graves in the burial ground in the woods. That happened to match exactly the number of old pipe crosses somebody planted in neat rows on a hidden corner of campus sometime in the 1990s.

We knew there were more graves than the state's top law enforcement agency could find.

"The historical records are incomplete," I read aloud, "and often provide conflicting information."

This we knew, and it was what made the whole thing suspect. School records might read, "runaway" or "died off campus," but the death certificate for the same boy would read, "blunt trauma to the head" or "shot by person unknown."

Seven boys died after running away from the school. Some records simply read: "Exposure." Others were even more vague: "Unknown reason." One document listed the cause of death as: "Hit by car." Getting hit by a car wouldn't be suspect, but the boy died in the 1930s, when few people in the county owned cars. Equivocal deaths, we call them, and they occur frequently. They're inquiries that are open to interpretation. They may appear to be a homicide or accidental death, but for various reasons, the facts are missing or misleading.

"We pieced together school records that indicate that forty-five individuals are buried on school grounds. Thirty-one were shipped home to families or buried in other locations. And twenty-two remain unknown."

Unknown. Twenty-two boys died in the care and custody of the state of Florida, in the United States of America, and no one working for the state could point to those boys' specific graves nor say with any certainty whether they were buried on the campus at all.

"Eight percent of boys died following attempted escapes," I read. "Twenty-three percent of boys died within the first three months of being remanded to the school." Half of those died within their first month.

"We suspect there could be more burials there," I continued. "Through fieldwork analysis using ground-penetrating radar (GPR) and test trenches, we estimate fifty burials."

And this was the reason for all the fuss, the reason the press was here, the reason politicians got involved.

Boys died, but no one could say for sure how many, or which boy's remains were in the bottom of which grave. And, as we were learning, most of them were Black boys.

Systemic racism, exclusion, and segregation were a fact of life for all citizens in Florida through the late 1960s. Basic rights of citizenship, justice, freedom of movement, and accountability were denied to anyone labeled "colored." Their marginalization is evident in who lived and who died, which of the deaths were investigated or even reported to the state, and who were issued death certificates. We had found that nearly 70 percent of the boys buried at the school were African American. In other words, seven out of every ten kids who were buried at Dozier were Black without counting the seven white boys who died chained to their beds in a single incident when the white dormitory burned down in 1914. The school consistently underreported the number of deaths that occurred in their biennial reports to the state. William McKinley, a Black boy, died from unknown causes on July 19, 1915, and his death was never even reported to state authorities. We found references to the deaths of at least fourteen other "colored" boys, but the school records didn't contain their names or specific information about their identities or causes of death, including burial locations.

In fact, many of the boys who died after trying to escape from the school were never reported either.

So, while the state's own investigation identified only thirty-one burials on-site, we now had records for forty-five. In addition, field-work showed the possibility of fifty graves.

Plainly put, the families of the boys who died wanted us to do more fieldwork in the areas surrounding Boot Hill. They wanted answers. We believed it was their fundamental right to know the truth.

We would need the press's help to push that message out. There were dozens of politicians who could put a stop to our work. We had to change the narrative from a criminal investigation to one of restorative justice and to help the public understand that this was a human rights issue. Denying justice to some puts us all at risk.

I had tucked that news—the most important point—into the middle of a list of scientific-sounding recommendations on what should be done next. Rookie mistake.

"Recognizing the historical significance of civil rights issues in Florida, and in the area of juvenile justice, and the rights of families to have accountability and transparency as an important aspect of restorative justice, we make the following recommendations," I read aloud to the bathroom mirror. "Additional fieldwork in the areas around Boot Hill, including test excavations in areas that were marked by GPR anomalies; we recommend horizontal clearing by mechanical excavation to the primary burial area in order to identify specific individual graves and get a very accurate account; excavation and skeletal autopsy for forensic pathological and anthropological analysis to determine the health, activities, cause of death, and identification for reinterment and repatriation to the families; and additional research and interviews of all the various stakeholders there."

That was indeed a mouthful. A professional opinion. I wondered if I should put it more plainly. Something like this:

When you think of Florida, you might think of sugar-sand beaches and citrus trees, space shuttles and Disney World, but this state has a dark and shameful history of crushing poverty, racism and racial violence, and an unjust legal system, and if we ever hope to heal from those sins of the past, we need to know the truth. And finding the truth at the Dozier School for Boys means getting dirty, means stripping off the topsoil so we can see what is underneath. It means digging down until we find the bones of dead boys, then carefully bringing them up from the earth and taking them to my lab so we can determine who they are and how they died. It means giving the remains of those boys to the families who had been robbed of them decades before.

We'd been working for a year on the campus of what was now being called the North Florida Youth Development Center, just the latest feel-good name for a juvenile prison that opened in 1900. Every time the place was scandalized in the ensuing century, some bureaucrats decided it was time to change the name and they rebranded. The state-run reformatory had been called the Florida State Reform School, the Florida Industrial School for Boys, the Florida School for Boys, and, more recently, the Arthur G. Dozier School for Boys, this last one being its name for most of its existence. Though the name changed, the people who ran it did not. Nor did its culture of cruelty.

The Dozier customs did not come out of nowhere. They seemed to be following a script. I had no idea how entangled in it I would become.

The old men mingling among the press outside called the place Dozier. Some of them even remembered the school's namesake, Arthur G. Dozier. Some of them remembered Dozier swinging the strap that split their backsides open.

The men, now in their sixties and seventies, called themselves the White House Boys, after the building in which they were abused by

Dozier and a dozen other men who ran the school. Whether you were white or Black, you took your beating in the White House. These men were the reason we were all here.

They would not let the state of Florida forget its sin, and they were far from ready to forgive. Their nightmares kept them vigilant. They remembered classmates disappearing. They remembered bunkmates returning from beatings with distended bellies, and some being dragged away for discipline and never returning at all.

When they finally spoke up and told the newspaper reporters about the blood spattered on the walls of the White House, about the pain and suffering that started when they were boys at Dozier and chased them like demons into adulthood, kept them up at night, made them sleep with the lights on, the state opened an investigation to try to learn if any crimes had been committed. Investigators from the Florida Department of Law Enforcement knocked the cobwebs off old records and taped interviews with gray-haired former wards and feeble old guards, but they could find no evidence of crime to prosecute.

The White House Boys thought the investigation was a whitewash. They wanted vengeance. They wanted reparations. They wanted apologies. They wanted the forgotten to once again be remembered.

They wanted the elected leaders of Florida to admit that the stories they told were true.

It wasn't enough that you could hear the truth in their voices and see the pain on their faces. Government is often cold and void of empathy. Without provable facts, what happened at Dozier was folklore.

This is where science came in. Where others might see a hole in the ground, I see a story.

There is one way to know for certain what is buried beneath the earth's surface.

You dig a hole.

And so we took what we'd learned in the past year—that the state of Florida said thirty-one boys were buried in the little reform school burial ground, that our ground-penetrating radar (GPR) showed there were at least fifty graves, that our research told us there could be many more—and we dug a shallow trench. We didn't have permission yet to dig deep.

We started with a test trench: twenty inches wide, twenty inches deep, three yards long.

Much of Florida soil is soft, like sugar sand. In the panhandle, though—fifty miles north of the Gulf of Mexico, twenty miles south of the Alabama line—the earth is hard, red clay.

And so when walls of the long and skinny test trench showed a mixture of coffee-colored topsoil and hard, red clay, we knew that someone had dug here many years before us.

The trenches confirmed what our ground-penetrating radar showed us: these were burials, and there were more than the school records indicated.

The crowd outside the restroom was growing. It was almost time. I made more finger circles.

"Not all the burials are accounted for," I repeated. "We pieced together school records that indicate that forty-five individuals are buried on school grounds. Thirty-one were shipped home to families or buried in other locations. And twenty-two remain unknown."

The families of some of those boys were gathering outside as well.

Ovell Krell was out there. Her brother died in custody, and her mother never forgot.

Richard Varnadoe was out there, too. His brothers, who Glen had told me about, were healthy when the sheriff took them away. One of them was dead a month later. The school said he died of pneumonia, but the family never believed it.

Finger circles. One last look in the mirror.

"Without doing a full excavation," I said, "we can't say exactly what's there."

With that, I took a breath and walked through the door and into the hot lights of my first press conference for Dozier. Before the whole thing was over, I would do thirty-five more.

Chapter 2

NEW LIGHT

Four years before, in late October 2008, five old men stood under a perfect blue sky on the campus of the Dozier School for Boys, in front of a low-slung cinder-block building that they sometimes visited, against their will, kicking and screaming, in their nightmares.

The men—Dick Colon, Robert Straley, Michael O'McCarthy, Bill Haynes, and Roger Kiser—were locked up here when they were boys, and each of them held a special grudge against this place. They blamed it for their broken dreams, for their sleepless nights, for haunting them.

When they were boys, they were prisoners here. Though set free decades ago, they found themselves prisoners still.

They had bad backs and carried photos of their grandchildren in their wallets, and they all remembered the same things about this place where they'd gathered: chunks of vomit or bits of lip or tongue on the pillow they were forced to bite, the way the springs on the metal cot squeaked with each blow of the strap. They remembered walking into the little building called the White House, in bare feet and pajamas, shaking with fear. They remembered the scream of a rusty old ventilation fan in the ceiling, and the cries of the boys piercing the night.

They'd come from places like Montgomery, Alabama, and Brunswick,

Georgia, and Clearwater, Florida, places where they had tried to make homes and build lives.

Dick Colon, a sixty-five-year-old electrical company owner from Baltimore, was tormented by memories from his time at the Dozier school—he had a vague, distant memory of walking into the school's laundry room, seeing a boy's body tumbling inside an industrial dryer, and doing nothing to help. Michael O'McCarthy, a writer and political activist from the Florida Keys who was beaten so badly he was treated at the school infirmary, stood nearby. Then there was Roger Kiser, a *Chicken Soup for the Soul* contributor who lived in a mobile home in Brunswick, Georgia, and wanted revenge. Bill Haynes had been sent to the school after allegedly stealing a bicycle, and when he saw the sprawling, manicured campus, he thought it would be better than home. That idyllic notion fell apart when he took his first beating in the White House.

Robert Straley stood on the end. He was the most mild-mannered among them, but for decades he had dealt with blackout spells during which he entertained violent ideations of vengeance. They came on out of the blue sometimes, like seizures, and he would wake up sweating, overcome by anger, his fists balled into hard knots. He felt at times like he had a demon inside him, fighting to cut loose.

Robert grew up in a small house by a lake in rural Central Florida, the son of a strict mother and an absent, one-eyed father. When he hit puberty, Robert started running away to escape his mother's draconian rules. The police always brought him home, but when he turned thirteen and went joyriding with two friends who had stolen a relative's car, his mother refused to take him back. "I don't care what you do with him," she told the officers, "but he's not coming back here. I don't want him."

The authorities shipped him off to reform school in Marianna, hundreds of miles from home.

Lately, Robert had been experiencing public blackouts more frequently, brought on, he thought, by the grainy video clips he had seen on the evening news of the death of a child named Martin Lee Anderson at a boot camp in the Florida panhandle. The local sheriff had claimed that fourteen-year-old Anderson had dropped dead during mandatory exercise. The problem with that was a surveillance video, which showed guards pushing the boy even after he had collapsed, as well as a nurse nearby doing nothing to help. When Anderson didn't obey their orders to stand, the guards piled on top of him, one of them covering the boy's mouth with a cloth until his squirming body stopped moving and went limp. The local medical examiner performed an autopsy and concluded the death was natural and related to sickle cell trait, more common in African Americans. A second medical examiner's autopsy—ordered by the governor—confirmed what many suspected, that Anderson's death was "caused by suffocation due to actions of the guards at the boot camp. The suffocation was caused by manual occlusion of the mouth, in concert with forced inhalation of ammonia fumes that caused spasm of the vocal cords resulting in internal blockage of the upper airway."

Under mounting pressure from protesters and national media, the state closed all five of its juvenile boot camps, gave Anderson's family $7.4 million, and finally brought manslaughter charges against the guards and nurse. The case was headed to trial. In the heart of the Florida panhandle, though, not even a second investigation and a special prosecutor would win a conviction.

Robert saw himself in the young Black boy, and the video triggered flashbacks to his own time in state custody. The blackouts came on strong and unexpected and pulled rage up into his throat.

Worse, the news coverage triggered a recurring nightmare he'd had since he was a boy, all of his 105 pounds, locked up at Dozier. In it, he felt a man sit down on the edge of his bed. A man who would rob him of his innocence. A monster.

He was here to confront that monster, come what may. He could no longer escape.

Robert and the other men now called themselves the White House Boys.

They found each other online, as each man had logged on to search for information about the Florida School for Boys, for something that suggested they weren't the only ones haunted by the Florida School for Boys. They had found Roger Kiser's amateur website, and he added their memories and photos.

Using Michael O'McCarthy's press contacts, the White House Boys enlisted the help of an investigative reporter at the *Miami Herald* named Carol Marbin Miller, who had long challenged the way Florida treated its child inmates. In the wake of Martin Lee Anderson's death, the state's Department of Juvenile Justice was trying to improve, so administrators lifted the veil of secrecy around Dozier and other programs and allowed Miller and the *Herald* to review old records and tour the facility, surrounded by woods in rural Jackson County. Miller reported on the century-long history of abuse and neglect at the facility, writing that an investigative committee in 1903—three years after the reformatory opened—found that the lofty experiment had already gone horribly wrong. "We found them in irons, just like common criminals, which in the judgment of your committee is not the meaning of a state reform school," a state senate inspection committee wrote, calling the school "nothing more nor less than a prison." Another committee visiting the school seven years later found that the "inmates were at times unnecessarily and brutally punished, the instrument of punishment being a leather strap fastened to a wooden handle." The school fired the superintendent, but the beatings never stopped.

IN THE SCHOOL's first two decades of operation, investigators sent from Tallahassee found that its administrators hired out boys to work with state convicts. They found students who were brutally beaten. A fire killed at least eight boys and two staff members who were stuck inside a burning dormitory. A grand jury found that the men who should've been watching the boys when the dorm caught fire were actually in town on a "pleasure bent." Yet another superintendent got fired, but the trouble did not stop. There were reports of inadequate medical care, overcrowding, rodent infestations, sickness, and the murders of students allegedly by their peers.

In its second decade, the reform school even hired a publicist to try to generate more positive coverage and keep the stories of escapes and lawlessness under wraps. The school also put its best foot forward every Christmas, when thousands of families from across the panhandle and lower Georgia and Alabama drove from miles around to see elaborate light displays, plywood nativity scenes, and waving Santas built by the wards.

While the school opened with a dozen or so children in 1900, by the mid-1950s, the overcrowded school housed around nine hundred boys, most of them Black, and had become the largest reform school in the country, and it was still growing. Reporters continued to shine light on the school's criminal abuse in exposés that outraged Floridians.

In 1958, the *Miami News* published a three-part series on the beatings called "Marianna's Two Faces." The stories by muckraking journalist Jane Wood reported that seven psychologists had resigned in a two-year period in objection to the "routine beating of boys."

"They are beatings delivered with the full force of a grown man," one of the psychologists, Dr. Eugene Byrd, told Wood. "They wear out the straps on the boys." Byrd, who also testified to the abuse before a US Senate subcommittee, said fifteen to twenty boys were beaten in the White House every Saturday. The only thing the staff disputed was the severity of the beatings. "I don't think you can paddle a boy hard enough to do any good without leaving some discoloration," the assistant superintendent told the newspaper.

Florida law at the time prohibited those kinds of beatings for adults in prison, but it still allowed whipping children with straps even though guidelines for juvenile lockups from the Children's Bureau of the US Department of Health said that "corporal punishment should not be tolerated in any form." A contemporary study of 250 boys committed to Marianna showed they had received 691 whippings among them—and most of the beatings were administered on the younger boys. The governor of Florida set up a committee to investigate, but the superintendent, Arthur G. Dozier, for whom the school was later named, said spanking was better for the boys than solitary confinement.

In 1964, a reporter for the *Miami Herald* visited Dozier and quickly heard about the White House. "It is not on the tour," wrote reporter Joy Reese Shaw, hinting at the secrecy. "Nobody likes to talk about what goes on inside—and when they do, the sting of the whip seems to split through the words." A learning-disabled Miami boy sent to the school for bicycle theft told Shaw that he'd been whipped seven times while serving his eleven-month sentence.

Four years later, a state supervisor for the Marianna school witnessed a beating so sickening that he wrote a letter of complaint to his boss: "At the time the strap was being wielded by a man who was at least 6 feet, 3 inches and weighed well over 200 pounds . . . The child quivers and writhes . . ." A former cottage father—a man who lived on the second floor of a dormitory and oversaw day-to-day activities of the boys—sent a letter describing beatings he had witnessed, writing, "The belt falls between eight and 100 times. After about the tenth stroke, the seams of the sturdiest blue jeans begin to separate and numerous times the boys' skin is broken to the extent that stitches are required." One supervisor at Marianna described a boy's buttocks as "bleeding profusely; the skin was broken, and the color of his buttocks was green, blue, red and purplish . . . It reminded me of the Dark Ages."

Corporal punishment was finally outlawed in 1968, but the new superintendent of the reform school told state legislators that bringing back the strap would cut down on runaways. When that man, Lennox Williams, was fired for his archaic belief, the townsfolk in Marianna spoke up in his defense. Among those arguing for the belt were a state senator, a state representative, the mayor, the superintendent of schools, and the local newspaper publisher. Williams was reinstated and went on to become the longest-serving superintendent in the school's history, facing down scandal after scandal. Superintendents like Williams ran the entire operation, answering directly to a board of managers who answered directly to the governor himself.

When tough-talking Florida governor Claude Kirk showed up at the Dozier school in 1968 for a look around, he found holes in the leaking ceilings, bucket toilets, tight quarters, and no heat at all in the cold North Florida winters. "If one of your kids were kept in such circumstances, you'd be up there with rifles," he told reporters. A US Department of Health official said the school was a "monstrosity," and several judges who visited Marianna vowed to never send another troubled child to the facility. An award-winning *Christian Science Monitor* reporter working on a story about juvenile detention found a boy named Jim in solitary confinement who had eaten a lightbulb and used the diffuser from a fixture to shred his arm. "No one seemed to care," the reporter wrote in a story headlined "Bulldoze Them to the Ground."

The school administration promised reform over and over, but nothing changed. In 1978, a child advocate named Jack Levine visited and found a confinement building at the rear of campus that reeked from the stench of sweat and urine. Inside, Levine discovered a cell, with a lock so rusty that a guard had to whack it with a Holy Bible to break it open. Inside, Levine found a small, shirtless, and scared boy who had been pulling his hair out and had no idea how long he'd been locked in there. The scene compelled Levine to report the school to the American Civil Liberties Union (ACLU), which in 1983 filed a class-action lawsuit against the school for holding boys in solitary confinement for three weeks or longer and hog-tying them facedown as a method of restraint and punishment. When the state settled the suit rather than going to trial in 1987, Florida agreed to cap the inmate population and outlaw hog-tying. The department secretary called it progress.

THE WHITE HOUSE BOYS knew none of this. They knew only what they had each experienced, and they knew there must be more men who carried the same terrible baggage.

Stepping forward to publicly tell their stories was only the latest scandal in a century of them.

In 2008, as they began to organize, they approached the state, seeking official acknowledgment that they had been abused and hoping to find some resolution along the way. They found an advocate in a former state legislator who now worked for the state's Department of Juvenile Justice, a man named Gus Barreiro. He set up a ceremony to close and seal the White House, and he even ordered a plaque to be mounted on the building:

IN MEMORY OF THE CHILDREN WHO PASSED THESE
DOORS, WE ACKNOWLEDGE THEIR TRIBULATIONS AND
OFFER OUR HOPE THAT THEY HAVE FOUND SOME
MEASURE OF PEACE.
MAY THIS BUILDING STAND AS A REMINDER OF THE NEED
TO REMAIN VIGILANT IN PROTECTING OUR CHILDREN AS
WE HELP THEM SEEK A BRIGHTER FUTURE.
MOREOVER, WE OFFER THE REASSURANCE THAT WE ARE
DEDICATED TO SERVING AND PROTECTING THE YOUTH
WHO ENTER THIS CAMPUS, AND HELPING THEM TO
TRANSFORM THEIR LIVES.

Besides the men, a small crowd gathered that Tuesday morning including state officials, school staff, and a few television crews and newspaper reporters.

Bill Haynes, now a sixty-five-year-old corrections officer, who drove down from Alabama, stepped in front of the microphone.

"I have tried to understand why as a child in need of supervision I had to be beaten in such a brutal and sadistic manner," he told the small crowd and the television cameras. "My experience at FSB has mentally scarred me."

One after the next, the five men told the stories that haunted them.

"There was blood splattered all over the walls," said sixty-five-year-old Michael O'McCarthy.

The birds sang in the pine trees as the men told of their miseries.

"When I walked out of this building . . . when I looked in the mirror, I couldn't tell who I was, I was so bloodied," said sixty-two-year-old Roger Kiser.

Inside the buildings scattered across the campus, a new batch of incarcerated boys watched the commotion through the windows. The staff wouldn't let them outside, so they wondered what the fuss was about. They, too, were being abused and neglected, but the world wouldn't know about it, not then.

"They were monsters," said Robert Straley. "Oh, my God, the things they did."

When the ceremony ended, the men led the television cameras across County Road 276, to Boot Hill, where thirty-one pipe crosses in crooked rows marked the final resting place for an unknown number of boys. Some of the men knelt down to pray as camera shutters clicked. A few of them remembered seeing the burial ground when they were imprisoned as boys, and some recalled guards using the graveyard as a sort of morbid threat—if you don't behave, you could wind up there.

Newspapers across the country ran the story the following day.

Charlie Crist, the Republican governor of Florida, called for an investigation into the school and the small graveyard on the property. He ordered the Florida Department of Law Enforcement to find out who or what was buried in the graves beneath those pipe crosses, to identify any remains and determine whether any crimes occurred.

"Justice always cries out for a conclusion, and this is no different," the governor told reporters. "If there's an opportunity to find out exactly what happened there, to be able to verify if there were these kinds of horrible atrocities . . . we have a duty to do so."

Reporters across the Sunshine State began working on localized stories, too. Men scattered all over Florida and other parts of the South came out of the woodwork to say that they, too, had been brutally beaten, and some of them said that they remembered classmates who had been dragged to the White House and were never seen again.

George Goewey of St. Petersburg remembered how the one-armed man who often doled out beatings would swing the strap from below his waist, and it would scrape the wall and then the ceiling before raining hell on his backside, so he could time the pain.

John Brodnax of Pinellas County remembered being beaten by seven different men.

Jerry Cooper from Cape Coral recalled getting 135 lashes one night in 1960, when he was sixteen, and he paid for a lie-detector test to prove he was telling the truth. He said he received the beating from men who took turns with the strap. He passed out from the pain, and when he woke, he was on the floorboard of a state car, his back and buttocks swollen, his nightgown spattered with blood. His cottage father instructed Jerry to cake Vaseline on his open wounds and wrap them with two towels tied in place by a bedsheet.

A woman named Monica Adams showed reporters a diary kept by her tortured husband, who had died four years before.

After I saw these straps—long ones, thick ones, short ones—they reminded me of razor straps on the side of barber chairs . . . I knew something horrible was going to happen to me. I was taken into a room and placed on a small bed about 3 ft wide, maybe 5 or 6 feet long. The bed was near the floor and had a filthy mattress on it. I was told to hold on to the end of the bed and not move or cry out. And then I remember the sound of something cutting the air, followed by a pain I can't describe. The most horrible pain a human being can imagine. It hurt so terribly bad. I would try and move to get up from the bed. God, Please make them stop beating me. But they beat me and beat me so bad.

One man had a story about a boy who was taken to the White House for punishment and didn't come back. Yet another remembered a kid who died from exposure while hiding under a cottage.

Within a few months, more than three hundred men had contacted a lawyer, who agreed to bring a lawsuit against the school and whatever old guards were still alive, pro bono. That the state seemed willing to investigate the abuse—to even explore criminal charges if the evidence was there—impressed some of the former wards, who thought they'd be turned away.

"This is a big occasion for the state of Florida," Michael O'McCarthy told the Associated Press. "Rarely do state or federal governments like to admit that they have committed this type of egregious, destructive kinds of crimes, especially to children."

For the first time, some of the men who had been so scarred by their experiences at the school were feeling hopeful, on the edge of the justice they'd longed for. The governor seemed sincere in his call for accountability. The leaders of the still-open reform school seemed eager to address the past abuse and help the men find healing. The state's premier police agency had already begun interviewing former wards and old guards and combing through archives and school records to identify the inmates buried at Boot Hill.

Their hope was fleeting, though. In May 2009, after a six-month investigation, the FDLE agents issued a report that said they found records to indicate that twenty-nine boys and two men had been buried at Boot Hill since the school opened in 1900—a body count that matched exactly the number of pipe crosses planted in the little clearing.

"There is no evidence to suggest that the School or its staff made any attempts to conceal and/or contributed to the deaths of these individuals," the report read.

However, the report also noted that the special agents relied heavily, and sometimes exclusively, on incomplete and deteriorated records kept by school officials, the same men accused of beatings and rape.

In addition, the investigators didn't know the exact location of any of the remains. The graves were completely unmarked for years, until a superintendent asked a Boy Scout troop to honor the dead with concrete crosses. The same man supplied the number of graves—thirty-one—based on folklore and a little research. Two decades after the markers were placed, part of the cemetery was destroyed by a tree-planting operation and so another superintendent ordered pipe crosses. The problem was that workers had no reference point, so they placed them based on how they thought they should be arranged.

The special agents also stopped short of trying to exhume any remains or dig shallow exploratory trenches to see if anyone had dug holes there before. They may not have even known that the process called "ground-truthing" by archaeologists and forensic anthropologists was a relatively easy way to learn whether the earth had been disturbed in the past. They also didn't try using ground-penetrating radar to capture an accurate count of how many actual graves had been dug over the years, or where they were. The FDLE chief of executive investigations told reporters that the "hundreds" of witnesses the agents had interviewed "did not provide any first-hand knowledge . . . that would refute the information provided in these records."

Their report concluded: "In all cases, the deceased were accounted for in official documentation. There is no evidence to suggest that the School or its staff made any attempts to conceal and/or contributed to the deaths of these individuals. There is no evidence to support that an unidentified perpetrator exists or existed that was responsible for any of these individual's deaths. Therefore, from witness testimonies, records that were examined and all information currently available, FDLE determined that there was no indication of a criminal predicate to warrant further investigation into this matter. The investigation pertaining to the School's Cemetery will be closed due to lack of evidence as defined by Florida Statutes."

The report asked more questions than it answered, and it left many loose ends.

No matter. It was presented with a level of finality, as though the case was closed barring the discovery of a smoking gun.

The school's biennial report for 1911 and 1912 lists one death, the first on record, but no name and no burial information. Two staff members and eight boys died in a dormitory fire in 1914. A telegram to a dead boy's mother read: "Bodies charred beyond recognition. Will be buried here. Greatest sympathy to family." Three more boys, all Black, died in 1915, but there was no cause of death or location of burial. Three more Black boys died in 1916. No information besides names and "deceased." Nine more died in 1918, five white and four Black, but no other information was given. On it went, until the last recorded death, a drowning in the Chipola River in 1973.

"There is no evidence to suggest that the school or staff caused or contributed to any of these deaths," FDLE commissioner Gerald Bailey told reporters.

After the press conference, reporters wondered among themselves whether Bailey was clueless or protecting a sacred state institution that had become, for better or worse, a symbol of the state's regard for juvenile justice.

That investigators relied on school records was a major problem. In the end, the FDLE determined that eighty-one people died at the school over the years, but the official records placed thirty-one in the cemetery on the hill. Where were the other fifty?

Investigators couldn't say whether those fifty bodies were shipped to the boys' hometowns, buried in a municipal or church cemetery in Marianna, or buried on school grounds, perhaps in some other cemetery besides Boot Hill.

And as the story spread like wildfire across the country, the families of boys who died in custody were coming forward with their own stories of loss and of longing for answers.

Among those families was a woman named Ovell Krell, who was a kid when her brother was shipped off to Dozier.

HIS KIN CALLED him George Owen. He was naturally musical and loved to listen as the Saturday-night sounds came rolling out of the local juke joint. The Depression strangled Central Florida, but George Owen Smith would throw his head back and try to sing it away. He was afraid of the dark, so he'd whistle Gene Autry songs while he walked, as if country music could keep him safe.

His family knew him to be a bit restless, a wanderer who would sometimes leave his small town in Central Florida for Gasparilla Island on the west coast, without telling a soul, and he'd return full of stories about fishing in the Gulf of Mexico with his grandpa.

One day in late 1940, when he was all of fourteen years old, George Owen left home and didn't come back. His family got word that he'd been arrested in Tavares—auto theft, for riding in a stolen car—and a judge had sentenced him to serve time at the Florida Industrial School for Boys.

George Owen sent a letter home, to let his folks know that he'd arrived at the reform school and that he was fine. Then weeks passed with no word. The next they heard, he'd escaped and made it all the way to Bartow, fifteen miles from home.

When his next letter arrived, George Owen wrote an ominous line: "I got what was coming to me," he wrote.

Then the letters stopped, no matter how many stamps his mama licked.

Frances Smith wrote to the school's superintendent, Millard Davidson, in December 1940, asking for an update on her son. Davidson wrote back saying that the boy had run away again, that no one knew where George Owen was. "So far we have been unable to get any information concerning his whereabouts," said his letter, dated January 1, 1941.

Frances wrote back, telling him she was embarking on the 350-mile drive and would be at the school in two days to search for her son. That letter apparently arrived in Marianna around January 23, 1941. That was when the Smiths heard the news from a priest in Auburndale. He was apologetic and said the school had found George Owen, that her son was dead.

A friend drove them to the stately campus, with its manicured lawns and tall pine trees, and they passed hundreds of boys marching in lines and working in the fields. Davidson told the family that George Owen's remains were found under a house in Marianna. They identified him by his dental records and the markings on his clothes and the color of the scattered tufts of his hair, he said.

The superintendent led the family through the woods to a clearing, to a patch of fresh-turned earth.

Even at twelve years old, George Owen's sister Ovell knew something wasn't right. Her brother went missing, then just before the family arrived to help look, he was allegedly found under a house and buried before his own parents can pay their respects?

The Smiths met with another boy in the presence of the superintendent.

The boy told them that he and George Owen had escaped, that headlights caught them as they were walking toward town and they froze in their tracks. Then George Owen ran. The last time the boy saw George Owen, he told the family, he was running across an open field, and men were shooting at him.

A man named James Young remembered being at the school with George Owen. James recalled years later that George Owen got a beating from guards and swore it'd never happen again. "Ain't one of you gonna lay another hand on me," he remembered George Owen saying. "I'm never going back to that White House."

The next the boys heard, George Owen was dead.

"Then it was hushed," James said. "We didn't say anything about it."

Frances Smith never believed her boy was dead. Every night for forty years, she sat on the stoop of her home in Auburndale, listening for him to come whistling through the woods.

Ovell witnessed her mother's unending grief. She later said that she lost a brother *and* a mother when George Owen died.

Her story was heartbreaking, but she wasn't asking for sympathy. She wanted answers, and now that the state's oldest reformatory was in the headlines again, she was compelled to add her voice to a growing chorus of bereaved family members calling for justice. She reached out to reporters at the *St. Petersburg Times*, the largest newspaper in the state, and the *Times* ran a story about her. She'd grown up and gotten married and joined the police department in Lakeland, in Central Florida, not far from where she grew up. She was one of the first female officers in Florida, and she served for two decades. She knew the truth from a lie.

She couldn't understand what happened to her brother. Why would he crawl under a house? Why would he not come out, even if he were starving or ill? What kind of fourteen-year-old boy lies down and dies?

She kept all the letters between her mother and the school superintendent, thinking they might be useful someday. When she learned of the FDLE investigation, she wrote a letter to the agents but got no response.

The detectives' report said that her brother had "escaped from the school in September of 1940 and his remains were found in January 1941 under the Marianna residence of Ms. Ella Pierce. After a coroner's inquest, no cause of death could be determined due to the extreme decomposition of the body." He was buried on Boot Hill with the others, the report said, one of five children whose death certificate lists no known cause.

"I think they should dig further," she told the newspaper. "I stake my life that there was a conspiracy."

Chapter 3

GRAVEYARD

When my friend, a writer named Jon Jefferson, approached me about setting up a meeting with the investigative reporter Ben Montgomery in early 2011, I'd heard a little about the Dozier School for Boys and I'd seen a few newspaper stories, but the idea of getting involved wasn't on my radar.

Jon had written a fiction book called *The Bone Yard* (under the pen name Jefferson Bass), which he based on the story of the Dozier school, and he'd met with Ben, who was still working on a series for the *St. Petersburg Times* (which became the *Tampa Bay Times* in 2011) called "For Their Own Good." In 2010, Ben (along his coauthor and photographer) was named a Pulitzer Prize finalist for the series. The three of us met in the cafeteria at the University of South Florida, where I teach, and Ben gave me a stack of stories he and a colleague had written for the *Times* about the burials at Boot Hill, about Ovell Krell and George Owen, and about a man named Richard Varnadoe, whose brothers were sent to Marianna in 1934, one of whom died about a month after arriving. The school officials told the Varnadoe family that Thomas had died after a bout of pneumonia, but the family doubted it. Worse, the boy was buried on the school grounds before the family could fetch

his remains. "I would just like to have some closure," Richard Varnadoe, eighty, told the *Times*, "and I'd like if someone could find his
remains and dig him up and get him down here where we could give
him a proper funeral and bury him close to family."

Ben and his colleagues had been ringing the bell on the injustice
at Dozier since 2009, and he worked for an independent paper that
had exposed scandals at the school for decades, including a seminal
piece in 1964 called "Hell's 1,400 Acres." I'd read the modern news
articles before, but I had my hands full teaching class, working with
police on unsolved cold cases, and trying to finish a research project
on murdered women dumped and left for dead. The stories gnawed
at me, though.

Sitting at my desk one morning with a large coffee, I read the stories
Ben handed me about the White House Boys and the beatings they endured, the torture and sexual abuse, the indentured servitude, and even
the allegations of murder in the 1950s and 1960s. I found their blog
posts online. One of the former wards called Dozier "a concentration
camp for little boys."

I read about Robert Straley, who had been making a living selling
glow sticks and novelty items at carnivals and state fairs. He traveled
the country and was a prolific writer. As he aged, he found himself
suffering from acute depression that he tied to the abuse he suffered
at the reform school. Robert was working closely on research with
Michael O'McCarthy and another former student, Roger Kiser, who
had been deemed "incorrigible" and sent to Dozier in 1959 for running away from an orphanage. Robert said that he and Roger started
corresponding and eventually decided that the only way to drag this
out into the open was to establish a trail of abuse—otherwise it was
two old men telling horror stories.

I got the sense that while the school's founding purpose was to
rehabilitate and educate boys who were arrested for serious crimes, it
quickly evolved into a much-feared penal institution and work camp,
many of whose inmates had been sent there for things like "incorrigibility," "truancy," or "dependency." Some were sent to Dozier for

"smoking in school." In some cases, the boys' only offenses were being abandoned children, orphans, or wards of the state.

I started to research the numerous state investigations—I found six in the school's first thirteen years alone—which included reports of abuses such as brutal whippings, shackling children to walls, and leasing children to area businesses for peonage work that brought profit to the school and the Marianna community. At first, girls were sent to the reform school, too. I couldn't learn much about them since those records disappeared in the 1914 fire. Early legislative investigations into the school revealed that the male staff improperly treated the girls, but the lack of detail left me to guess at what kind of horrors that meant.

From its start, school leaders lobbied to increase the number of boys sent there and asked for control over their release dates, rather than leaving sentencing up to the judges who convicted the boys. What bothered me most was this simple question of demand: How many children were convicted of crimes in the 1890s, sparking the need for such an institution? Yes, reformers wanted to save them from the convict lease system. But towns competed for the school and rallied to donate the land and funding. Fourteen hundred acres and $400 from the people of Jackson County won the bid. I wondered what the turn-of-the-century lawmakers in Tallahassee thought those men would do with one hundred boys on fourteen hundred acres.

I thought maybe my friend Rich could help. We'd worked together before on clandestine grave searches for the police in missing person's cases when leads came in about possible murders and burial or dump sites.

Dr. Richard Estabrook, a veteran archaeologist in Florida for more than thirty years, lugged Matilda—the name he gave to the remote sensing tool for ground-penetrating radar—to many of our crime scenes. Rich was an experienced and dedicated Florida archaeologist who spent most of his time on historic cemetery preservation. Though he was way more comfortable with lithics like arrowheads than he was with dead bodies, he was always willing to help and always up for an adventure.

I called after reading as much as I could find about the school. The stories begged a slew of questions, but first among them was this: Is it true?

I wondered the same thing. It wasn't that I had any doubt about the prevalence of child abuse or murder. I know the heinous atrocities men and women inflict on one another from my years of forensics work, but this level of institutional abuse right here in Florida, an hour's drive from the state capital, with hundreds of men coming forward, was hard to imagine. How had it lasted so long? How had I never heard about it before?

When Rich answered the phone, I said, "This article in the *Times* talks about abuse and forced labor practices at the Dozier reform school in North Florida. Something about missing boys and an unmarked burial ground at the school. Have you heard of this place?"

He knew what I was talking about immediately.

"That place is notorious," he said. "Court cases and lawsuits . . . lots of history in Florida along these lines. If that's your interest, you should look at the state hospital—that's the worst—and then there are the turpentine companies. Have you heard about these?"

Rich was like an encyclopedia. Surprisingly, no, I didn't realize the prevalence of these abuses, nor could I have imagined that we were opening Pandora's box.

Florida used convicts to build railroads, cut lumber, mine and manufacture bricks, pick oranges, and harvest turpentine. Convicts were leased out to work in cotton fields. There was no state income tax in Florida to provide the most basic of services, such as prisons, so the convicted criminals created a labor pool that was exploited by the state and private industry for decades. It was a practice that gained momentum at the end of the Civil War, when enslaved people were freed. Florida needed to find a new way to obtain free labor. Enter convict leasing. By the turn of the century, labor camps were simultaneously notorious and tantamount to death sentences in many cases. Floggings and brutal whippings were standard forms of legal corporal punishment. They were throwbacks to the whipping sheds and labor bosses of rural plantation life throughout the Deep South. The labor boss was responsible for the inmate during his or her sentence, providing food, shelter, and medicine—or not. Rampant infectious disease, overcrowding, deplorable conditions, and a lack of medical attention were the norm. So many died, but inmates were dispensable. Most of the deaths were justified as acceptable hazards. Few men were ever held accountable or convicted of the deaths that occurred in their care, even in the more blatant and witnessed cases of death due to beatings or neglect.

"I was working on a site recently that is supposed to have a mass burial from a flu outbreak," Rich told me. "Indentured servitude was common also. But there were no prisons, so the convicts were pretty much used to anything, treatment-wise." He paused before adding, "You don't have to look too far to find injustice in Florida."

Now I was curious about the leasing system and its similarities to the system of slavery. I was hooked.

"I didn't realize this form of labor was so prevalent," I said. "I mean, I understand the problem historically—but in this series there are hundreds of men who are talking about having been abused, they are alive and lived it, and some people coming forward are the siblings of boys who died there, but the families don't know where their brothers are buried."

I tried to grasp the extent of what happened at this school: "It's not really an historic problem when the victims are here telling their stories, right? So is this a missing person's case or an issue of a historical cemetery that fell into abandonment?"

"There are lots of problems with convict treatment in the past and even today. You remember the boot camps," Rich said.

"You really should look at the state hospital," he continued. "They had thousands of deaths. And they had that casket factory."

A hospital with a casket factory?

I brought it back to Dozier. "I may not be able to get in," I told him. "It's still open, I think . . . or maybe it's closing. But at a minimum, don't you think we should document the cemetery? We could find the burials and mark them at least. Research the history."

As we spoke, I researched the laws on access to cemeteries on state property on my computer. We needed the right angle.

"I can see this is going to be political, but it's still just a cemetery, and burial grounds are protected, so why not investigate and record it like any other historic cemetery?" I said.

He knew exactly what I was thinking.

"If you can convince them to give you permission to go on the grounds," he said, "we can do this."

"What do we need to do to get an archaeology permit to document and preserve it?" I asked.

"You need an 1A-32 permit and permission from the landowner," Rich said. "If they tell you we can go on the property, then I can get the permit."

"But who owns the land?" I asked. "I get that it's the state, but who is that exactly?"

I imagined all the personal assistants I would have to call to figure this out.

"Since there's a jail nearby, maybe the land is managed by the Department of Corrections?"

I spend a good deal of time working with law enforcement, so I thought maybe it was best if I started by calling the jail.

"If that's the case, you may run into a whole slew of problems," Rich said. "There are some that may not want you to find out how many burials are there, you know? That can open a lot of questions, especially if men are out there saying more things happened to these kids than a raging fire or the flu outbreak."

"Right," I said.

The newspaper stories made it seem pretty clear this issue was closed for the state, since the FDLE investigation was over.

"I don't think you can just say we don't want to know the truth because we don't like it," I said. "It is what it is. And anyway, it has been more than fifty years since the last reported death. Why would you want to cover up someone else's dirty little secret? I can't accept that."

I was fired up. Rich knew it and laughed.

"You think there are more than thirty-one burials?" he said, goading me.

"I guarantee there aren't thirty-one," I said. "You're in cemeteries every day, same as me. How many are exact without any problems or errors?" I knew the answer: zero. If there was a cemetery that had a perfect record of keeping track of the dead, I'd never heard of it.

"Whether we can find the graves is another issue."

It all seemed simple enough. I needed to figure out who controlled the land and ask them if we could go on public property to document a historic cemetery. I needed to quietly build a team of people to help—students, colleagues, anybody who cared enough to make the five-hour drive to the panhandle and get a little dirty.

"If you do," Rich said, "just give me the letter from the land-owner. The permit will be no problem at all. Very standard."

"Perfect," I said. "So, you're in?"

"Yeah," he said. "I'm in."

No one knew for sure how many boys died or where they were buried.

We were going to find out.

IT DIDN'T SURPRISE me that Rich knew so much about the Dozier school. I liked to think of him as Mr. Florida Archaeology. He knew everything about Florida history and prehistory and was always my go-to guy.

Projects like this were multidisciplinary, requiring archival re-search, fieldwork, interviews with former staff and wards—I needed a good team to make this work. I was teaching two classes with labs. I was buried in forensic cases and report writing. There was always—always—a cold case that needed fresh attention, in addition to invited lectures, departmental committees, student admissions, thesis reviews and revisions, manuscript editing, journal reviews, and faculty meetings. Most importantly, my own boys—Reid, who was three years old, and Sean, who was seven and already active in sports year-round—were my full-time job. We had lacrosse practice twice a week, and games on Saturday; flag football in the summer; birthday parties; school volunteer days; playdates; piano lessons; homework; not to mention diapers, laundry, cooking dinner every night, grocery shopping—the stuff that makes life run.

Then I met Robert Straley.

Robert had been invited to sit on a panel at a small local bookstore to talk about a project he'd been working on; he had teamed up with a Pulitzer Prize–winning journalist to publish an account of his own time at Dozier. I saw Robert's face change when he talked about his mother and the day he was sent to Dozier. He was in his late sixties, and it was obvious he was still hurting from the pain inflicted when he was thirteen. Not the physical pain; that was quickly overcome. But hurting from the disappointment and sadness he felt when his mother let him down. She said that she didn't want him back. He said that she was bipolar and that was why she agreed to let the truancy officer take him away. But the sorrow was still evident in his eyes. Most of all, Robert was sincere and thoughtful. I could tell right away that he was telling the truth. His face hid nothing. This old man still had the face of a child.

My own childhood consisted of a lot of paradoxes. Maybe that is why I am well suited to this work.

I wanted to be an anthropologist for as long as I can remember. Not that I was a studious child. Quite the opposite. Rather, I thought it meant traveling around the world and writing books, which seemed the perfect job to me. My mother, Marcia, had actually suggested it for me. I always sought adventure and freedom and rejected convention. I attended six different grade schools in as many years. By third grade, I often skipped school. Rather than walking myself there, I cut out and rode my bike around whatever town we lived in.

Our family moved around a lot. I lived at times in the country, on very rural farms, and, at other times, in cities. I often wandered off into cornfields, stayed lost for hours, and found my way back. Growing up in the country for me meant scouring dirt roads for agates (Minnesota has a lot of rocks, unlike Florida) and exploring the dilapidated ruins of old restaurants or barns. Any abandoned building was my playground—even old dumps offered up treasures if you knew where to look. I would climb on top of the heaps of trash and go to work, excavating and playing make-believe. It gave me the sense that anything was possible.

My father wasn't around much. I was raised by my grandparents and a young single mother. We lived with my grandparents until I was nearly five. My mother worked at a living history museum called Pioneer Park, in Annandale, Minnesota, where I spent my days playing dress-up in what felt like a life-size dollhouse—only it was an entire village. It had recently opened, and the village consisted of a dozen original pioneer buildings full of artifacts, from a one-room schoolhouse to livery and millinery shops. While my mother gave tours and negotiated for new artifacts from local antique dealers, I had free run of the place. My earliest childhood memories are waking up from naps on a pile of bear pelts in the log cabin and pointing out each wildflower on the nature trail as my mother talked about their medicinal values.

In middle school, my mom married, and Craig became a father and friend. Home morphed into stability and a quiet rural life. I spent nearly a thousand hours volunteering at the St. Cloud Hospital as a candy striper. In the early 1980s, the US was helping the mujahideen in Afghanistan as they fought against the invading Russians. Many Afghan soldiers and political leaders who were wounded were brought to American hospitals, including the one where I volunteered. There was one soldier who was young, cute, and flirtatious. I was drawn to his story, what he had been through, why he was fighting. I wanted to see it for myself. The nurses weren't keen on this budding friendship, but I knew when he smiled at me that my days living life in this little town in north-central Minnesota were numbered.

I loved volunteering at the hospital. It gave me a sense of purpose. I had always worked. Starting in fifth grade, I was a nanny for a neighbor with two small children. Every day after school I took care of the neighbor's kids and my little sister, Angie. I did this for more than a year, until we moved again. The father of that family would drop us off at the mall once a month with a handful of cash so that we could buy our own clothes.

My first real job was as a cocktail waitress when I was fifteen. My mother would drive me to a joint called the Side Bar in time for my shift, and she'd pick me up around 2:00 a.m.—I couldn't yet drive myself. I technically earned $2.02 an hour, but the tips were amazing—more money than I had ever seen. I also worked at a video store, a pizzeria, and a nursing home, the last a job I took shortly after my grandfather, Carl, died.

His death was the greatest loss I had felt. He was everything to me, a rock and a shelter, strong and full of conviction. He and my grandmother, Esther, the sweetest person I've ever known, lived next door to my family for a time. Every day after school was the same: he took me fishing from the dock on the lake behind his house, then we cleaned the fish, played cards, and had a daily prayer. We listened to Walter Cronkite, Paul Harvey, and Garrison Keillor on the radio— so very Minnesotan.

I wasn't overly interested in school, but I liked being a cheerleader, and I enjoyed the art club and performing in one-act plays. I once won a trophy for giving a speech about great speeches, which I found amusing and ironic.

I also got deep into the work of Dick Gregory, a Black writer, comedian, and civil rights activist. My debate teacher gave me his book, *Nigger: An Autobiography*, a blunt view of racist America. I carried it proudly around the high school halls my junior year. His words about fighting for civil rights and taking action to do the right thing simply because you knew it was right resonated with me.

I loved art and writing but felt called toward activism. Maybe my Lutheran upbringing deserved credit. That was what Connie Perpich suggested to me. She told me that growing up with a strong religious conviction gave you a moral foundation to stand up for what you believed, no matter what that was. Connie was the daughter-in-law of longtime Minnesota governor Rudy Perpich and worked as a lobbyist for Planned Parenthood for more than two decades. She had taken me under her wing as an intern and student political organizer in college. In the 1992 presidential primary, I campaigned hard for Tom Harkin, rather than the Southern Democrat Bill Clinton, due to Harkin's anti-NAFTA position. Minnesota didn't have the Democratic Party. It had the Democrat-Farmer-Labor Party. Growing up there meant labor rights were part of my worldview. The backseat of my car was always full of books, mostly thoughtful and important works by writers such as Charlotte Perkins Gilman, Margaret Sanger, Susan Faludi, Betty Friedan, Gloria Steinem, Marilyn French, and Toni Morrison.

My grandmother, Esther, had gone to school only through the eighth grade, which wasn't uncommon for Depression-era children who grew up on rural farms in Minnesota. Polish was her first language; even though she was born here, her parents could barely speak English. She learned it at school. She collected books for years about Abraham Lincoln. He was her favorite president. She believed ending slavery was the single greatest event in US history. At eighteen, she left home and worked at a children's home in Superior, Wisconsin. She saw firsthand how boys were sexually abused, a well-guarded secret among administrators there, so she renounced her faith in bitter disappointment. She went further by running off with a cowboy to elope and start a new life working on a cattle ranch in Colorado. It was almost a decade before her family would forgive her for it and accept her back. Throughout my life, she was adamant about two things: don't marry a Catholic, and always treat everyone as an equal.

After Carl's death, I reached out to my biological father, Charlie, who had left for California after my first birthday. I was sixteen when we reconnected, and we would visit each other often. He gave me some money for college and a lot of advice about "the way things really are." He told me he was sorry he had left, that he had felt forced to make that decision by his parents after my mother refused to marry him. She was only seventeen then, so it was probably the right call. We spent the weekends scouring flea markets in Marin County and around the San Francisco Bay Area for vintage hi-fi equipment. He started *Vacuum Tube Valley*, a magazine about tubes, amps, and all things hi-fi. Every guitar or radio tube and every old stereo, radio, or guitar amp that used a tube, he purchased. His collection was the largest in the country when he died in 2009. He left more than four hundred radios he had fully repaired and a mountaintop warehouse full of tubes. I still listen to recordings from the weekly radio shows he hosted, a mixture of jazz and old hippie politics. He would have loved that we fought our way through the Dozier project.

At first, he didn't like that I had decided to study anthropology in college. He repeatedly told me I would never find a job and that I needed to be more realistic. In fairness to him, nearly everyone told me that, apart from my mother. My teachers, my boyfriend's parents, everyone said the same thing . . . and I found it so basic. I couldn't understand what made their lives so special. Nor could I imagine trying to force my ideas about lifestyle on someone else, as they did. So, I ignored them all and after college followed my boyfriend to Washington, D.C. He had a job in telecom sales and was given an opportunity to move out east.

When I got to Virginia, I applied for two jobs: the Gap in Alexandria on King Street—it was very near to where I was living—and the anthropology department at the Smithsonian Institution's National Museum of Natural History. The museum was hiring osteologists who could do skeletal analysis of American Indian remains for repatriation. I had helped with exactly that as an undergrad during college, and my professor and mentor, Dr. Susan Myster, introduced me to her colleague Dr. Tony Falsetti, who ultimately recommended me for the position.

The Gap did not hire me. Fortunately, the Smithsonian did. I made the call to accept the position from a pay phone at the Fish Market on King Street. I loved Virginia and the D.C. area, the weight of all that history. I will never forget that call.

I feel most at home in museums, and working behind the walls of one of the best of them remains my favorite job. Whenever I need an escape or place to reflect and find some peace in my own life, I go find it at a museum. Art evokes emotion, and sometimes the best way to reset is to let it wash over you.

At the repatriation lab of the Smithsonian, I was the first one in the lab every morning and usually the last to leave. I dedicated myself to it. Day after day, I was immersed in skeletal analysis, working with diverse collections. It was an amazing education in skeletal variation. I got to work on materials from sites throughout the Great Plains and Alaska as I had with archaeological materials from Minnesota and the Dakotas while in college. After two years, my contract was terminated due to lack of funding, so I applied to graduate school. To have a career in anthropology, it was obvious I would need a doctoral degree. In pursuit of that goal, I started coursework for my master's degree at the University of Nebraska. Dr. Karl Reinhard, a Peruvian specialist, bioarchaeologist, and mummiologist, offered me a full ride. While I worked on my degree, I also interned at the local medical examiner's office. I attended autopsies every morning at 8:00 a.m. before my classes for the day began. I learned how to cut for autopsy and assisted in everything they'd let me be a part of. I did this for two years.

I studied anthropology and forensic science and went to crime scenes with the forensic pathologist Dr. Matthias Okoye. He made me outline the chapters of various forensic pathology textbooks as part of my internship. As we performed autopsies, he drilled me with questions about the readings he had assigned. Dr. Okoye was Nigerian and also held a law degree. He believed in teaching through the Socratic method. He would say, "Today, I will show you how to do this. Tomorrow, you will do it for yourself." We attended my first meeting of the American Academy of Forensic Sciences and published three papers together.

After graduating I went to Chicago to work with Dr. Mitra Kalelkar in the Cook County Medical Examiner's Office on a research project that looked extensively at gunfire injuries. The busy medical examiner's office had thousands of cases, and many of the victims had been shot, then recovered from those injuries only to be shot again and die. Dr. Kalelkar called them "old warriors." I felt at home living in downtown Chicago, like I had in D.C., and I could have made either city my home. Both places were temporary stops in my pursuit of a PhD. I soon left Chicago for Knoxville, in eastern Tennessee, which was a huge adjustment.

The University of Tennessee in Knoxville was the premier school to study forensic anthropology. It was home to the famous Body Farm established by Dr. Bill Bass. As grad students, we also worked cases for law enforcement all over eastern Tennessee, everything from skeletal remains found in the woods to sorting debris from a home with a meth lab that had blown up with victims allegedly trapped inside. To help pay for books I worked the night shift in the morgue as an autopsy technician.

The Chicago study would be the key to landing a job two years later with the United Nations in the Balkans, investigating war crimes. Clea Koff, whom I had met in the Nebraska program, was a close friend. She had recently written a book called *The Bone Woman*, about her work for the International Criminal Tribunal for Rwanda. Her father was British and her mother Tanzanian, so she approached her work in a very personal way. She showed me how forensics could be used for human rights work and encouraged me to apply for a job with the International Criminal Tribunal for the former Yugoslavia. When I interviewed for the job, I was asked a lot about the research I had done in Chicago, the in-depth study of gunfire injuries. That was the knowledge and experience they were looking for.

At its core, the job in the Balkans was to do trauma analysis, to piece together the skeletal injuries demonstrating the cause of death and patterns of injuries that could be used as evidence in trial. This was in 1999, and the war in Kosovo had recently ended. The victims were Muslims, killed by the Serb military and hired militias. Some had been shot in their homes or in fields or at work. Most had been shot multiple times with AK-47 rifles, which fragmented their bones into tiny pieces. Their bodies were buried and then exhumed by our forensic team, and the shattered bones had to be glued back together to determine the type and extent of injuries. I got the job and took a leave of absence from UT to go on missions to Kosovo, Bosnia, and

Croatia over the next two years.

I flew to Macedonia alone. The airport in Kosovo wasn't open yet, and so crossing the border meant meeting the United Nations caravan in Skopje. We were given a two-hour training on how to watch out for landmines. Basically, I was told to avoid stepping anywhere or touching anything that looked suspicious. I looked around me, having never before been in a war-torn city. I saw the garbage piles blockading sidewalks and roads—there was no sanitation service. I witnessed power outages that would last for days. I saw bomb craters in the middle of city streets and packs of dogs roaming the landscape. Everything I saw looked suspicious.

It was a job that required wearing many hats and usually working fifteen-hour days, which would foreshadow my eventual career in anthropology. We excavated graves and worked with military personnel from five different North Atlantic Treaty Organization (NATO) countries. NATO provided security but also the police and transitional justice system for the newly developing nation. We performed autopsies and skeletal analyses and talked to the families of missing persons. Sometimes we had to inform them of their loved one's identity and cause of death. I analyzed hundreds of remains. Later, as the chief forensic anthropologist, I oversaw the analyses and reports of all the others working with our massive international team.

In the Serb-controlled areas, snipers sometimes fired upon United Nations vehicles. In Croatia, protesters wanted the UN to leave, as the organization had set about prosecuting Croatian generals, viewed there as war heroes; protests ensued, and we became the enemy from multiple sides. It reminded me of a bumper sticker I saw once in Berkeley that read: "What is the difference between a terrorist and a freedom fighter?" Standing knee-deep in bodies, with protests coming from the side we were there trying to help, made me think about that bumper sticker and how perception was everything.

Before we could excavate, we had to show the NATO explosive ordnance team where to search for landmines or hidden explosives based on where we wanted to dig. I remember walking to a small graveyard on the side of a mountain in Kosovo and pointing out the area where we wanted to excavate. Years later, it occurred to me that as the one who led the way, I think I would have found any mines had they been there.

More than seven thousand men were killed in six days at Srebrenica, a silver-mining town in eastern Bosnia-Herzegovina established as a UN safe-haven. Countless other examples from the region and around the world would show the same. For me, security at home meant calling 911. But who do you call when it is your nation's military killing its own people? The civilians had been utterly helpless. Doing the hard work for war crimes prosecution did not restore their loss, but many of these civilians fled during the conflict, and they did not know what had happened to their children, or their fathers, or their husbands, and that meant the women and other survivors had yet to grieve.

Our work—informing them of what had happened, trying to bring them that harsh reality—was all they would ever know about the deaths of their family members. They wanted the truth. They needed it. That reinforced the idea that forensics and the court system could enforce human rights. I later took that idea to projects in Nigeria, Peru, and even Marianna, Florida.

In the war-torn Balkans—like with most conflicts around the world—the survivors were largely women. They were mothers and grandmothers. I connected with the grandmothers, who, despite great challenges of poverty and illiteracy, were now becoming politically active. They were hiring lawyers and lobbying politicians. They were engaging international media. It was all for one seemingly simple reason: so they could find their missing loved ones and bring them home.

I would always call my grandmother from Kosovo or anywhere else I later traveled, and she would say, "I am there with you. I am looking at the moon right now, look at it. See, we are looking at the same thing, so we are together."

Two years later, I went back to Tennessee to finish my degree. I knew by this point that I wanted to be a mother. I was dedicated to my work and as passionate about it as ever, but I felt like having a family gave me a reason to do the work. I put the international missions on hold when I became pregnant with my son Sean.

Soon, with a doctoral degree and a six-month-old baby whom I had barely put down, we moved. The boyfriend I had followed to D.C. became my husband, and his job was now bringing us to Tampa. It was supposed to be temporary. I wanted to spend as much time as possible with Sean, and I wanted to write a book about the work I did in the Balkans. Sean and I were inseparable for the first eighteen months of his life. I never had a babysitter, and I never had a need for one. He was one of those babies who would sleep as long as I held him. So, of course, I indulged him.

I loved to watch him sleep. His little face is the face I still see when I look at him, though he is now becoming a man and he towers over me. His is also the face I couldn't push from my mind when, in early 2012, I took my first road trip north on Interstate 75 to Marianna.

Chapter 4

THE BATTLE OF BOOT HILL

The state of Florida was absolutely fine with letting us map the cemetery, so long as the work stopped short of digging up bones.

To start, I applied for a $5,000 grant through the university for what I thought would be a few weeks of fieldwork with my team of students and colleagues. That would cover a simple survey of the burial ground with Rich's ground-penetrating radar to determine the location and identity of the graves. While I waited for the funding, I reached out to the FDLE agents who handled the investigation, hoping we could share information. I also began to contact the families of boys who wanted the remains of their brothers and uncles returned.

Robert Straley helped me by firing off an email to his growing list of former wards of the state, a group that had grown to include more than five hundred men who all shared similar experiences at the reform school.

"There are several conflicting stories about the location of graves and the cemeteries," Robert wrote. "We are trying to reach anyone who ever saw a burial, saw the cemetery, or attended a funeral. If you have direct, firsthand knowledge please let us know. Your information could be essential even if it seems basic."

Tips flooded back to him, and he turned over a handful of promising leads from men who remembered seeing a cemetery on what had been the white boys' side of campus.

Robert quickly became my friend. We had long talks, and he always made me feel like what I was doing was a good thing.

The five-hour drive to and from Marianna was rough. The drive was like the road itself, lonely and desolate. Five hours was too much time to reflect—too much time to replay all the criticism we were hearing. Word was starting to spread: outsiders bent on getting the facts were planning on poking around the Dozier school cemetery. The place had employed generations of locals, and many of them were proud of the time they had spent teaching young men right from wrong, even if those lessons were learned at the end of a leather strap.

Adding fuel to the fire was the fact that the state closed the school in June 2011, after 111 years of operation. Gone were more than two hundred jobs in a region that desperately needed them. The state cited budget concerns and a drop in demand for beds in juvenile lockups across the state, but the locals grumbled about the bad publicity from out-of-towners trying to stir up old trouble. Many accused the White House Boys of lying about their time at Dozier, either for publicity or to sell the books that some of them had written. The antagonism came from familiar quarters: the town's white power brokers, who wished to preserve their version of history. They said the boys were bad enough to be sent to the reformatory in the first place, so a little discipline was good for them and probably served to make them better citizens. It was only a matter of time before they started accusing me, too, of trying to profit off the tragic story of the systemic failure of the program.

Leading the criticism was a man named Dale Cox, a local armchair historian who took potshots on his blog and wrote stories arguing that nothing was amiss in the old graveyard. At the same time, the local weekly newspaper published columns that were critical of the White House Boys.

"The recent negative publicity about treatment of residents at Arthur G. Dozier School for Boys (formally Florida Industrial School for Boys) which has now spread to international proportions has generated outrage from many local residents who worked there during the era in question," wrote publisher Sid Riley in the *Jackson County Times*. "They feel that they are the victims of a 'witch hunt' motivated by media sensationalism and the personal greed of two former detainees of that reform school. Since the school was opened in 1900 there have been hundreds of thousands of man hours expended by thousands of hard-working employees who were dedicated to helping the wayward boys who were sent there. As a result of their work, thousands of Florida's troubled youth were positively influenced. Many of these former employees have now come forward in defense of the administration of that period, and the environment which existed on the campus of Dozier at that time."

The White House Boys had, in fact, brought an exploratory civil class-action lawsuit against the state and a former disciplinarian named Troy Tidwell, who was known to the boys as the One-Armed Man for the fact that he'd lost a limb at age six, when the shotgun he was leaning on accidentally went off. Their suit was eventually dismissed on a technicality, but not before Tidwell was made to answer questions during a four-hour videotaped deposition.

The White House Boys said Troy Tidwell, in his mid-eighties now, was a monster who forced them face-first on a cot, made them bite a pillow, and brought the strap he was holding down so hard that they could still feel the blows fifty years later. They said he enjoyed it. It didn't matter that he was a doting grandpa to his own kin, or that he liked to dance the foxtrot and flirt with the perfume-counter ladies at the mall in Dothan, Alabama. Hundreds of former wards thought the man should be locked away. However, the accused former guard called it state-sanctioned "spanking" and said he hit kids only six to ten times per infraction with a thick leather strap, but never hard enough to draw blood. He denied ever telling a boy to bite a pillow.

"And when you would spank these boys, how many times would you hit them with that leather strap?" a lawyer asked Tidwell during a deposition in 2009.

"I used my own judgment," he said. "If I gave him maybe six, it would be a minor offense—sometimes eight. And there's a possibility that maybe ten if it was serious enough."

"Never gave more than ten?"

"Not to my knowledge," the old man said. "I didn't want it. If you're at home and you take your belt off, and you hit the couch or mattress with your belt six, eight, or ten times, you know whether or not, if you use good judgment, whether that's enough for a spanking or not."

"When you spanked these boys, did you ever hit them thirty or forty . . ."

"No."

". . . or more times?"

"Never."

"Never happened?"

"I never did."

"Did you ever have any of the boys that when you were through spanking them were bloody from the spanking that they'd received?"

"No."

"You never . . ."

"Well, I had a chance to see some of the boys that were spanked, and it would sometimes be a blue spot on their buttocks, or pink, you know."

"Never saw any boys that had been through a spanking that were black and blue, bruised from the middle of the back . . ."

"Like I said, there were blue spots on their buttocks."

Sure, he said: sometimes they had to fetch two or three boys from the kitchen to come to the White House to hold the victim down. It was for their own good.

"I shouldn't take up your time like this," Tidwell told the lawyer for the White House Boys during his deposition, "but one boy in particular, he was a nice guy and he was planning on running one night, and his house leader called me and I went down and talked with him. He didn't run. He made his rank. He was like a teacher's aide in the classroom. A smart kid. But he came up in rank, went home, and went through school, ran for insurance commissioner. Did actually good there getting votes. And his last time coming by to see me, he was driving a Cadillac, shiny, nice suit of clothes, dressed real nice. Came in and visited me for a while. And when he started to leave, he pointed his finger, and he said, 'I want to tell you something, Mr. Tidwell. You're responsible for me being where I am today. If I had ran away like I had planned, I don't know what would have happened.'"

THE FIRST TIME I went to Marianna in 2012, I went alone. Along the way, I stopped in Tallahassee at the FDLE headquarters to meet with their investigators who wrote the Dozier reports in 2009. I hoped to leave with copies of the interview transcripts and other records I requested several weeks prior. After our meeting, I followed them an hour's drive west down Interstate 10 to Marianna.

We drove straight to Boot Hill, a small clearing at the end of a dirt road where thirty-one metal crosses stood in a very small clearing. At that time, only the fenced perimeter and around a mulberry tree were mowed per the instructions of the local jail warden. The jail was located down the hill from Boot Hill and the warden's mother made him mulberry pies, so he kept the trail to it cleared. Otherwise, the woods encroached on the burial ground's fence on all sides.

As we walked into the woods, the agents pointed to where they'd found a pile of broken concrete crosses from the 1960s—grave markers from a previous era that had been cast aside in the woods. The brush was tough to navigate through without a machete. I hacked my way into the thick of it. The agents seemed concerned for my well-being, walking behind me through the brush as sticks and thorns caught on our clothing and tangled in my hair. "Be careful," they continued to warn. "I am quite fine," I told them, laughing. Men often tell me that I don't look like someone who would do this kind of work. *What should I look like?* I often ask them. I think the blond highlights and manicured nails lead to false assumptions. They think I'm fragile. Men will smile and graciously open the door, then expect compliance with their expectations. It's fine until you show initiative or assume leadership. That's when things get difficult.

Even through the thick of it, the significance of the large oak tree was evident. I tried to make my way to it and confirmed with them: Is this where they found the crosses? Yes, piled here, and even more scattered throughout the area, they said.

"I bet the graves are here," I told them. "The trees give it away. Old cemeteries are landscaped like this, with oaks sometimes marking the entrance, or Southern cedars marking the perimeter."

They shrugged, unconvinced. Maybe, maybe not. No one would ever know, according to them.

I could tell they were skeptical. I was excited to find out if I was right. Science is just that: ask a question, devise a way to find the answer, execute the plan, and learn the answer. I wanted to come back with our crew and start on the fieldwork right away.

"Can the GPR find a bullet?" one agent asked me.

"If I was searching for a bullet, I would use a metal detector," I said.

The question came out of nowhere, and I wasn't sure what it meant, if they knew something they weren't saying. I explained how ground-penetrating radar worked and how metal detectors worked and the difference between the two.

"If you're searching for metal, especially near the surface, a high-quality metal detector is best. GPR data will reflect off metal, but the metal is an obstruction, and if there's a lot, the results are obscured," I said. "With GPR, we are looking at the consistency in soils, obtrusions into the natural stratigraphy or objects under the ground's surface that interrupt the signal. A disruption, if you will, but one in which the size, shape, and depth have to be interpreted. Is it a burial? A buried tree stump? A pop can? And so on."

"No, I mean could you see a bullet in a skull?" she persisted.

"Not with GPR," I said. People always asked that question. "There is no little body outline. You know how with fishing radar you see a little fish? Yeah, we do not have that. It would be awesome, but it doesn't work that way."

"But if there were metal," she asked, "like if they were chained, you would be able to see that?"

"It's possible," I explained, "if there are chains around or with the bodies that would stand out as clearly a lot of metal. Any time there is a container or objects with a body, there's more data to interpret."

Her questions gave me the impression there was more to the story than their report reflected, and we both knew it. The agents were bound to the confines of a criminal investigation, so the official scope and interpretations were limited.

What happened to the boys at the school was now a historical justice question. Our goal would be to find the facts about what happened, figure out who was involved, try to determine why it occurred, and find out where they were buried. It required a very different perspective and scope than the FDLE inquiry. We didn't have to work within the confines of a criminal investigation. We weren't concerned with statutes of limitations, or when certain acts like child rape became statutorily criminal.

We stomped out of the woods, climbed in our cars, and drove to the south campus, where we parked near the superintendent's old administration building. A representative from the Department of Juvenile Justice joined us for the remaining tour. They showed me the decrepit, old building where they found the ledgers and other records. Everyone on their team got sick following the time they spent in the musty basements, crawl spaces, and abandoned rooms. Mold grew on everything, especially the paper records. They had waded through it, room after room.

The buildings looked abandoned, as if everyone got up and left one day, which is actually what they did. The air conditioner was running, and the lights were on. The department was maintaining this part of the campus, pending its forthcoming sale. Even so, furniture, records, all the other things were left in place, and it felt odd, sort of postapocalyptic.

We walked the entire campus as the agents pointed out the buildings lining a long boulevard, split by a median, that stretched through the spine of the grounds. The main part of campus, the last big section in operation until June 2011, was surrounded by a tall chain-link fence topped with unspooled razor wire, and inside a booth at the entrance sat a security guard, an older white man who still operated the gate for the rare visitor. Right outside of the perimeter fence were thick North Florida woods and swamps, in all directions. All that space, extending beyond the interstate, had once been part of the school's fourteen hundred acres of rolling cotton fields, bucolic pastures, swamps, and clay mines.

I thought about the superintendent I'd read about in the archives, the one who in 1919 used school funds to purchase additional adjacent land in his own name. He sent young prisoners over to cut down the forests with axes, then sold the wood back to the school for a profit. I wondered where his parcel was. Was that what brought the property up to sixteen hundred acres for a few years? Were any parcels ever sold separately? They should have investigated the school as a RICO case—under the Racketeer Influenced and Corrupt Organizations Act—I told my tour guides, half joking.

The first and only security fence went up in 1981, which was why so many boys could escape or at least attempt to run away over the years. So many of them tried, repeatedly. The big old ledgers were full of the dates of their escapes, almost always followed in the next column by the dates of their captures. That must've taken so much courage, I thought, to be all of ten or twelve or fourteen years old, to wait for the right moment, probably under the cover of darkness, then make a break for it into the great unknown. So brave and so desperate, to run away into the middle of nowhere. I pictured my own sons locked away for skipping school—something I'd done when I was young—and hating this place or missing home so hard that they'd risk a beating in the White House for the chance to get away. Then, where did you run?

Boy hunting. That was what the men who ran the school called the search parties over the years. When a boy turned up missing at bed check or ducked off into the woods on some Saturday trip two miles into town, word spread across campus and all hands showed up to help look. I'd read that the cottage fathers often carried pistols on their hips or shotguns on their shoulders and they'd hatch a plan, then pile into pickups and creep down dirt roads for miles in every direction, headlights sweeping through thick woods—boy hunting.

They were helped by the natural and built landscape. The city of Marianna and Highway 90 sat to the north. The Chipola River was two miles east. For years, they called in trustees from nearby Apalachee Correctional, the adult prison. The Dozier kids called the trustees Dog Boys—they brought bloodhounds to help search—and the hardened prisoners who caught kids in the night could be especially vicious. I read testimony from former wards who tried to escape and wound up riding back to campus inside dog cages in the backs of pickup trucks.

The punishment for running, or even talking about trying to make a break for it, was almost always a beating in the White House. I tried not to imagine the rage that might be manifest in an adult disciplinarian who had been woken from his sleep and made to search for hours in the dark woods and swamps for an adolescent runaway, then administer spankings to teach the boy a lesson about running. I wondered if an especially brutal whipping taught the lesson the guards wanted to impart or if it just made a young ward more dedicated to getting away.

I'd heard the White House Boys talk about "Pukes." That was what they called the do-gooders and tattletales who reported would-be runaways to guards before they had a chance to make a break. Sometimes a Puke was right, and sometimes a Puke was lying for special privileges from the cottage fathers. The result was always the same: a trip to the White House—or the Ice Cream Factory, as some called it in the later years, on account of the whippings that went on inside.

We left the administration building and walked back over a slight hill to the edge of a row of structures. Across the small clearing and parking lot stood the White House, a low-slung, sturdy building with thick walls. We couldn't go inside—no one had a key. It was sealed, they said, ever since those five old men called the White House Boys held their ceremony and told stories about the torture they faced inside. Our tour guide told me they'd ask around about who might have a key and let me know. I didn't want to look inside. I felt like I already had.

Many of the buildings, including the cottages, were structurally unsafe, collapsing, the roofs caving in. The tiles and shingles were made of asbestos, and mold seemed to be growing on every surface. I was warned to watch my step, to stay out of certain buildings. Danger was the theme. I felt like they were trying to scare me off.

We ate lunch after, off campus, and the FDLE agents told me more about their quest to try to retrieve records from the storage pits. A box of letters had been found in the attic of one of the chapels, sent in the early 1900s from parents who were demanding the release of their children, complaining to the governor about the treatment of their children or the condition of the reformatory.

Where were the letters now? I asked. I would love to see them and document them as part of the project, I said.

Destroyed, said the employee. They had no evidentiary value. Anything not deemed to have investigative use had been destroyed.

I was devastated. Personal letters no doubt would have told the stories of mothers and fathers reacting to the school's practices, pleading with state leaders for mercy—and now they'd been destroyed in the state's final chapter on the reform school it created and protected.

One important exception: the original ledgers listing the personal information—names, parents' names, home addresses, arrival and departure dates—for the thousands of boys as they were admitted to the school upon arrival. The ledgers—printed by the Evans and Cogswell Company, the same South Carolina company that had printed Confederate currency during the Civil War—were hauled to the state archives in Tallahassee, along with a few other historical records the archivists requested.

What about the original printing press? I wondered. The school had at one time handled all document printing services for the government in Tallahassee on state-of-the-art printing presses. The school even published its own newspaper, *Yellow Jacket*. Boys ran a brickmaking plant as well, and at full tilt it could produce more than twenty thousand bricks a day.

All the printing shop equipment, where had it been taken? They were not sure. Many of the buildings had been full of equipment and records, but following the FDLE investigation, and once the school closed in 2011, lots of things sort of disappeared.

I checked into a hotel along Interstate 10, and the next morning I drove to the Jackson County Sheriff's Office for an appointment with the sheriff. I met instead with a major named Donnie Branch, who was stern and didn't smile. We met alone in his office. I felt uncomfortable. It wasn't the sort of response I usually got working with law enforcement. I told him we were going to be using ground-penetrating radar to locate and document the burial ground at the old Dozier school. I mentioned the letter I sent to the sheriff's office on University of South Florida letterhead requesting copies of any records regarding any interaction between his agency and the school. I was particularly interested in reading the reports they would have for each of their death investigations. There were cases where boys either died at the school or while trying to run away, and the sheriff's office responded. That was true for George Owen Smith, among others. Each death investigation would have produced a report, or at a minimum, a few pages of notes. For example, the sheriff's office investigated the murder of a ward named Earl Wilson, a crime for which four other boys were arrested, convicted by a jury, and sentenced to life in prison. I provided a list of the cases I had inquired about for their records.

I also used the opportunity to invite his detectives and crime scene investigators to join us on-site, for a training day, if they wanted to learn how to use ground-penetrating radar and other skills that might help when they worked outdoor homicide scenes or searched for clandestine burials in missing person's cases. We did this all the time, working with agencies around Central Florida.

Branch told me that the Jackson County Sheriff's Office never responded to any case involving the school, as it was not their jurisdiction. He said they never went on the school property, and that he had never been there.

"These are historic cases, before 1960, before our time," I said. "The records would probably be in archives someplace, right?"

The sheriff's office did not have archives, he said, and anyway, sheriff's deputies had never investigated a death at that school or a death related to it.

"Strange that the local paper always mentions sheriff's deputies being on scene, or investigating, or interviewing some witness?" I pressed with a smile and tilted my head.

His office was less than two miles from the school in a town with only one main road. The reform school was the largest employer for more than a hundred years, and the local sheriff provided security and transportation for thousands of boys over the years. What was more, thousands of boys had run away, only to be caught all over the county and brought back to campus, sometimes by the sheriff's deputies themselves. One such boy, who was local, was shot in his own home after running away.

The old newspapers and coroner's reports list sheriff's deputies among those present at the scenes where boys died off campus. Sheriff Barkley Gause led the investigation himself into the death of George Owen Smith when his body was reported found in Marianna after running away from the school in 1940.

The conviction of Frank Murphy for the murder of Eddie Black in 1949, both of whom were incarcerated at the reform school where Black's death occurred, was vacated in 1973 because Sheriff Ernst Barnes questioned the fourteen-year old alone before his trial and coerced an involuntary confession through threats he made to him.

All these cases were listed by name in the letter I sent requesting the reports. Yet, with a blank stare, showing no emotion at all, Branch repeated himself: The sheriff's office had no role. They were never there.

He recommended that I speak with the police chief, who happened to be a local history enthusiast. I asked where the county archives were located, and Branch told me they kept old records in the basement of the courthouse. Again, I was to go through the police chief for any records, even those of the county and sheriff's offices.

It made no sense. City police chiefs did not work for the county nor did they oversee the sheriff's records. City and county governments were separate entities. I knew I was being handled. I went to my car. *Where the hell was I?*

The school opened in 1900, when fewer than nine hundred people lived in the county seat. Even today, the police department has only seventeen sworn officers for Marianna's some 7,000 residents, and the school is outside the city limits, squarely in the county's jurisdiction. I knew for a fact that in 1934, the sheriff's actual office was in the county courthouse in the heart of the city, because a mob lynched a Black man and hanged him from an oak tree outside the sheriff's window. If one thing is true about law enforcement, it is that jurisdiction is critical to missing person's cases. If a person goes missing from one or another jurisdiction, and it is unclear exactly where he or she was last seen, reports might not be filed or properly investigated. You have to know where one jurisdiction begins and another ends.

I drove to the courthouse, looking for the keeper of the town's written history. There I met an archivist. She was an older woman, petite, but not a wallflower. I gave her a list of the records I was looking for: coroner's reports, sheriff and police reports, court records with specific names and dates. The trial of the murder of Earl Wilson, the discovery of the body of George Owen Smith, and so on.

I explained I was looking for information about the deaths of some of the children who died at the reform school, and that their families were looking to find their graves. I also told her we were documenting Boot Hill as a historic burial ground.

"Inmates," she corrected me sharply. She disapproved. The tone in her voice said it more clearly than her words. "They were inmates. Not children. These boys were not sent here for singing too loud in the church choir."

She told me she did not have any of the records I asked for and suggested I speak with the police chief.

Coincidence?

I suspected Branch had already called her, as they clearly seemed to be reading from the same script. So, I told her I just met with Major Branch at the sheriff's office and that he sent me here, as she was the best person to help me.

I conceded that, of course, everyone sent to the reform school was an inmate, sentenced by a judge. Nonetheless, their families would like to visit their graves. In my head, I prayed for patience and wondered if there was any way to win her over.

"Seems understandable they would want to know where the graves are?" I asked. "Right?"

No. She did not believe most of them had families.

"They was throwaways," she replied, refusing to budge. She was not going to concede the slightest bit of empathy. I would come to experience that same reaction over and over. Resolved in her opinion, she came across as angry. I just wasn't sure how much of it stemmed from my presence.

Throwaway children. That was the phrase used in the FDLE report. Whose narrative is this? I wondered.

For the record: I do not believe we throw away children.

Resolved that I was not going to leave empty-handed, I smiled again, pausing to ask another question, seemingly oblivious to her mounting frustration in the hope that acting aloof would disarm her.

"If you could kindly just check for the coroner's reports, there must be something, and I could check it off my list?" I tilted my head this time when I smiled again, beseeching her.

She let out a deep sigh and said nothing, then disappeared around a corner as I stood there. I waited, unsure what was happening. She came back with a file. It was the inquest from the 1914 fire. That was all she could find, she said. As I read it and took pictures of the yellowed, handwritten documents, she talked about other notable men who came from the area and a fire that killed workers at a sawmill. She said those were historical projects that deserved my attention, more interesting and important than the one I was doing. She lit up talking about those other examples and offered to share a lot of information if I wanted those files; they would be no trouble to find.

I thanked her and told her that perhaps I would, someday. I was ready to go home.

On my way out of town, I again drove back past the abandoned buildings on the school grounds, and everything about Dozier and the highway leading to it felt haunted. Not haunted like slamming doors and fragmented visions of ghosts, though there were plenty of stories like that. I mean the haunting one feels in a place gripped with so much trauma that it lingers even after everyone is gone. The worn pavers of an old road that were molded by all those who passed over it. Rusty bunk beds had been crammed into abandoned dorm rooms where boys slept two to a bed. Windowsills had been carved with initials, dates, hometowns, stick figures, and sailboats. I thought about the thousands of children who had passed through, as well as those who never made it home.

It was hard not to fixate on the fear the boys must have felt riding for hours from South Florida to that isolated town. That was what haunted me—their fear. Hundreds of miles of nothing but forest and fields, the same Florida blur for hours and hours, as if they were a million miles away from home. Most of the boys had never been away from home before being sentenced. It was one of the first questions I asked the men I spoke with. They traversed that journey not knowing what awaited them.

I knew their fates, and I couldn't think about it without feeling my stomach churn.

One of the men I'd grown friendly with asked, "Why didn't anyone come for me?"

His question was rhetorical.

"No one saved us," he added. "No one came. Until you."

Many of the men who were abused at the school had a deep need to confide their experiences. They shared their stories of violence and being raped. They shared their suffering and fear. Some recalled that the guards threatened them as they left Dozier.

We know where you live, and if you ever tell, we'll come find you.

So they never told anyone. Sitting beside me, crying and shaking, they confided their truth. They felt safe enough to do so.

Doing this work was a privilege. It was also a heavy weight to carry. I don't know how to listen and research and learn from people who have been through such tragedy without connecting to them. I came to care deeply about their quest for justice. The obstacles put in their way needlessly by people who had other motives offended me. Feeling the survivors' trembling hands squeeze mine as they told me their story was a view into what was truly evil. That door, once opened, was never really shut. I can't erase what I have seen or heard. If I allow myself to think about it, it feels overwhelming and sad. Relive the moment we shared. Inhale the musty, dank smell of the buildings in ruins. Feel the coldness and wet inside the concrete cells of the White House. The nausea in my stomach with Robert Straley as we walked around the "rape room," a dank basement, and his memory of his time down there, a nightmare from which he was never free.

Their injuries were not my own. This was my job, to find the missing, to search for graves, and to excavate the bones of those who didn't survive. To be good at this job—to be really good at it—passion and empathy must guide the way. Separation must also exist, though. It can be both an opening and a darkness. To seek the truth but find such horror—to search for a grave and then hold the crumbling bones of a child in your hand.

I've done this type of work for more than twenty years, and never has the family of someone who was missing or murdered told me they didn't want to know the details. No one chooses ignorance. They want to know.

No one can ever make it right. No restitution is enough. The deed cannot be undone. Justice itself is elusive.

There can be acceptance, though, and that is what carries one forward. I've learned that only truth can enable healing, and that's what led me to Boot Hill.

Chapter 5

"SATAN HAS HIS SEAT"

My team and I probably looked like farmers at planting season as we mapped the site and created large grids to run remote sensing. Rich Estabrook walked behind the GPR, a contraption that looked like a jogging stroller. I followed him. Ground-penetrating radar was an excellent tool for finding buried archaeological sites, including detecting burial shafts. The GPR recorded hundreds of subsurface images every inch, and Rich watched the monitor, noting places where the radar picked up changes.

"We've got an anomaly right here," he said, pointing with his toe.

I pushed little orange flags into the earth in spots where the machine detected that the ground had been disturbed.

Inmates from the nearby county jail helped us clear trees and underbrush, opening a clearing around the old oak I'd seen last time I visited, north of the pipe crosses. When we had run the GPR over the newly cleared land and studied the data, it seemed clear that the burials weren't limited to the initial clearing. More lay in the woods. So, we had to clear more land.

I told the students who had joined us to dig a shallow trench about a foot deep, a standard archaeological procedure called "ground-truthing," a way to peek into the earth without disturbing any remains.

They grabbed shovels and started digging a trench five and a half meters long and a half meter wide. They used hand tools to smooth the walls of the narrow trench, revealing different colors in the soil where someone had dug a hole in this spot nearly a century before us. This was definitely a burial, but we didn't know just how deep we'd have to dig to find it.

The work was slow, and everything had to be documented and augmented by archival research and interviews. We researched the deeper history of the school, as well as the system that would create such a place.

CALLED "THE CITY of Southern Charm," Marianna is the kind of place where preachers still pack churches—Baptist and Methodist churches are largest—and reenactors re-create the local Civil War battle like clockwork and sing "Dixie" at gatherings of the Sons of Confederate Veterans. The county had been settled by whites who were among the last American frontiersmen and -women, and the slow development and lack of cities meant the Southern frontier mores held strong.

Before the War between the States, giant plantations sprung up across Jackson County and enslaved people provided much of the field labor in the wealthy agricultural hub, with cotton fields for miles in every direction. That changed in September 1864, after a fight known as the Battle of Marianna. Confederate blood was spilled on Lafayette Street, and among the advancing Yankees were the 82nd and 86th Regiments, US Colored Infantry. They set fire to houses and to St. Luke's Episcopal Church and laid waste to a local home guard of old men and boys known as the Cradle and Grave Company. A quarter of the male population of Marianna died that day. When the Union soldiers left, heading west for Pensacola, behind them marched six hundred formerly enslaved men, women, and children who were freed after the fighting.

Reconstruction shook Jackson County. In 1865, Florida governor John Milton, who owned a sixty-three-hundred-acre plantation and enslaved over three hundred people there, gave his final address to the state legislature, saying he believed that "death would be preferable to reunion." He went home to his big plot in Jackson County and shot himself in the head.

Following the Civil War, the white establishment struggled with the new reality of a shattered class system. Their power hung in the balance. Sheriff's offices sprung up around the state to protect white citizens from violent militias and maintain peace. It was said that the threat of violence was so great, mothers preferred to send their sons to fight in the war.

In my own family, this held true when my great-great-grandfather joined the calvary for the US Army. His mother was so fearful he would be killed by Missouri bushwhackers, the pro-Confederate militia, that she insisted he join the US Army at fifteen, and she lied about his age for him.

Between 1869 and 1871, as the federal government began granting unclaimed land to more and more formerly enslaved Black citizens, vigilante killings ensued and communities descended into disorder and furious outbursts of violence against Black citizens.

Throughout the South, more than four hundred thousand acres of abandoned or federally confiscated land was granted to forty thousand freed people. The Southern Homestead Act of 1866 and Freedmen's Bureau helped distribute land and loan money for farming. In the years that followed, there was a significant increase in Black land ownership, farmland ownership, and business development. By 1910, over fifteen million acres or fourteen percent of American farms were owned by 210,000 Black landowners. However, the lack of documentation for citizenship and land ownership made it difficult for freed people to acquire and maintain their land. White violence helped enforce Jim Crow policies, forcing people from their land. By some estimates, more than 150 people died in Jackson County in the three years that became known as the Jackson County War, an emblem of the residue of postwar hatred and greed that endured for generations. Jackson was notorious for being the most violent Reconstruction-era county in Florida.

As more sheriff's offices opened around the state, their duties expanded to include things like collecting taxes. The law was viewed as inefficient, and townsmen saw it as their duty to exact their brand of justice. Whitecap societies, largely comprised of poor rural farmers, organized under the auspices of keeping law and order. These mobs of vigilantes started lynching suspected lawbreakers and exacting other acts of violence against Black individuals and businesses, and eventually grew into the Ku Klux Klan, making the way for spectacle lynchings that would draw in thousands of people from beyond the local community.

Popular works such as *The Clansman: A Historical Romance of the Ku Klux Klan* by Thomas Dixon documented the rise of the Klan and created an image of freed Blacks as violent savages who were going to rise up and oppress and rape whites. What most terrified the white establishment was the idea that eventually Blacks would rule over whites, a notion fostered by Dixon, who claimed that eighteen million Southerners supported his belief in the need for segregation. The adaptation of his book into the film *The Birth of a Nation* was the longest film made at that time. It glamorized the Klan. The message in it was simple and clear: the KKK had to protect white Southerners by maintaining law and order through segregation and by any means necessary.

With only a fledgling law enforcement system in place, the door was left open for white hysteria and mob rule, and both grew like wildfire. The stark reality was that the increasing violence was being inflicted by white men against African Americans and their communities. Nationwide, more than four thousand Black men and women were lynched between the end of the Civil War and the beginning of World War II. Entire towns and communities of African Americans were wiped from the map in massive violent riots like those that occurred in Rosewood, Ocoee, and Marianna, Florida.

In *A People's History of Florida: 1513–1876*, Adam Wasserman wrote,

"Throughout the Reconstruction, Jackson County was the main site [in Florida] of political unrest and class struggle between planters and black laborers . . . Jackson County [was] so thoroughly dominated by the Klan at every institutional level as to render the county and state governments completely powerless to stop them."

"The sheriff of Jackson County, Thomas M. West, complained that public sentiment was so strongly opposed to him as sheriff that he did not feel safe to go outside of town and serve any legal process whatsoever. His life was constantly threatened. He was even openly assaulted in the streets of Marianna, severely beaten to the near-point of death," wrote Wasserman. In testimony to congressional hearings about the KKK, state senator Charles Pearce said, "Satan has his seat; he reigns in Jackson County."

Lynchings were not random acts of violence. Nor were they simply vigilante justice in the face of emerging law enforcement systems. Lynchings were organized practices, which served to inflict widespread fear into Black and white communities to maintain power by the ruling elite.

The Klan and former Confederate veterans aimed their violent acts at the Republican Party, which supported Black liberation and equality. According to Wasserman, more than 150 Republican leaders and prominent African Americans were killed. No one was ever arrested for those murders either.

Over the next sixty years, there would be nine recorded lynchings in Jackson County, but one stood apart.

A tree growing on the edge of the courthouse lawn stands as a reminder of the 1934 lynching of Claude Neal, an illiterate farmhand who was accused of raping and killing a white neighbor. When the girl's body was found, the Jackson County sheriff arrested Neal and secreted him from jail to try to protect him from the pursuing mob. After a week, a group of vigilantes known as the Committee of Six found and abducted Neal from a jail in Brewton, Alabama, and announced in the newspapers a lynching party. The Committee of Six tortured Neal as a crowd gathered at the dead girl's farm. Reporters estimated that five thousand people turned out from nine Southern states, their cars lining dirt roads in both directions. The rural whites cursed when they learned that the kidnappers had accidentally tortured Neal to death; many drove from hundreds of miles away in hopes that they could have a hand in the killing.

When the Committee of Six delivered Neal's corpse to the mob, people took fingers and toes as souvenirs and hanged the body from a tree in the courthouse square, then posed for photographs. Before the National Guard could arrive, the whites set fire to Black homes and businesses and chased Black residents from the city.

Coincidentally, the lynching and riots came within twenty-four hours of the death of Thomas Varnadoe, Glen Varnadoe's uncle, at the reform school less than two miles away. Despite the violence on October 26 and 27, churches reported strong attendance on Sunday, October 28. A newsman from Montgomery, Alabama, reported the same day, "Marianna goes on her placid way apparently unaware of the drama that has attracted the attention of a nation." Howard Kester, a Southern liberal who showed up to investigate the lynching for the National Association for the Advancement of Colored People (NAACP), noted, "On the whole the lynching was accepted . . . as a righteous act."

The spectacle lynching of Claude Neal resulted not only in his death but in injuries to more than two hundred African Americans throughout the community, who were forced from their homes, and businesses that were burned to the ground. Burning the structures made it harder for Black families to return to their property. Republicans and those who supported African American rights were all targets.

By the end of the nineteenth century, newly created laws enacted by a Democrat-controlled legislature in Florida as well as elsewhere throughout the South resulted in complete oppression of Blacks under restrictive laws known as the Black Codes, or Jim Crow, and they mandated segregation at every level. The Democratic Party during this period of Florida's history was focused on ensuring white power and control and negating civil rights for Blacks, especially freedmen.

Florida was the first state in the country to segregate its railroad cars. In his book *Arc of Justice*, Kevin Boyle wrote, "The legislature made it a crime to teach black and white children in the same classroom." Segregation permeated every aspect of life in Florida, and so no understanding of the unmarked burial ground can be understood without considering its impact: 74 percent of the boys buried at Boot Hill were Black.

Florida relied on the convict lease system to house and maintain individuals convicted of crimes. This system placed men, women, and children together into labor camps. In his book, *One Dies, Get Another: Convict Leasing in the American South, 1866–1928*, Matthew Mancini wrote: "Vagrancy was a widespread 'offense' in the South throughout the late nineteenth and early twentieth centuries, one that frequently led to outright peonage, but in Florida it was most pervasive."

The Jim Crow laws were enacted to control the movement and wealth of Blacks following emancipation. Vagrancy laws made it illegal to not have employment or a home address. Apprenticeship laws sent orphans and the children of poor families to work for plantations and labor bosses. The government denied citizenship to Blacks by refusing to issue birth and, later, death certificates. These codes were made possible by a loophole in the Thirteenth Amendment: "Neither slavery nor involuntary servitude, *except as a punishment for crime whereof the party shall have been duly convicted.*"

And here it was, the perfect recipe for the reform school we had come to investigate, and an explanation for how five-year-old children could be sentenced for crimes by a judge.

State legislatures worked to create an expanding body of Jim Crow laws, while ensuring cheap and easy labor. Mancini wrote, "Florida had 208 prisoners in January 1883, 291 two years later . . . There were 530 convicts in 1895 and 1,071 by 1904. There can be little doubt that part of the growth can be attributed to the assiduous enterprise of the [labor agents] . . . hired to pay the fines of vagrants and transport them to the stockades."

More than 90 percent of the leases were Black men.

Douglas A. Blackmon, in his book *Slavery by Another Name*, wrote,

"By 1900, the South's judicial system had been wholly reconfigured to make one of its primary purposes the coercion of African Americans to comply with the social customs and labor demands of whites."

Labor bosses worked for business owners from various industries who paid the fees of those convicted, or sometimes worked through labor agents who had control of the individuals for a period of one year or more.

The reform school was established to pluck children out of that system, to turn them into good and productive citizens, but it soon became its own labor enterprise.

It often went like this: A boy was picked up by a sheriff or his deputy and brought before a judge. No lawyers represented the boy. The authorities rarely if ever notified the boy's parents. None of those protections came until civil rights legislation, a century after emancipation. The labor agent paid the fine, and the defendant was sentenced for a minimum of a year. The labor boss covered housing, food, and maintenance of the convict, who worked to pay off the court fees, plus all expenses charged to him, such as housing and food.

At the reform school, once boys were to be released, the parents were told to send money for bus fare home. Those who could not afford it were not released. The boys were hired out by the school to local plantations or other industries to work for their bus ticket while accruing more expenses in the form of their room and board, falling more and more into debt. It was a vicious cycle designed to keep the wheel of cheap labor turning.

The men who ran the convict lease programs were not sworn law enforcement, yet they could legally discipline convicts in their care, even legally shoot and kill convicts who tried to escape. The same was true for the reform school.

The convict lease labor camps became notorious for deplorable conditions, the spread of infectious disease, and deaths due to brutal treatment such as flogging. Floggings often occurred at the hands of the whipping boss and were reminiscent of life on the plantations. In 1899, a House of Representatives investigative committee reported the convict labor camps were "a system of cruelty and inhumanity." One foreman was reported to have "beat sick men that died," and "some would be so badly beaten that they could not lay on their back for weeks."

Most of the deaths in the convict lease system were undocumented and underreported. The dead were often buried in folk burial grounds at the edges of fields without markers. In some cases, small wooden crosses were planted near the heads of the graves. Cedar trees often lined the entrance of unmarked burial grounds, leaving clues in the landscape. Burial shrouds were often used so their clothing could be given to the next convict.

A turning point came when a sixteen-year-old boy, whose autopsy report stated, "Death from Torture," died in 1887 from a whipping received in a convict labor camp. Public attention over this death and others at the camps grew, as did demands for reform and that children be taken out of the convict lease system. Calls for reform grew louder with the publication of J. C. Powell's *The American Siberia* in 1891, which described the brutal conditions of labor camps. It was in this environment that the idea for a reform and training school in Florida developed.

The death of Martin Talbert, a twenty-two-year-old South Dakota man on vacation in Florida, eventually led to the ban on leasing convicts in 1923. Shortly after he was sent to a labor camp after being arrested for vagrancy, witnesses reported he was beaten to death with a leather whip, though no one was ever charged in his murder. His family was told he died of an infection—malaria. They created a national outcry for reform.

Though Florida was among the last of the Southern states to outlaw the convict lease system for adults, reform or industrial schools for convicted juveniles were exempt. The use of child labor continued until labor laws forced reform in the 1960s, providing the first real protections for minors.

When Florida's leaders began looking for land on which to build a reformatory for children, up stepped offspring of former Florida governor John Milton, the staunch Confederate and slave owner who had killed himself near the end of the war. William H. Milton, who would later serve as superintendent of the school, offered the state more land and money than anyone else.

The reformatory opened on January 1, 1900, on a large plot south of Marianna. Farming on school property was profitable thanks to the free labor, and soon officials at the predominantly Black "school," under Milton's leadership, were asking the state for ways to make the boys' sentences longer. "Having so few inmates makes the crop come in slow," one superintendent wrote in 1906. We learned that Milton asked the governor to authorize that "incorrigible children be sent, without conviction, for an indefinite period, leaving the term to be fixed by the management."

Whatever idealistic notions citizens had for the program were overshadowed by the greed of the school's operators.

MEANWHILE, OUR LIST of names of boys who died in custody grew, and we carefully scrutinized the circumstances of their deaths. Dozens of men came forward to tell us what they remembered about the boys who died, how they were buried, and to share stories and memories about additional graves outside the Boot Hill area.

Scores of White House Boys believed there were two burial grounds when the school was segregated. Black boys and white boys had separate dorms and cafeterias and campuses. Nearly every facet of life was divided, all but where the beatings were administered. So wouldn't it make sense if they were buried in different cemeteries? We followed every lead. We paid particular attention to a field north of Boot Hill and an area south of the dining hall on the south campus. We weren't certain there were burials outside of Boot Hill, but we did believe there was sufficient evidence to search those areas.

Ovell Krell, who came to campus with her parents in 1941, immediately following the reported discovery of George Owen's body under a residence in Marianna, recalled specifically leaving the administration building with Superintendent Millard Davidson, who showed them George Owen's grave in a small burial ground near a wooded area to the south. That was nowhere near Boot Hill. She remembered seeing two rows of graves in front of a wooded area. Her brother's grave was topped by a fresh mound of dirt, and the burial ground had no markers or crosses.

There was no evidence that the graves were originally marked, since we couldn't find any historic markers, plot maps, or information about the specific locations.

We interviewed another former inmate, Philip Marchesani, who remembered seeing boxes of letters from parents asking about their children, letters to the children themselves, and maps of the school. All of it was inside a box, he said, stored in the attic of the chapel on the north campus in the 1960s. He told us that the maps were marked with two separate burial areas.

We knew about those letters from families, which the state had destroyed, but they didn't say whether the maps were recovered. It frustrated me that we never had a chance to go through the boxes of materials.

Since we suspected there was possibly another cemetery, we asked the state for permission to explore the south side of campus using GPR. They said no.

Almost immediately, Glen Varnadoe, who had made a promise to his dying sister to find their uncle's remains and repatriate them to the family plot, filed a complaint for declaratory and injunctive relief, asking the court to stop the planned sale of the property until someone could tell him where his uncle was buried so the family could relocate the remains. "There is substantial confusion and doubt whether Thomas' remains are buried on the North Campus or the South Campus that is being sold," his complaint read. "There is no valid reasonable basis for the DEP and the DJJ to refuse to provide the Varnadoes with access to Thomas' remains and allow the Varnadoes to disinter and relocate Thomas' remains to the family burial plot."

The state reversed its decision the next day.

"After careful consideration, we will work with the researchers on how best to provide them access to the site," Department of Juvenile Justice secretary Wansley Walters told reporters.

Glen Varnadoe had been writing letters to every political leader in Florida he could think of in preparation for what he knew might be a fight. He heard back from US senator Bill Nelson, the former astronaut who had been in Congress for more than a decade. Nelson, we'd later learn, had been such a successful politician undoubtedly for the fact that he understood people and pressure points. He brought the press and knew how to spread his message, which would prove incredibly helpful.

"I'm quite pleased that the state has chosen the path they have taken," Glen told the press. "I think it's the right thing to do, and I'm very pleased with the outcome. I think in the next 120 days, Dr. Kimmerle and her team will discover burial plots on the south campus and possibly in more than one location."

Injunction in place, we were free to explore the south side of the campus.

Glen's lawyer, Bob Bolt, was also a pilot, so he offered to fly Ovell Krell and her son to Dozier to meet us on-site and walk the property. We wanted Ovell to show us where the superintendent had taken her that day, the field in which he said George Owen was buried.

Ovell and I had talked on the phone before, but we met for the first time in person that day at the campus. Ovell seemed much younger at heart than her age betrayed. She wore sneakers and was full of energy. We made brief introductions and then got to business.

We went to the superintendent's office—the same building she entered with her parents in 1941, when she was twelve. She studied it and walked around the building. She went inside, then came out, declaring it was not the same building. At first, I thought her memory was deficient. Landscapes looked different years later. It had been seventy-one years, after all. She kept walking around the building and looking intensely at every aspect of it, inside and out.

"This is it, but the front is different," she finally said. "It had a different entrance."

We all studied it more closely. She was right. The front had an addition and a new facade that now covered the original entrance. The modification was evident in the bricks and materials. She knew. We all felt a sense of relief.

We walked outside along the main road to the industrial buildings, north, toward what had been the "colored" campus. She remembered walking, not driving, to the burials. She recognized the fields and trees but did not recall walking through the then-segregated part of campus.

The questions lingered. The tour was emotional for Ovell. She and George Owen were close growing up. She remembered the two of them listening through the scrub pines at night for the sounds of the South Florida Ramblers wafting out of the local juke joint. She remembered that George Owen made his first guitar out of a cigar box because their daddy couldn't afford to buy him the real thing in the throes of the Great Depression.

Ovell's son talked about growing up knowing that his mother was *always* searching for her brother. Families can carry that weight for generations. If your person is missing, the entire world feels empty.

We drove her to Boot Hill so she could see the metal crosses.

"Some marker," she scoffed. "I knew he was lying."

She didn't know if George Owen would be there, nor whether it was the same location she saw as a child. The school made their attempt to commemorate the burials only after disturbing some of the graves while planting pine trees in the 1980s. They didn't erect any markers in the 1940s, even though the superintendent assured Ovell's family they would.

I would see Ovell again and again over the next year, as we held town hall meetings and press conferences about our progress. She came anytime we called, eager to help, to talk to reporters and show her support.

More families of boys who had been buried on school grounds had stepped up to demand the remains of their brothers and uncles. Glen Varnadoe and Ovell Krell were joined by Cherry Wilson, Robert Stephens, and Charles Evans, as well as the families of Lee Goolsby, Joseph Weatherbee, Earl Morris, Loyd Dutton, Grady Huff, Waldo Drew, and Thomas Curry.

They wanted to know what had happened. They wanted to know why their relatives weren't given proper burials.

Only by actually excavating the graves would there be a chance to find some answers. It was becoming clear that if we wanted answers, we'd have to dig more than test trenches.

The crew of talented and energetic graduate students were joined by detectives and crime scene personnel from the Hillsborough County Sheriff's Office, who were helping out by learning how to find clandestine graves using GPR themselves. We were happy to have the extra muscle, and their presence made lunchtime at Marianna's greasy spoons slightly more comfortable. We still felt the eyes upon us everywhere we went. One night we went to eat at a local haunt, and our waiter, an older white man, blurted out, "Gravediggers," loud enough for everyone in the restaurant to hear. Later, as he poured water for the table, he leaned in close. "I think you are doing a good thing," he said. "It needs to be done. I just can't let people around here know it."

We scanned and documented several acres of property using GPR, and we conducted a pedestrian survey of a few hundred more acres. We started doing archival research at the state archives and university libraries, and we studied historic photographs and maps of the property, reconstructing where every road and building had been over the last century. We tied all this information to location data using geographic information system (GIS) mapping and layered it into Google Earth Pro, so we could stand anywhere on the property and use our phones and tablets to toggle between the past and the present, noting how the landscape had changed.

Then, using tracking apps, we recorded and superimposed our own footprint—the paths we searched, the holes we dug—onto a new layer. We immediately uploaded photos throughout the search so that as we continued our fieldwork at the site over several years, all that data plus the historic information was at our fingertips. When we processed and studied the data, it became clear. As we suspected, the state's number of burials was also wrong. Now we had physical proof.

The GPR time-slice images showed there were at least fifty burials—far more than the state's top law enforcement agency thought—in the area around Boot Hill, many of them strewn throughout the surrounding woods.

I wasn't planning on making any kind of grand announcement about our findings outside of a press release, but the story had grown, and behind the scenes, pressure came from all sides. The communications department at the University of South Florida had been fielding calls from reporters across the country—around the world, even—so they wanted to capitalize on the attention and keep everyone focused on our message. I deferred to the public relations team of Lara Wade and Vickie Chachere—they knew what they were doing. Vickie had been a reporter out of Tallahassee and covered several stories about Dozier, long before the White House Boys came forward. Lara and Vickie also knew that when it comes to politics, public opinion makes the difference. So, before I knew it, I was twirling my fingers and rehearsing my speech in the mirror of the granite bathroom of the Patel Center in Tampa, before stepping in front of a bank of television cameras to say that we had found fifty graves, nineteen more than the state said were there.

AS SOON AS our findings were broadcast on television and in Florida's newspapers, Florida agriculture commissioner Adam Putnam asked FDLE to review our report and explain the disparities. The state's law enforcement agency issued a statement the following week:

The USF report is an academic research study which is different than FDLE's criminal investigation into the Dozier School. While both have value, each has a different standard and scope.

In 2008, FDLE was directed by then Governor Charlie Crist to investigate the 32 unidentified graves that were marked by white, metal crosses and determine the identity of the deceased in those graves and if any crimes were committed.

USF used ground penetrating radar to identify "probable" and "possible" grave shafts. Ground penetrating radar is used to identify anomalies below the ground. These may or may not be graves. "Probable" and "possible" information has limited or no value in an investigation when "possible" information cannot be further investigated.

FDLE identified 85 student deaths: 31 buried in the cemetery, 31 in other locations and 23 in unknown locations. USF identified 98 student deaths: 45 buried in the cemetery, 31 in other locations and 22 in unknown locations.

The USF study included 11 students who died of influenza. Unable to identify these students by name, FDLE did not include this information in its count because it may have duplicated deaths already listed. Two additional students appear to have been double-counted. FDLE identified one student as being buried in an unknown location while USF listed the student as being buried at the school.

Should additional evidence dictate an expansion of our original charge, FDLE is ready and willing to reopen its investigation of the Dozier School.

It seemed lost on them, the fact that there was more that could be done to investigate the circumstances of deaths and burials.

Why not bring in forensic anthropologists, who search for clandestine burials? We do this regularly for law enforcement in missing person's cases and use remote sensing and excavation methods. Or, rather than accept that children died in a fire, try to investigate the fire. Who died? Why? Why were there three investigations and controversy immediately following, in 1914? How were white and Black boys cared for during the flu epidemics in 1918 and 1932? Did they receive the same medical treatment and care? Even in cases of accidental or natural deaths, there are issues of culpability. These children were in the care of the state of Florida. How did the state do when it came to protecting their safety and well-being?

Private meetings between Glen Varnadoe and the attorney general's office stalled any hope Glen had for support. He asked Attorney General Pam Bondi to enlist a special investigator to explore the case, to find his uncle.

However, since this was not a criminal investigation, that option was not open to him. It felt like we were racing the clock. The state was determined to sell the boys' school property. Local leaders wanted the whole thing over with. Tourism officials complained to the press that we hurt the local economy and no tourists wanted to visit Jackson County. Backstage, the entire issue became increasingly politicized, pitting panhandle lawmakers against those advocating for excavation. A front-page story in a Sunday edition of the New York Times didn't ease the tension as 2012 turned into 2013.

"The scattered graves bear no markings: no names, no loving sentiment. The only hint of a cemetery are the white crosses that the state planted in the 1990s, belatedly and haphazardly," reporter Lizette Alvarez wrote. "From the time it opened in 1900, as the state's first home for wayward children, until it closed in 2011, as a residential center for high-risk youths, Dozier became synonymous with beatings, abuse, forced labor, neglect and, in some cases, death. It survived Congressional hearings, state hearings and state investigations. Each one turned the spotlight on horrific conditions, and little changed."

As word spread that we'd found fifty burials, there were many people who thought we predicted too many graves, that we misinterpreted tree roots or buried mules for human burials.

Local officials maintained there were only thirty-one burials, as the markers suggested. What the critics failed to appreciate was that we ground-truthed the results from remote sensing. As scientists, we didn't conjure up an answer and accept it. We validated it. Through this process we used GPR to collect data about the layers of soil and what was buried within them. Then we dug shallow trenches several meters long through the site, transecting the anomalies to validate the results. Through this process we dug deep enough to look at the soil, but not so deep that we intruded into a burial.

This process allowed us to look at the color and density of the soil, as well as look for stains or cultural materials that informed us whether this was a human burial, a fence post, buried garbage, or something else. This process of ground-truthing went on for months and required a half-dozen trips from Tampa to Marianna, through the rain and soupy heat of Florida summers.

We also turned up names of boys who died but whose deaths were never reported to the state by school officials nor to the public by the state once they did find out. Most never even made the newspapers. A lot of boys died after running away. Some died after being paroled to local plantations for labor. Others died of illness in overcrowded living conditions, without adequate food or medicine. All these deaths made the state culpable.

These findings stood in stark contrast to the FDLE position that "there is no evidence to suggest that the School or its staff made any attempts to conceal and/or contributed to the deaths of these individuals."

The most disturbing thing was that during this era of racial segregation and Jim Crow laws, far more Black boys were sent to the school and died than white boys.

I wasn't prepared for the backlash against our initial findings. We did good work. I thought that perhaps some people really wanted us to be wrong, because what does it mean to be right? To have fifty children buried in unmarked graves without records of who they were and how they died suggested that mistakes were made. The one-hundred-year-old headlines calling for the governor to take responsibility seemed timeless.

"How certain are you?" they all asked. Reporters, politicians, the state archaeologist, the Florida cabinet, the local medical examiner, on and on. How sure were we that we had fifty graves? Sure enough that I stood up at a press conference and made the statement.

The local medical examiner who had to answer to the Jackson County board of commissioners seemed especially concerned.

"What if you don't find anything?" he asked. "Maybe nothing is preserved at all. Not bones or even an outline of the grave? I know of exhumations by medical examiners down by the Glades that were only about ten to twenty years old and there was nothing preserved at all."

His questions sounded to me like predictions.

So what if we did find nothing? What harm was there in trying? I didn't really understand his question. I told him that finding *nothing* wasn't a possibility. How do you convince people of that when you can't show the physical evidence buried in the ground? The very act of burying human remains and caskets means the soil is disturbed because the topsoil layers, rich with nutrients from the leaves and plants that nourish the topsoil, black in color as a result, are pushed to the deeper layers of white and tan-colored sand, along with the red clay, and the layers become mixed and mottled when you fill in the hole. This mixing of colors from the different soil layers (called *stratigraphy*) lasts for thousands of years. All the bodies and artifacts—the nails, wood, metal, bone, enamel—may decompose in the soil, but for all traces of any disturbance to disappear beyond recognition in less than a hundred years is extremely unlikely and not something I've ever witnessed. You simply cannot undig a hole.

I tried to explain that we could already see the rectangular outlines of burials in the top layers of the soil in our shallow trenches. If nothing else, we could remove all the topsoil and count the number of graves by soil staining. Of course, that may prove burials, but it wouldn't prove who or what was buried there. Some of the local critics claimed the burials were trash, or mules, or dogs, or peacocks, or other pets—anything but children. The local blogger Dale Cox claimed to have known all along that there were more than thirty-one boys buried there. Suddenly, everyone in Marianna seemed to have information about the little burial ground.

Charles Evans, born and raised in Marianna, knew his uncle and cousin were buried at the school, but he'd never seen the grave site, not

even during his many times on the school grounds. His dead relatives—
Bennett and Charles, both white—worked at the school and died while
reportedly trying to save each other during the 1914 fire.

Charles was named after his dead cousin. He'd always assumed the
cemetery was like any other in town, with flowers and headstones.
Maybe it was in the woods and slightly overgrown, but he always
pictured markers and nice landscaping. The rest of the Dozier school
grounds were well manicured. As a child he attended the Christmas
lights parade the school hosted each year, and it had been elaborate
and meticulous. His family called Bennett and Charles heroes, and
Charles believed they had an honorable resting place.

I met Charles at the burial site after we started fieldwork. He drove
up the makeshift dirt road behind the county jail at the edge of the
clearing and shook his head.

"Why would the state allow this?" he asked me. He gestured at
the gnarly and weedy expanse of land before him, sweeping his hand
in the air in an exaggerated broad stroke. "They had so much money
and so many convicts. Why couldn't they keep it up? Where are the
damn headstones? I don't see a single marker."

He turned to face me. "Have you found any markers? Do you
know where my uncle and cousin are buried?"

I walked with him around the clearing, pointing out where we
had found unmarked burials.

"Most are on the north end," I told him. "Here," I said, pointing
out the roadway. "We've asked people to stop parking their cars and
turning around in this space because we're finding a lot of burials
under this road."

"Nothing's marked," he said. This time his voice was as thin as
the reedy quack grass that had formed a heavy mat across the hill.

"We can find your uncle," I told him. "And your cousin, too. But
I need your permission to continue our work."

"Yes, you should find him," he said.

His response was a huge relief.

Charles had first been contacted by a local newspaper reporter working on a story about our efforts, and he seemed to oppose digging up the cemetery. His objection had the potential to derail the entire project. The next of kin always have a right to move a burial when needed. Likewise, if Charles Evans—the known next of kin for local white men buried at Boot Hill—had been against the excavation of his relatives' remains, that could have cast a shadow over the requests made by others.

The other families were asking the state to allow us to go even further than we expected. Beyond ground-truthing, they wanted full excavation and identification of the dead. They wanted us to bring their brothers home and to bury them in family plots, next to their parents' graves.

Local leaders seemed to be bent on making sure that never happened. They didn't want the truth dug up. They most certainly didn't want to keep talking about what had happened in their community, under their watch and at the hands of some of their own kinfolk.

Charles told us that the reporter had asked him if he wanted his dead uncle dug up, and he had responded with a loud "Hell, no." He thought his uncle's grave was marked and that it was about to be desecrated by a bunch of money-hungry outsiders and academics. So at first he spoke out against our effort.

Now that he'd seen the burial ground, marked by flags in the woods, now that he'd met me and we'd walked the land together, he not only understood how the other families who had been speaking out felt, he was also ready to sign on to our effort to uncover the truth.

Charles would visit the site with us once more—but that time he'd come to provide support and to let us take his DNA with a buccal swab in hopes we would be able to match it to his uncle and cousin and give them a proper burial.

Chapter 6

A MEETING WITH THE CHIEF

The state was perfectly fine letting us map the cemetery. We used ground-penetrating radar to discover similar folk cemeteries and clandestine burials for the police frequently. It wasn't invasive, and there was no better way to collect that type of evidence or see what was a possible grave shaft.

When we analyzed the GPR data and discovered fifty graves, and quite possibly more sprinkled in the woods around the cemetery, our work on campus was brought to a halt. Local politicians were clamoring to state leaders. The scope of the mystery had grown, and the findings generated headlines in newspapers and on websites around the world. Suddenly, it felt like a million people were watching our tedious, scientific process unfold.

We took our cue from the families of the dead and formally requested permission to excavate the graves so we might identify the boys. Senator Bill Nelson called a press conference in February 2013 to help garner support for the project.

"I'm just here to make sure that this investigation continues," the longtime Democratic lawmaker said, calling on the state of Florida to keep funding the project. "So continue the investigation, locate the graves, exhume what remains are there, try to have identification of the remains through whatever evidence and DNA, and then bring in the appropriate law enforcement in order to determine if there were crimes committed."

Ovell Krell and Glen Varnadoe flanked Nelson at the briefing. I sat beside Ovell.

"These are the folks that are the courageous ones," Nelson said.

On the opposite side of the political aisle, Florida attorney general Pam Bondi, a rising-star Republican, had lent us her support as well. Bondi's office filed a petition on behalf of the District 14 medical examiner Dr. Michael Hunter to allow him to exhume human remains on the site of the Dozier school for up to a year. They were seeking a court order in Marianna, in the Fourteenth Judicial Circuit.

Under normal circumstances, when unknown or clandestine burials are found, the local law enforcement agency with jurisdiction obtains permission from the landowner and a search warrant to excavate. This was complicated by the fact that there was a historic burial ground located there. Yet it was an undocumented burial ground consisting of juveniles in state custody, and none of the graves were marked.

Today all deaths in custody are investigated and autopsied, even when inmates are executed through capital punishment, which may seem redundant. Local law enforcement was not about to open an investigation, so the attorney general's office was lending support to the local medical examiner.

"The deaths that occurred at Dozier School for Boys in Marianna are cloaked in mystery, and the surviving family members deserve a thorough examination of the site," Bondi said. "I am committed to doing everything within my power to support investigative efforts to help resolve unanswered questions and bring closure to the families who lost loved ones."

Hunter's petition was based on the speculation that some of the deaths could have been the result of excessive corporal punishment, that the records shed little light regarding the cause of death of each child, and often even less regarding the disposition and location of the remains.

The petition addressed our most salient suspicions. We had learned so much, but every new fact begged more questions.

Former wards Johnnie Walthour and Woodrow Williams both told us that they were present for three burials at the Boot Hill cemetery between 1951 and 1952, but the school's records document only one, the burial of Billey Jackson. Other circumstantial evidence from the state archives suggested that there was another funeral at the school in the 1950s besides Jackson's.

Billey Jackson's death was suspicious, too. His death certificate said he died of pyelonephritis, a urinary tract infection that affects the kidneys. Both Johnnie Walthour and Woodrow Williams told us that approximately two weeks prior to Billey's death, the Black boy had attempted to escape but had been caught and was so badly beaten in the White House that his stomach was distended. Shortly after, he was hospitalized but never returned, except to be buried by Johnnie and other boys at the school. Caskets were made in the school's carpentry shop and driven up to the burial ground in a tractor-drawn wagon.

The petition also cited the death of George Owen Smith. No death certificate was issued for George Owen either. George Owen wasn't the only student who ran away and then died under mysterious circumstances.

Thomas Curry ran away from the school and allegedly died of a "wound to the forehead, skull crushed from unknown cause."

Robert Hewett ran away in 1960 and died of "gunshot wounds in the chest inflicted by person or persons unknown."

The petition to exhume cited Thomas Varnadoe, too, whose death on October 26, 1934, came thirty-four days after he arrived. The school's records said Thomas died of pneumonia with a possible contributing cause of anemia. The reform school's student-run newspaper stated that Thomas was very sickly when he arrived and his funeral was well attended by other students. Thomas's family, however, has consistently disputed that Thomas was a sickly child, and Thomas's brother, Hubert, who was also an inmate at the school when Thomas died, stated that the newspaper article was false and the only people at Thomas's funeral were Hubert, a preacher, and the man who dug Thomas's grave.

The petition to exhume explained that if remains were found, Hunter would assume control and, in the event we found evidence of a crime, call in law enforcement. We had found the family members of thirteen of the Dozier dead so far, but if we couldn't identify remains or find family members, then the state would take them for appropriate and respectful disposition either at Boot Hill or some other site.

"There is a need to determine who these people are and how they died," Hunter wrote, "to answer questions for families, to allow families the choice of where their relatives are to rest, and to ensure history is as accurate as possible."

Meanwhile, the local historian who had been defending the Dozier school practices and history on his blog tapped out an email to the Marianna police chief. He didn't name names, but it seemed obvious who he was talking about.

To Chief Baggett, Dale Cox wrote:

I hope this finds you doing well? I tried to give you a call around lunchtime but missed you.

I have a question for you about the University of South Florida and the Dozier School cemetery. I believe that Florida Statutes prohibit the disturbance of a human grave. Last summer, USF had a permit from the state archaeologist to conduct ground penetrating radar research at the cemetery. That permit, however, did not include authority to conduct excavations or disturb the graves.

At the time I questioned numerous state officials by email and received responses from them, assuring me that no excavations would take place.

However, video on the USF website clearly shows them digging in the cemetery. In addition, their report on the Dozier cemetery includes photographs of excavations at the site. Would that not be a criminal violation of state law? I believe it is a 3rd degree felony to disturb a human grave without authority:

872.02 Injuring or removing tomb or monument; disturbing contents of grave or tomb; penalties.—

(1) A person who willfully and knowingly destroys, mutilates, defaces, injures, or removes any tomb, monument, gravestone, burial mound, earthen or shell monument containing human skeletal remains or associated burial artifacts, or other structure or thing placed or designed for a memorial of the dead, or any fence, railing, curb, or other thing intended for the protection or ornamentation of any tomb, monument, gravestone, burial mound, earthen or shell monument containing human skeletal remains or associated burial artifacts, or other structure before mentioned, or for any enclosure for the burial of the dead, or willfully destroys, mutilates, removes, cuts, breaks, or injures any tree, shrub, or plant placed or being within any such enclosure, commits a felony of the third degree, punishable as provided in s. 775.082, s. 775.083, or s. 775.084.

There are exceptions to the statute for archaeologists, but I believe they would still have to have had a permit to do any digging in the cemetery there and their permit did not allow excavations.

If they violated state law, I feel they should be charged. I'm providing this for your information, but if you need extra information or someone to file a complaint, let me know!

Best,

Dale Cox

Cox seemed determined to undermine our work, even though he'd been wrong about the number of graves several times. In 2009, he was confident there were thirty-one burials, like state investigators said. This was, of course, before we found more. Then he changed his story.

He told Ben Montgomery from the *St. Petersburg Times* that he wasn't motivated by money, and he wasn't writing a book about the school as he had about the Claude Neal lynching. Despite these denials, a few years later, he self-published a book called *Death at Dozier School:*

The Attempted Assassination of an American City. Cox told Montgomery that he was simply speaking up for elderly citizens of Jackson County who felt like they didn't have a voice in rebutting the abuse claims.

He also told Montgomery that he first learned of the cemetery in the mid-1980s, when he worked on a story for a local television station. Cox was the same man who coincidentally claimed to have interviewed two of the men who lynched Claude Neal, though he would not reveal their identities. Neal's death remains an open homicide, investigated as recently as 2013 by the FBI through the Emmett Till Antilynching Act.

Montgomery found an email Cox sent to state lawmakers, asking them to stop us from even using GPR to map Boot Hill. "It strikes me as appalling and odd that taxpayer dollars would be spent on digging up graves that another taxpayer investigation has determined are in no way related to the allegations made against the school," he wrote, referring to FDLE's 2009 investigation. "Is there no way that funding for the project can be withdrawn or eliminated by the State Legislature? Marianna has suffered the loss of jobs and undeserved notoriety during a severe recession due to this fiasco and surely as taxpayers we shouldn't be called upon to fund the digging up of graves too."

The local weekly newspaper seemed to have its own mission, calling our inquiry a "greed-motivated waste of money" and launching a series to dispute some of the allegations made by the White House Boys. They complained that the negative attention had cost Jackson County, population forty-nine thousand, at least two hundred jobs and $14.5 million in annual spending when the Dozier school was shuttered. All that came at a time when the rural county had one of the highest unemployment rates in the state.

The antagonism wasn't altogether unexpected. Anytime there's an effort at truth and reconciliation in a small town where the bright light of publicity shines on some dark deed, the powerful people in town try to control their truth—or at least the thing that's true to them.

The reform school, with its manicured facade, required a lot of imagination. Imagination that it could be different, that justice could be found. This idea stood in sharp contrast to the belief system tightly guarded by those who opposed our investigation. The Dozier culture did not come from nowhere—there was a script behind it, and that moral imperative set the stage for conflict. It was science versus belief. No facts or data will change a belief that is valued and nurtured, in spite of all evidence to suggest otherwise. In this case, it was a code of conduct built on a foundation for which cruelty and inequality could be repeatedly justified, contrasted against notions of equality and transparency.

They knew Marianna to be a good and decent place, and they had a hard time believing the men who ran the school could be friendly and cordial at church or Otto's Diner or the Waffle Iron, then head out to the school to hurt kids. They could've been ignorant, or they could've been complicit. It was an open secret that the strap used in the beatings was made by a guy named Presley on Market Street.

INTERSTATE 10 CUT south of town, where a cluster of chain hotels and restaurants and a Walmart Supercenter had sprung up around the busiest exit, edging the city toward modern America.

Locals told reporters that the White House Boys were exaggerating to pressure the state to pay them off.

"Unfortunately, you can throw mud and dirt further than you can throw clean sand," wrote a columnist for the *Jackson County Times*. "These claims have not been proven or substantiated, but much national media attention has been generated which includes very negative publicity for our community."

Glen Varnadoe wondered whether something sinister was motivating the opponents.

"My biggest question is: What do they have to hide?" he asked.

He wondered if there was something connecting his uncle's death to the Claude Neal lynching at the same time, and the ensuing white mob violence. Three days before the Neal lynching and Thomas's death, a headline in the local paper read, "Ku Klux Klan May Ride Again, Jackson County Citizens May Rally to Fiery Cross to Protect Womanhood."

Without some direct connection, it was all speculation.

There were locals who supported what we were doing. In fact, my colleagues and I were invited to attend a family reunion and birthday party for Allie Mae Neal, who was three when her father was lynched in 1934. Her family has no idea where, or even if, he was buried.

Our most vocal support came from Black ministers, local white farmers, and the NAACP. They all wanted to help us find the truth. They knew that families had a fundamental human right to the remains of their loved ones who died in state custody. It's why the US government spends millions to find and bring home soldiers who die overseas. It's why American Indian tribes demand their ancestors' remains when developers discover ancient burial grounds. We have a right to memorialize.

Around the time the White House Boys were starting to organize, the year that Martin Lee Anderson was held down by seven guards and a nurse as he suffocated to death, the United Nations General Assembly affirmed the right of victims to know the truth about the circumstances of an enforced disappearance and the fate of the disappeared person. Considered a human rights issue, it was affirmed that family members could seek, receive, and impart information toward this end and was generally thought of simply as "The Right to Know."

Now Cox, with whom I had spoken only once, was encouraging my arrest. We had not broken the law, of course. Would that even matter? I wondered.

I dashed off a letter to the attorney general's office, to make them aware. Then I called the Hillsborough County sheriff David Gee, whose deputies were assigned to assist us. Were they being investigated, too?

"The facts are that what we have uncovered are children's graves that are under brush and trees, among trash, and without this effort they would have been lost forever," I wrote. "What we are doing is the exact opposite of what Mr. Cox alleges. We are finding and preserving graves and we are doing this at the behest of families of the children buried there and interested state parties. Several of these same families have visited the site with us and helped to fund the project. Families have a right to know what happened to their brothers and access to their graves, and we support their rights."

The digging Dale Cox saw was ground-truthing.

The story of my possible pending arrest as reported by at least one panhandle television station made me equal parts sad, angry, and ill, all at a time when the stress of this project and working long days was wearing me down. The irony was that they were accusing us of destroying graves that they said didn't exist. Which was it?

Hayes Baggett, the chief of police in Marianna, turned Cox's complaint over to the regional state attorney, Glenn Hess. Hess was a helicopter pilot in the Vietnam War before getting into law and becoming a judge, then a prosecutor. When he took office in 2008, he instituted a new dress code and a guiding principle: *Do the right thing.*

Hess passed the case to his research attorneys, who read the information from Dale Cox and reviewed the videos Cox was referring to on the university's website. His researchers reviewed legal cases back to the 1800s and found none that applied to what was going on at the reform school. Historically, laws protecting grave sites were meant to thwart grave robbers. Unearthing a casket without permission, for instance, was a felony crime with a maximum penalty of fifteen years behind bars. Destroying a cemetery plot was criminal mischief punishable by up to five years.

More current statutes that protected cemeteries mainly addressed policy goals of historic and cultural preservation.

"It is apparent that the University of South Florida activities at Dozier had not been contemplated by our lawmakers," Hess wrote in a letter to Chief Baggett.

Hess's researchers did find a statute that applied in Florida law, one that provided an exemption to those authorized by the Department of State to work in cemeteries—in other words, us. We had a permit to do what we were doing.

The two questions Hess thought worth addressing were: Did the trenches we dug exceed the authorized activities under the permit? And did those trenches violate state statute?

The statute addressed specific acts, like destruction, mutilation, defacement, injury, or removal. The act of digging was not mentioned in the statute. If the digging destroyed something, the statute might apply. We destroyed nothing.

As to the other charge—did our trenching violate the archaeological research permit we were operating under?—the question was moot. Violating a permit is not a crime. Besides, the senior archaeologist at the state's Division of Historical Resources explained to Chief Baggett that digging was an activity covered by the permit.

It all seemed so asinine. That anybody would waste time on the issue blew me away, but it was absolutely no fun to have your future freedom in the hands of a panhandle prosecutor. In his letter to the chief, he wrote: "Insofar as the answers to the foregoing questions are negative, no charges appear to be viable at this time."

What he wrote next sent a clear message: we were being put on notice.

"Mr. Cox is to be commended for his concerns and for his diligence. Please make a copy of this letter available to him."

The chief finally relented. The attorney general's office met with him, the medical examiner, and Cox to tell them we had broken no laws. Chief Baggett told the newspapers that he had spoken with state officials, including State Attorney Glenn Hess, and decided not to investigate.

"I'm not interested in wasting one taxpayer penny on a witch hunt," he said.

The events—not only the discourse that showed opposition, but the official government refusal to find justice for boys in a swirling mess of testimony and inconsistencies—made me feel vulnerable. Powerless, even. These boys and their families—whose crimes had essentially been poverty and race—had no recourse if we couldn't press forward. The weight of the injustice was palpable. No wonder it was so delayed.

It ultimately didn't matter how many people in Marianna tried to stop our work. All we needed was the permission of circuit court judge William Wright. As spring set in, we waited for his ruling. I looked into Judge Wright's background, to see if there were any connections between him and the Dozier school. Many Jackson County residents were connected when it came to the history of the school. It turned out his wife may have been part of the effort to mark the little burial ground in the 1990s and helped the school erect the crosses, according to one informed local who was warming up to us and now providing local insights.

Then came his ruling. Judge Wright rejected our petition in May.

"Counsel for the Petitioner has failed to meet the threshold for an order granting exhumation in a civil case, if one is needed under the circumstances," the judge wrote.

The court said our report, included with the petition, didn't give any details about what physical evidence we were likely to find that would help in the identification process or when determining the cause of death.

"Any further excavation by USF will be with State permission on State property," Judge Wright wrote. "The Medical Examiner does not need a court order to carry out his statutory duties if human remains are found."

He noted that the exhumations had to be done in pursuit of a possible criminal investigation, not as fishing expeditions.

"The last known burial was in 1952, more than sixty years ago," he wrote. "There is correspondence indicating that some bodies may have been buried without a casket, and there is no indication that any of the bodies were embalmed."

The judge's order also pointed out that the statute of limitations would bar prosecution of any crimes other than homicide.

"Although Petitioner's counsel speculates that burials may have occurred after 1952, he concedes that a criminal homicide investigation is unlikely. It is not expected that USF will find evidence which would support prosecution for homicide and the Interim Report does not indicate what evidence is likely to be found."

And he concluded with an ominous warning, citing a 1949 court case: "Regardless of the authority to continue this investigation, Florida officials should proceed with caution and pay heed to *Currier v. Woodlawn Cemetery*: '*The quiet of the grave, the repose of the dead, are not lightly to be disturbed. Good and substantial reasons must be shown before disinterment is to be sanctioned.*'"

Chapter 7

"HELL ON EARTH"

In April 2014, while we tried to decide what to do next, the Jackson County board of commissioners held a public meeting to allow people to talk about what was happening at the Dozier school. The commissioners were trying to decide whether to weigh in, either in favor or opposed to our project, as an official governing body—not that it would have mattered, but it might've earned them some votes when it came time for reelection.

The room was packed, and during a period when the commissioners heard public comments, a man named Dale Landry stood to speak. Landry, a cigar-chomping regional vice president of the NAACP, was one of our most active supporters and saw the issue through a prism of race and justice, and he was completely unafraid to say what he thought. Even though he didn't live in Jackson County, he wanted his voice— and the opinion of the powerful NAACP as a group—heard loud and clear by the white people in Jackson County.

Landry had toured the reform school campus recently with Senator Bill Nelson. The men walked through the White House. To make a point about complicity, Landry, who had traveled the world while serving in the military, compared the White House to a Nazi gas chamber at Dachau, Germany, suggesting that those who lived near the concentration camp did not know of the atrocities until the camp was liberated and they had a chance to see the place for themselves and better understand what had happened there.

"I propose to you that many people in Jackson County did not know what was going on," Landry told the commissioners. "This is not an indictment of Jackson County." It seemed lost on the commissioners that he was trying to give them a way forward.

Dale Cox, who had received the Jackson County Chamber of Commerce's Citizen of the Year award in 2012, reacted in anger.

"What kind of a situation are we in when people are comparing Marianna to Dachau? That is absolutely ridiculous!" he said, interrupting the meeting. "Dozier school is no more Dachau than I'm Santa Claus!"

Dachau was actually an interesting comparison.

My students and I had been puzzling out the details of a fire that ravaged the school in 1914 and stood as the prime example of the dysfunctional and deadly legacy of a sordid state-run institution.

We used every primary source we could find to try to gain focus on a clear picture of what happened. An accurate death toll was elusive and illustrated the challenges we faced throughout our research.

On that night in 1914, as the floor beneath them gave way to the flames, the boys' screams could be heard throughout the yard, even over the roar of the fire and the shouted commands of men who desperately fought to put it out. Those who were there on-site that night told reporters, state investigators, and the coroner what they saw: the silhouettes of boys chained, locked in dark cell chambers, were visible to witnesses below through the large windows, where they watched in horror as the boys fell with each collapsing floor. Neighbors gossiped about the origins of the fire and the young, seemingly unfit man who ran the school. Decades later, when researchers came from Florida State University to ask them questions, they could still describe the smell of burned remains and the revulsion in their hearts. One woman reported at that time, that decades after the deadly blaze, her father would wake up hearing the boys' cries.

Was it an accident? Some called what happened a black eye and an embarrassment for the state of Florida. Legislators who had warned the year before that the dorm was at risk for a major calamity called the tragedy avoidable. When Governor Park Trammell ignored the public call to take responsibility in 1914 and close the school, his constituents cried injustice, a public outrage that reverberated in the halls of the capital for the next century. Daily newspapers captured the dramatic reactions of the boys' grief-stricken mothers, who were notified by telegram that the remains of their sons were burned beyond recognition and buried on the grounds of the reform school where they'd died.

That's what they were told, anyway. There was more to the story.

THIS IS WHAT we could piece together.

On a cold November night, Mr. O. G. Martson woke to a loud roar. A fire had broken out as nearly one hundred children slept in their beds. Martson, a longtime staff member at the school, was charged with caring for the boys. He lived among them in a large dormitory on the south side of the reformatory. Martson would later tell authorities and state investigators what happened next.

Within moments of hearing the noise, he found that the kitchen located on the first floor was in flames. The fire quickly spread along the freshly painted, oil-soaked wooden walls and staircase. Martson raised the alarm by going from room to room to wake everyone, then quickly went in search of keys to untether the boys he knew were chained in isolation cells on the third floor.

Several of the men who worked and lived at the school, including Superintendent William H. Bell, were absent. The smell of fresh paint mixed with smoke as the handful of staff available hustled to rush the boys outside to safety. Oily paint rags strewn throughout the kitchen would later be blamed in large part for the ferocity of the fire. Flames quickly overtook the central staircase, forcing the staff to shuffle the ninety-eight children and young men ranging in age from five to twenty-one years old toward the ends of the hall.

As the flames spread up the central staircase, their escape was blocked.

George Robinson, who had worked every job from yardman to nurse to farm manager to undertaker, directed boys to turn toward the ends of the hall. New doors had been installed at each end with side staircases on the outside of the building, leading to exits below.

Those doors were locked with chains. Not wanting to wait for keys that should have been located in the kitchen, the men and older boys tried to break through the doors. Pounding and prying, they were able to break the chain's metal latch from the wall and the door swung open.

They had to move fast. Smoke filled the air and their lungs. If they didn't flee at that point, they would all perish. The boys rushed into the blustery night, barefooted.

The fire escapes weren't the only locked doors, though. The boys still trapped on the third flood were accessible only via the central staircase, and the new fire escapes didn't extend to the third floor. Martson went in search of those keys when he first sounded the alarm, but they were with Superintendent Bell. Nobody could find Bell.

There was no way to reach those still trapped.

The taste of ash floating in the air was bitter. Outside, the chaos grew. Volunteer firefighters arrived in their horse-drawn Model A Ford with a booster pump, but the dorm was already overtaken with smoke and flames.

From the ground, the volunteers, boys, and staff could see those still trapped through the windows above and listened to their cries for help as the floors beneath them gave way. Those trapped inside toppled to their deaths. There was little that the firefighters could do to quell the fire, and quickly they turned to spectators. Helpless and defeated, the school's staff would watch the ruins smolder for days before picking apart and demolishing the debris left behind.

In 1913, less than a year before the fire, the sixth legislative investigative committee since 1901 had reported on the state of the institution and the deplorable conditions of the children.

The committee reported that all the windows were heavily barred and that only one doorway led from the hallway to the staircase. Concerned for the safety of the children housed there, they warned that if there were a fire, no one could escape the second or third floors of the building.

There were no escape exits and the practice of chaining children to walls to keep them from running away was a guaranteed risk should a fire break out in the facility. Committee recommendations called for the construction of escape exits, which was later signed into law on June 5, 1913. The committee also recommended the facility end the practice of chaining children for restraint—which was the same recommendation they made in every single legislative investigation since 1903. Every year, school officials ignored the recommendation.

The youngest boy found in chains was five years old. What would prompt the court to sentence a five-year-old to a reform school for delinquency? School officials counterargued the chains were necessary to keep boys from running away and that modifications to the buildings were too costly. By law, only children convicted of crimes, not orphans, were sent to the reformatory.

Attendance records from the 1930s show that African American boys as young as five years old were convicted of delinquency by the courts, but in contrast, some of the white boys during this same period of time and of the same young age were orphaned and sent to the school without criminal charges.

Following the scathing legislative review of the conditions of the grounds, the treatment of the children, and the possible malfeasance, William Milton, who had been instrumental in bringing the school to Marianna and ran it since it opened, was finally replaced. His nephew John had been replaced by Bell, who lived on the grounds and ran day-to-day operations. Bell, in his early twenties, was a former delinquent himself, whose father was able to use political connections in order to land him the job in Marianna.

A compromise was quickly reached between the state and school officials. The dorm for "colored" boys would be left unchanged, thereby saving money. Only state funds appropriated from the legislature to modify the housing for white boys were needed to add fire doors and additional staircases on each end of the building up to the second floor—a modification that undoubtedly saved countless lives that night, as it was the dorm for white boys that caught on fire. Not so for those trapped on the third floor.

The *Miami Herald* reported that boys climbed through skylights to reach safety from the third floor to the roof. Based on the construction of the building, witness statements, and what was determined through the state investigation, it's more than likely that staff attempted to reach the boys on the third floor by cutting a hole in the roof. The third-story floor would have been accessible from the new roofing added over the fire escapes only months before. A witness named Bowles also reported in a later interview that George Robinson, the longtime school employee who also served as their undertaker, attempted to free boys locked in the third-floor isolation cells by climbing onto the roof to cut a hole in it and drop a set of keys down. Would such keys be for the chains that tethered them to the walls? It's unclear how keys to locks on the outside of their doors would have led to an escape.

Neither the existence of skylights nor attempts to access trapped boys via the roof are discussed in other records, so it is unknown if the versions of events told by school administrators were constructed to defend officials as they fought to keep the school open amid growing public outcry that the school should be shut down permanently.

George Robinson and his wife were employees of the school at the time of the fire. George was also the son-in-law of M. S. Knight, who would later take over running the school in the 1920s after a long tenure at the Florida State Hospital. Most likely it was George Robinson who signed many of the death certificates and prepared the remains and buried the caskets of those who died in the fire. Did he know how many victims he was burying?

Even though they were shoeless, some boys tried to run away the night of the fire. The weather that night was bitter cold. Local residents didn't open their doors to take in the children. As young as they were—they were still convicts. If their own parents didn't want them, why should they? At least that was the view of many residents who lived around the rural campus. As the county archivist said, the boys were nothing but throwaways.

The community needed the school—and the jobs it brought along with state funding. The institution quickly grew into an integral component of the local economy through farming, agriculture production, document printing, and brickmaking.

That dependence also grew into contempt at times, and townies developed strong feelings against those boys who were not local, not part of the community. They sometimes saw them marching into town on Saturdays to go to the movies. Other times, they saw them hiding in roadside ditches. Sometimes, they saw the wards in the newspaper after they'd been caught trying to escape in a stolen vehicle or on foot.

The boys were seen as a burden, according to some residents who said it tarnished the prosperous image the community tried to project.

Run as some boys may have tried, there was really nowhere for them to go. Across the road, Department 2 housed the "colored" boys. It was already overcrowded, typically sleeping two boys to a bunk.

A dorm designed to sleep 64 housed 190 boys that night. The structure was the same size and layout as the dorm that burned but with twice as many boys sleeping there and no fire escapes. The surviving 84 white boys were "marched to the colored campus and crowded into the dorms," where they stayed until new dormitories could be built.

The practices of segregation were well established and permeated every aspect of daily life for everyone—white and Black. So if school officials violated the law and housed them together, they didn't record it. Many parents arrived to bring their boys home as the public outcry for justice grew louder. Whether the school would rebuild remained in question. They estimated the damage to be $100,000, or roughly $2.7 million today.

The story of the reform school could've ended there, in the smoking heap of the state's failed experiment. It did not. The school would rebuild and continue to grow over the next fifty years. The fire that killed boys who could not escape its spread would become a symbol of how school leaders dealt with a century of scandal.

Bend the story. Twist the facts. Lose the records. Bury the evidence.

IF YOU GATHER all the evidence and reconstruct the fire and the few days that followed, you can see the protective spin start to take shape.

We know for a fact that the night of the fire, the crowd grew as more hands arrived to help, and those on the ground below clearly saw boys burning to death behind the barred windows. D. B. Vickery, assistant superintendent, was also unable to reach the boys who were trapped; for him, being forced to watch helplessly as the boys tried to escape the flames was torture. Many years later he told his daughter that he could still hear their screams.

The dark cells were for isolation—a form of punishment that could be delivered for any infraction of the rules, or for illness, or for runaway attempts, falling behind the workload, or not following orders. Strict discipline such as whippings, beatings, isolation, and iron chains were a ubiquitous part of the boys' reform. At least five boys were locked up in the dark cells on the third floor during the fire.

Harry Wells, who was cold in the night's wind, had reached safety outside the burning dorm but ran back inside to grab his blanket, according to school officials who later tried to explain his death. The board of managers reported that Harry was "demented," perhaps offering an explanation as to why he would enter a burning building. Nothing was said publicly of the fact that children with disabilities were sent to reform school or convicted of delinquency. Perhaps that was a sign of the times. The school existed in an era before our understanding or concepts about learning disabilities.

Joseph Weatherbee, who was seventeen years old, also allegedly reentered the dormitory to go to the third floor to look for Super-intendent Bell, who Joseph thought was inside sleeping. The tele-gram to Joseph's mother is one of the surviving documents from this incident.

The board's report stated that Charles Evans and his father, Ben-nett, both employees, were trapped inside. Bennett didn't exit with the rest. He was inside looking for Charles. The two men searched for each other amid the flames until it was too late.

Speculation, rumors, and theories spread across the crowd that night like a child's game of Telephone. What started the fire? Perhaps it was arson? There had been threats from angry parents who wanted their boys released. Kerosene lanterns hung in the hallways. Dyna-mite was stored under the stairwell, used to blast the compact clay for mining to make bricks, remove tree stumps, and clear the lands for cotton and peanut fields. Notably, the wood stove in the kitchen stood propped up on only three legs. It was broken, as were most things around the emerging industrial complex—maybe a metaphor for the school itself. Then there were the oily rags, which had been used to clean up the place following the recent addition of stairwells. Debate ensued about what caused the fire, but perhaps the real question was why the dorm hadn't burned down a lot sooner.

When he got out of prison himself, George Coldwell came to pick up his son a few days before the fire. On November 13, Coldwell de-manded his son be released and for the reformatory to hand him over. The boy had already tried to escape once. As a local from nearby Lau-rel Hill, Coldwell knew the reputation of the school and its practice of convict labor—hiring the boys out to local plantations, brickmakers, and naval companies. He also knew the trumped-up charges against boys—such as trespassing, truancy, or incorrigibility—that could be levied against poor folks who didn't have the means to defend their boys. He demanded the release of his son, and when school leaders refused, he threatened to blow up the school. Five days later, the in-dustrial school dormitory burned to the ground.

Coldwell was arrested about the time the fire began making national headlines. It wasn't the first threat like this school officials received. Angry parents routinely stormed the school grounds, wrote letters to the governor, and talked to journalists about the inhumane conditions and treatment of the young inmates.

How many casualties? No one knew exactly, as the coroner, school board of managers, staff, families, newspapers, and legislative committee all reported different names and numbers of casualties.

So, who died in the fire? With so much activity—parents coming for children, the records being destroyed, and growing public scrutiny—counting the dead was anything but simple. Three investigations led to three reports, and each offered different names of those who perished and different causes for the fire.

The board of managers issued a report by its president, William Milton, the same day as the coroner's report was made public. The board of managers' report, of course, sought to absolve the managers of blame.

Milton didn't disclose that his nephew, John Milton Jr., an employee of the school, had served on the coroner's jury—a body of citizens assembled to help a coroner on an inquest—and was a primary witness. He had been superintendent until 1913, when Bell took over, and had a great deal of clout in the community. His report stated that per the legislative act in 1913, the school had added two fire escape doors. He acknowledged the doors were always locked but stated the keys were kept in the main office on the first floor, to which all the staff had access.

According to Milton's report, the boys filed out in an orderly fashion and did not encounter smoke. There were no injuries and only six deaths. Two were the staff—the Evans men—who were trying to help save the other children. One was a "demented boy" who reentered the building in search of a blanket; one was a boy who reentered the building believing the superintendent was inside in an attempt to rescue him; and two other boys were trying to save the others.

In the school's version, all who perished were heroes, credited with saving lives.

The Florida legislative committee conducted its own investigation, independent of the coroner and the reform school's board of managers.

The committee found that there had been no fire drills or preventative measures for safety. There were no watchmen on duty. The administrators, including the superintendent and several staff members, were away from the school at the time of the fire. Witnesses said all the doors had been locked, including the fire escapes. A woman identified as Mrs. McBride, who lived near the school, told state investigators that Superintendent Bell had the only set of keys when he left the school and went to town that night. As a result of the state's investigation, Superintendent Bell was terminated.

It wasn't enough. Floridians cried out for more accountability.

"CREMATION OF INMATES WAS DUE TO NEGLIGENCE," read a headline in the *Tampa Tribune*.

"'HELL ON EARTH' THE CHARACTERIZATION OF STATE REFORM SCHOOL," the *Miami News* reported.

"MARIANNA FIRE WAS PREVENTABLE," shouted the *Tampa Times*.

According to the *Pensacola Journal*, prior attempts to burn down the dormitory had been made several months earlier. The board of managers tried to make it seem like arson caused the fire by blaming Coldwell, but a grand jury later exonerated him in light of evidence provided by witnesses and the staff of the school, which, consequently, allowed him to take his son home.

THE MANGLED FALLEN debris smoldered into the morning daylight, and what remained of the building was demolished. W. S. Bowles arrived at the school the following morning with his father, who also worked there. Bowles said that only unidentified charred trunks of bodies containing unburned hearts were recovered. When a body is burned, it will turn black in color, appearing charred. The fire destroys the outer tissues first and works its way inward until it is consumed in its entirety. If the fire is interrupted, the internal structures could still retain their color and texture, appearing pink, as Bowles described. Typically, within a structure like the dormitory, the building collapses and debris falling on the remains can cause additional fractures or damage to the tissues. So, the description by Bowles may not have been far-fetched. He later reported that one of the workers killed was identified by a blue patch of material from his clothing, a worker's uniform.

Given this description, we could expect to find the torsos of all the victims buried at Boot Hill. The bones from the rib cage and vertebrae should have been intact and in anatomical order. This was what we were prepared to look for.

How many bodies should we look for, though?

Six deaths were reported by Milton, the president of the board of managers.

Seven deaths were reported in the state legislative report.

Nine boys are listed as victims of the fire in an article in the *Idaho Statesman*, which aligned with the numbers reported by the school.

Ten deaths were reported by the coroner, including eight boys and two adult staff.

The board of managers said that those who weren't list as deceased ran away the night of the fire.

Among the child fatalities, nine boys were noted as missing: Clifford Jeffords, Earl Morris, Harry Wells, Joseph Weatherbee, Waldo Drew, Walter Fisher, Louis Haffin, Clarence Parrot, and S. Barnett. The board claimed witnesses saw Earl Morris outside the building following the fire, after which he must have run away.

In the cases of Waldo and Earl, the families maintained that the boys died in the fire and never came home, according to newspaper reports in the years that followed the fire.

We also tracked down living relatives for both boys, and they each hold to this day that the boys perished in that fire, and neither ever came home again.

We would have to excavate to find out for sure.

■ ■ ■

AFTER JUDGE WRIGHT denied our petition, we sought permission from the next logical place: Florida's Bureau of Archaeological Research. They responded to our request for an archaeological permit to excavate the burials with a list of questions, which we answered. Then came the denial, which was a hard no.

Secretary of State Ken Detzner said that he understood the importance of telling the story of the Dozier school, but "the Department of State does not have the statutory authority to fulfill your request.

"The [Bureau of Archaeological Research's] existing statutory authority to grant archaeological research permits is restricted to the recovery of objects of historical or archaeological value, not human remains, absent a danger to the grave site that actually threatens the loss or damage of those remains."

Some of the graves were already lost.

The White House Boys were livid. They'd been striving for answers since 2008, and sixty of the old men had already died without knowing the truth about the burial ground. The Black Boys of Dozier, a group formed to fight for the interests of African American wards, had held vigils, town hall meetings, and protests for months in Marianna.

"This is an example of yet another attempt to cover up the truth," Robert Straley told a reporter. "This time I do not believe the people of Florida will stand for it. You cannot find this many bodies and simply walk away."

Leaders of the NAACP were mad as hell, too.

"They're liars," said Dale Landry. Landry had even met with Detzner in his office. The secretary of state was glad that USF wanted to lead the exhumation at Dozier, Landry said. Otherwise, the state itself might have to do it.

"He's playing a game of double talk," Landry said. "The NAACP is extremely angry. We're talking about a site where there were atrocities done in America, on state property—on both black and white boys."

Senator Nelson called it a classic runaround.

Miami Herald columnist Fred Grimm responded with a column blasting the "inexplicable" decision, writing that "the limitations Detzner imposed on the archeologists assured that those 'surviving family members' will never know that their relatives' bodies had been buried in the old reform school's Boot Hill."

Grimm wrote what I knew to be true, that our findings "lent support to the assertions by former inmates, survivors of Dozier's brutal regime, who have long claimed that the number of the dead was much higher—that boys had been killed by guards and tossed into unmarked graves."

This may sound like a confusing and complicated issue, and it was, but we were right. To read what Grimm pointed out so plainly was confirmation that our findings weren't going to be brushed aside and lost in a bureaucratic process nobody cared to unpack.

Grimm didn't let it go unnoticed that Detzner had been a Tallahassee beer lobbyist before Republican governor Rick Scott appointed him to be secretary of state, so his warning to us that "under Florida law, human bodies are not objects to be dug up for research purposes" was patronizing. Dozens of books have been written about bioarchaeology, a subfield of anthropology that specifically excavates and researches ancient and historic cemeteries. Where was the rest of the archaeological community? I wondered.

Grimm cited the letter from USF deputy general counsel Gerard Solis, who said that we agreed with the sentiment, even if it was paternalistic. "The purpose of USF's work at Dozier," Solis wrote, "is not to excavate bodies for research as an academic end in itself; but rather it is engaged research intended to locate unmarked human burials and identify any human remains."

"Put another way," Solis added tartly, "USF researchers are not at Dozier to get ideas for a journal article, but to return lost human remains to their families" and that "archaeologists in Florida often excavate and relocate human remains" using permits issued by the Department of State's Division of Historical Resources, including for "human skeletal analysis."

Grimm continued: "Those permits don't usually capture the attention of the secretary. So why now? Why did Detzner pick this case to suddenly rewrite agency policies?"

Maybe Senator Bill Nelson was right, that the state had the authority, but their refusal to issue permits was a dodge.

"It is a dodge," Grimm wrote. "And it's a mystery why Scott and Detzner decided to obstruct efforts to identify the forgotten boys. The awful abuse suffered by the inmates of the Dozier school happened years before Scott took office. Yet he and his appointee chose to shut down the investigation. If nothing else, it seems like clumsy politics. None of the state's other leading politicians have objected to Professor Kimmerle's work at Dozier."

The South Florida columnist wrote that the only grumbling about it was coming from Jackson County, "the rural, insular enclave that supplied the guards who administered the brutal beatings and surreptitious burials."

While it's hard to imagine that rural Jackson County has enough political influence to stop this investigation, it's worth noting that Gov. Scott was up in Jackson County on Sunday to support a Republican county commission candidate. Or it may be that Scott is worried about lawsuits—about the families suing once the dead boys are identified, though that prospect hasn't bothered Pam Bondi, whose office would be faced with defending any civil suits.

Would former governors Charlie Crist or Bob Martinez or Jeb Bush or Lawton Chiles or Bob Graham have done something? Would they have seized the issue and done right by those boys and their families? Crist ordered a fresh investigation in 2008. Former governor Claude Kirk had even provided future governors a template for dealing with sadistic cruelty when he made a surprise visit to the school in 1968 and emerged outraged, saying, "If one of your kids were kept in such circumstances, you'd be up there with rifles."

"Instead of obstructing this investigation," Grimm concluded,

"Gov. Scott and Secretary Detzner should have hurried to that forsaken campus, shovels in hand, to be with Professor Kimmerle, promising answers, justice and names for those forgotten boys."

I'd never met Fred Grimm, but to have that kind of support from one of the top writers in Florida newspapers was the boost we needed to keep going. Little did we know the backlash was coming, and it was coming from an unexpected place: academia.

Dr. William Lees is an archaeologist, the executive director of the Florida Public Archaeology Network, and a professor at the University of West Florida, located in a part of the state long known as Floribama, for its Deep South sentiment. Lees wrote a blog post supporting Detzner's decision, to shame us among the academic community, as if we did not know or value the history and ethics concerning burial grounds.

"It is ironic, I think," Lees wrote, "that these boys may have suffered at the hands of the state when they were alive, and now, as they lie buried, the hands of a state university once again threaten their peace."

What gave the dead peace? Was it burial itself? Or was it justice?

I tried to think of a religious story, folklore, or even a ghost story that depicted someone who died unjustly as lying quietly in a peaceful grave but came up with none. The state had every duty to return the children in its custody home to their families, safely and alive.

The fact that they died in custody, regardless of their cause of the death, meant the state still had a responsibility to return their remains.

The boys were buried without consent. They were buried before their families were notified. They were buried in an unmarked burial ground, analogous to the fields used for burying dead convicts throughout Florida's convict lease system. To us they seemed more like clandestine burials for throwaway children than peaceful graves.

Lees's post prompted a range of responses, including one from Dale Landry, who poignantly illustrated that the archaeological community had not been a voice for Black heritage. When presented with a case that was about historic justice, they were failing again.

Lees argued that the Dozier burials were analogous to Native American burial grounds, which were protected under federal law, but it was clear that the context, history, and justification for the Dozier investigation was lost on him.

"Private individuals as well delighted at excavating Native American graves and displayed collections in storefront windows and in private homes," Lees wrote. "At the time, these native people had no voice. They were not unlike the young men buried at Dozier. Because they had no voice, archaeologists thought it was OK to excavate (and maybe study) and store these human remains. But the Native American community has found their voice, and has successfully advocated for the respectful treatment of their dead."

That voice was about the living, though. The living had rights, and that was lost on those in the archaeological community who stood in opposition to the Dozier investigation.

Lees was right that American Indian Nations fought and won the right to repatriate the skeletal remains, sacred objects, and other objects of cultural patrimony taken from them and their ancient burial grounds and housed at universities and museums across the country.

The question was, though: Was the Native American Graves Protection and Repatriation Act a sacred vow to never excavate anyone or forfeit future claims they may have to justice? The Rosebud Sioux didn't think so, even though it was now being used against them. "How is it the Army cannot change its ruling that a nation has no claim to its dead?" asked Peter Gibb, a researcher for the Rosebud Sioux Tribe. Perhaps they didn't want to disturb the peaceful graves? The Indians were engaged in a new battle with the US Army, this time to have the graves of their nation's children excavated from the burial ground at the infamous Indian Industrial School in Carlisle, Pennsylvania, where more than 450 children died after being taken forcibly from their homes in a federal program of assimilation—part of the "Kill the Indian, Save the Man" myth. The US Army was denying their petitions to have the remains excavated. "We talk about historical trauma," said Russell Eagle Bear, the tribe's historic-preservation officer. "A hundred and thirty years later, this still has an impact on our youth. We're trying to make peace with those spirits and bring them home." They wanted to bring their children home, spirit and body.

Lees went on to compare our investigation to cases where cemeteries are moved for construction, as they continuously have been throughout Florida, but omitted a critical difference between the two scenarios: when historic burials were found during construction, they were routinely exhumed and moved to another location, which was allowed under state law. All that the law required was notification to the proper authorities and a licensed funeral home director, when it wasn't a forensics case.

Many African American burial grounds had been destroyed as a result of predatory land practices that redlined American cities from the 1930 to the 1950s, enabling city governments, housing and sports authorities, and highway developers to confiscate African American–owned property through eminent domain, forcing active cemeteries into a state of abandonment. Within a few years, the cemeteries disappeared from the landscape and written records. In some cases they were excavated and moved for development. Within the Tampa Bay area alone, this happened repeatedly with the construction of parking garages, sports arenas, condominium developments, schools, and public housing projects. In 2017, a private firm excavated and moved burials for a high-end condo and hotel development, from a well-known and highly documented burial ground containing the remains of African Americans, Cubans, Native Americans, white pioneers, and US military personnel.

"This has resulted in the adoption of Federal laws to protect Native American graves, and in the creation of laws in states such as Florida that make it policy to treat all human remains with respect," Lees wrote. "This included leaving them undisturbed unless there is compelling scientific reason to do otherwise, and securing the agreement and cooperation of descendants or descent groups. When human remains are disturbed during construction or through natural processes of erosion, a specific and respectful process is triggered through state and, in some cases, Federal laws."

It seemed archaeological ethics could be a game of splitting hairs.

Due to a lack of documentation about who specifically was buried in the Tampa cemetery, archaeologists deferred to US military records, as they had occupied the land area as a military fort starting in 1824 and therefore spoke as the former landowners. Construction disturbed the same cemetery, and ninety-nine burials were relocated in 1980. The forensic anthropological report at the time said 57 percent of those individuals were not Native American. At least two were African Americans and nine were white settlers, but the other thirty-one skeletal remains were too poorly preserved to assess their ancestry or anything about their age and sex. In spite of that, during the excavation and removal of burials in 2018, only the Seminoles and US military were considered stakeholders. Once again, the African American community was left out of the discussion.

"The ethics accepted by the professional archaeologist today gives precedence to leaving graves undisturbed and allows excavation only when disturbed through construction or nature, or under the most extraordinary circumstances," Lees wrote. "I doubt, in terms of archaeological knowledge, such extraordinary circumstances exist at the Dozier School for Boys, no matter how unfortunate the story of these young men may be. If it is a story of crime, then while archaeological methods might contribute to an investigation, it is not research covered under the archaeological research permit process. I applaud Secretary Detzner, Director Bendus, and State Archaeologist Mary Glowacki for understanding this and for standing by what to me is the proper decision to deny USF a state archaeological research permit for excavation of human bodies from the Dozier School . . . I experienced this change in professional ethics regarding human remains first hand, and am personally dismayed that some anthropologists at the University of South Florida, in a program for which I have great respect, do not appear to understand this history and the current position of archaeological ethics regarding human burials."

In response to Lees's public statement, Dale Landry wrote back, imploring Lees to hear the African American voices who demanded to know the truth, who desperately fought to shed light on the dark corners of segregation and its repercussions, still felt today. Segregation was a practice that not only discriminated against an entire group of people, it erased Black people from history, denying their very existence through the exclusion of birth and death certificates and the whitewashing of their history and their roles in creating the cities and states of this nation.

Landry called Lees's post "interesting and somewhat questionable."

"As you are aware," he wrote, "the Industrial School was segregated during much of its existence and only around the time it was named Dozier was it an integrated facility. The burial ground dates back to the era of the segregation period. According to the practice in that time, people of color were buried separately from the dominant culture, Caucasians. It is believed that many that may be buried in the burial ground may be African American youth, however that fact is not confirmed. Further, given much of the testimony (both from research and interviews) there are a lot of unanswered questions regarding the cause of death for many of them. Finally, there is the manner of burials, some traditional, some in shallow graves, and others unknown."

Landry said it was a "graveyard of unanswered questions."

"For many Floridians, especially African Americans, we want to know what happened there and are concerned about how these youth and people died and why they were buried under such conditions," he wrote. "In closing I would like to simply state there is a small culture of people whose roots are here in Northwest Florida, Pensacola to Lake City, that are afraid about what may be revealed through the research being conducted by USF. As an anthropologist, Dr. Lees, hopefully you understand and hear the 'Voice' of the African American community and express the importance of voices to Secretary Detzner and both you and he support our call for the continued research by the USF team."

■ ■ ■

BACK IN TAMPA, we met with the university's legal team and the attorney general's office to try to come up with a third option. We decided to appeal. It seemed to us like the secretary of state misunderstood his authority under state law.

The two channels for investigation we attempted had failed. As a matter of historic justice, Boot Hill did not fit neatly into either box. The medicolegal system accessed through the medical examiner and law enforcement failed to win a court order, and the secretary of state was caviling on issuing an archaeological research permit. It seemed our last hope rested with the most powerful statewide elected leaders in Tallahassee. As the property owners, they had a right to remove burials on their land. So that was what we asked them to do.

It meant convincing the governor and Florida cabinet to better understand the loss and the anguish tied up in a century of tragedy at this state-run institution. It seemed, more and more, like our last shot rested with the governor.

Christian Wells, Antoinette Jackson, and I wrote a summary appeal to him.

> The children who died were chained to their beds and locked in rooms called "dark cells" on the third floor of the dormitory. . . . While it may be the desire of a handful of Jackson County politicians to bury the past, the thousands of victims and their families associated with this institution and the rippling effects it has had on the juvenile justice system in Florida will not disappear as easily as the children who died there. Too many people have been personally affected by the institution and the consequences of a system initially built on racism for the profit of a few. These effects can still be seen in our justice system today. With this most recent act by the Secretary it appears to us that the State is running away from this issue when in fact it should run toward this opportunity to bring resolution and justice to us all, as Floridians.

How we treat people in life and how we treat them in death is not just a reflection of who we were then but is also a reflection of who we are now. While we understand that we could appeal or re-file the petition and add even more pages of documentation citing examples, precedent-setting cases, and scientific reasoning on how this effort is within our capacity and the law . . . it is apparent that it is not a matter of capacity, but of political will and as such, no amount of logic can compete. So, on the eve of the 100-year anniversary of the fire that killed so many innocent victims, we are asking you as Governor of the State of Florida to fix the responsibility. Unlike so many governors before you, who put their own political and financial incentives before justice, sometimes to the detriment of their own political careers, you have an opportunity. The story of Dozier is in desperate need of a hero. Please help us fulfill the mission we have been tasked to do and bring resolution to a tragedy that will not otherwise simply disappear.

We felt like this appeal was our best shot, but in the end we never even had to send it.

A memorial service at Boot Hill in the 1950s. The only documented death and burial after 1950 in the school's records was Billey Jackson's, in 1952. Witnesses who attended Jackson's funeral did not recognize the people in this photo or recall a service of this size. They also said there were two other burials at Boot Hill circa 1951–52, thus contradicting the official record.

Inside one of the small isolation cells within the White House, where the doors and windows were once barred. All boys, regardless of their perceived race, were brought to this building for punishment.

FLORIDA INDUSTRIAL SCHOOL FOR BOYS
COLORED

Barrow Press 2585

DATE	NAME OF BOY	D—P—R	SENTENCE	EXPIRATION	No. Boys Present
7/15	Chas. Lowry	Escaped			169
7/18	John Austin	Ret.			170
7/19	Wm. McKinley	Dead.			169
8/19	Tom Cole	Escaped			168
7/19	Tom Cole	Ret.			169
7/19	John Austin	Escaped			168
7/20	Ben Williams	Dismissed			167
7/24	Jas. Wilson	Escaped			166
7/25	Grant Dukes	Ret.			
" "	Aron Clark				

The ledger maintained by the school recorded each boy's name, his offense, and dates of entry and release. It also showed dates when any of the boys tried to run away and the dates of their capture. During the flu epidemic in 1918, the release date column for many boys said "mother carried him home." It's unknown if this meant they were ill or deceased.

A speaker from the Black Boys of Dozier at a press conference in front of the old dorms on the former north side of the reform school. Protesters gathered as he spoke about his experience while incarcerated at the school and urged state leaders to allow the excavation of the burial ground.

US senator Bill Nelson (D-Florida), Ovell Krell (George Owen's sister), and I look at historic maps of the property to jog Ovell's memory about the location of the burial ground. She was brought there in 1941 when her parents planned to visit the school to look for Owen after he ran away. Instead, they were notified that his body was found under a house two miles away from school grounds. He was buried on the school property before the family could arrive to claim his body.

Ben Montgomery, a reporter from the *St. Petersburg Times*, interviews Glen Varnadoe. Glen's father and his uncle, Thomas Varnadoe, were sent to Dozier in 1934 for having trespassed in a neighbor's yard, but Thomas never came home and remained missing.

Boot Hill Burial Ground. Christian Wells, University of South Florida (USF) archaeologist, records changes in the soil seen in the test trench in search of graves. The trench was used to ground-truth results interpreted from ground-penetrating radar (GPR) data, yet was shallow enough not to disturb any burial present. The crosses were put up to commemorate the thirty-one children the school officials said died here. The crosses did not correspond to the graves, which were spread out under the road and in the woods. We found more graves than names of boys who should have been buried there.

The crew excavates a burial. The team divides the tasks of troweling, recording, measuring, and bagging to expose the remains, collect evidence, and carefully preserve all of the findings.

Mike Hurley and I look for bone fragments as fire hoses force water and soil through two screen layers of mesh. Anything larger than one eighth of an inch remains on top of the screen surface for analysis: burned brick and glass, buttons, marbles, broken ceramics, and bone.

The excavation is well under way. Sheriff David Gee, from Hillsborough County, flew his helicopter up to visit the site and crew. Students flagged material artifacts and bones as they were unearthed from this shallow grave.

Yellow numbers and blue flags help mark the bones and artifacts, such as nails and coffin wood, through the mud and water on the bottom of the first grave.

This rusted belt buckle recovered from the grave was compared to historic photographs from the school to date the grave. That would help us determine who was buried there.

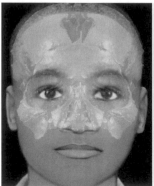

A facial approximation was created from reconstructed cranial fragments. The bones are glued back together and scanned. A digital face is drawn over the bones, following their anatomy to create a close likeness of the boy.

An excavated grave reveals the remains of a small boy with his arms across his chest. Boys as young as five were sent to the school in its early days.

A radiograph of a mandible excavated from Boot Hill showing the partial dental eruption of a nine-to-eleven-year-old child. We had so little to work with to identify remains, but every piece of evidence told a story.

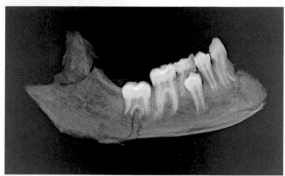

Marbles and buttons recovered from the excavation. The marbles—the only objects found resembling a toy—reminded all of us of the innocence of youth.

My sons, Reid and Sean, cool off during excavation of the dormitory, which burned in the early days of the school. Having the boys around made the work all the more significant and meaningful.

My colleague Dr. Greg Berg flags burials revealed by dark soil stains against the red clay after the Gradall excavator removed the topsoil.

Aerial view of the Boot Hill cemetery on the 1,400-acre campus during excavation. We ultimately uncovered fifty-five graves.

Last day of excavation, and I was glad this phase was done. I had no idea then that there was much more work to be done. I'd spend several more years working on the project.

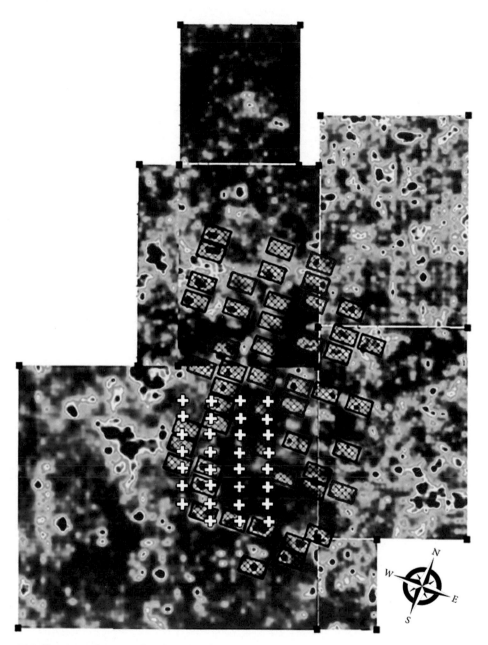

This illustration shows results of a ground-penetrating radar image overlaid with white crosses as they were arranged and rectangular boxes of the burials excavated. Only thirteen of the graves were in the area marked by the crosses when we started and even they did not line up.

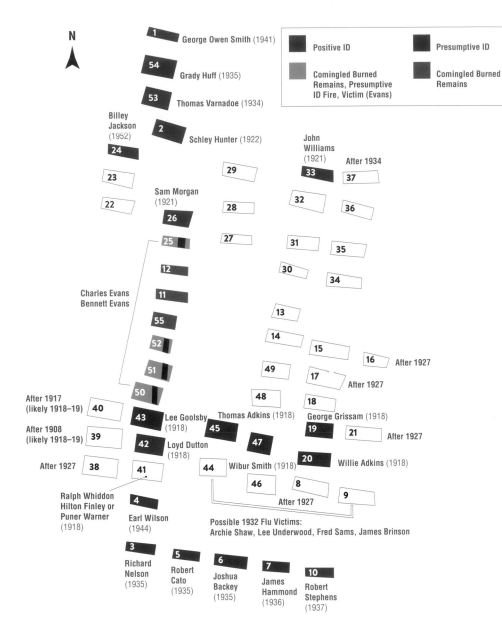

Site diagram showing burials excavated and names of those identified.

Chapter 8

"WE CAN'T FORGET . . . WHAT HAPPENED IN JACKSON COUNTY"

Richard Varnadoe was five years old when his two brothers were pried away from his mother and sent hundreds of miles away to the reformatory in Marianna on trumped-up trespassing charges. One came home scarred and afraid, and the other never came home at all. Dead of pneumonia, the school officials said. Case closed.

In June 2013, Richard was eighty-four years old when he opened his mouth to let a crime scene investigator with the Hillsborough County Sheriff's Office swab the inside of his cheek in order to collect his DNA, hoping it could be used to identify the remains of a brother lost for the last seventy-nine years.

I watched from nearby as television cameras from a dozen news stations zoomed in close.

Glen Varnadoe sat next to his uncle and put his arm around the old man's shoulder.

"I am hoping to find enough remains to identify him and get him back and put him with Mother," Richard Varnadoe told the TV cameras.

Seated nearby was Ovell Krell, also eighty-four and hoping to recover the remains of her brother George Owen Smith.

"It's been seventy-something years," Ovell told the reporters. "Of course, I'm hoping for closure for myself."

Sitting with Ovell and Richard and Glen was Robert Stephens, a welder from Tampa who was named after the uncle who reform school officials said was killed by another boy in 1937. Stephens had gotten a phone call from his sister, Priscilla Stephens Kruize, a few days before. She told him that an uncle they'd never met had died at the Dozier school under mysterious circumstances and that University of South Florida researchers wanted the family to submit a DNA sample to see if they could identify the remains of his young uncle.

Based on old records, we knew that fourteen-year-old Robert Stephens had been committed to the school in 1936 under the name Robert Seinous for breaking and entering. He was ordered to serve a sentence of two years, or until legally discharged.

About ten months later, on July 15, 1937, not long after he turned fifteen, Robert was found dead. A death certificate was signed by the reform school physician, Dr. Nathaniel Baltzell. The portion of the death certificate that left space for autopsy information was blank, so it's unclear whether one was performed.

The old school ledgers show that Robert Seinous—who we now know was Stephens—was "stabbed to death by another inmate, Leroy Taylor." Under "cause of death," the boy's death certificate read, "Knife wound following hemorrhage."

We found court records at the Jackson County clerk's office that showed Leroy Taylor was indicted on a charge of first-degree murder but later pleaded guilty to second-degree murder.

Robert was buried in "Marianna, Florida," but there's no indication of where that might've been. Since his mother was from Quincy, not far away, we suspected he was buried at Boot Hill. We needed his family's DNA if we ever hoped to confirm whether his remains were in one of the unmarked graves.

So here sat his relative, looking a little nervous as the television cameras captured him opening his mouth for the crime scene tech to take a buccal swab. His goal, said Stephens, was "to find the truth."

I was hoping this would work. We all did. Hoping that if the public saw images of these good and decent people stepping up to reclaim their pasts, they'd be compelled to support them. We didn't know it then, but the Stephens link would bring a whole family together and allow us to meet even more relatives, including a civil rights icon named John Due and a novelist named Tananarive Due, inspiring people who were interested in their family legacy, even if Robert Stephens's short life was a footnote in the history of the state of Florida. Kruize had learned about him only three weeks before.

"We can't forget and try to whitewash what happened in Jackson County in the 1930s," John Due said.

We hoped, too, that then governor Rick Scott and the Florida cabinet would see the same people and be compelled to allow us to excavate.

If they said no, there was no other real recourse.

It felt like we were trapped between worlds. This was not a modern crime scene, and it was not a dig in ancient Rome. Of all the systems in place for investigations, archaeological excavations, cemetery exhumations, criminal homicides—nothing fit. Every door was being shut. This was the challenge with historic justice initiatives. Our systems were not well equipped to redress past abuses.

It seemed to me that if we were going to do this, to excavate and identify the unknown boys, we ultimately needed the missing person's system to work for us. We needed a way to test DNA samples and compare our pool of unknown persons to the pool of potential family members.

The National Institute of Justice would eventually agree to fund us for this purpose.

David Gee, the sheriff of Hillsborough County, which encompasses the city of Tampa, also agreed. I worked with Gee and his deputies many times before. He was helping us tremendously by sending detectives and crime scene investigators on every trip to Dozier. They benefited from the scientific training, and they helped us by working hard as part of the crew. Gee, a lawman and sharp politician, personally helped navigate the murky waters of our relationship with the law enforcement officials in Jackson County. Our relationship with the Jackson County Sheriff's Office changed for the better thanks to Gee's help. Jackson County sheriff Lou Roberts was an earnest man who spoke about this project along with me to a group Florida sheriffs at their annual conference. He also provided security for us at the Dozier site, which was comforting, even if one of his deputies liked to eat boiled peanuts out of a tin can. Roberts seemed to be caught in a difficult situation, having to also live in Jackson County and answer to his constituents, many of whom, it turned out, did support us but felt like they could not say anything. To show him our gratitude, we brought our crew and the GPR to help him on one of his cold cases while we were there, searching a backyard for buried evidence.

WE KNEW A lot of the families, as they had started seeking answers and demanding excavation from the state before we were involved. Unfortunately, we didn't have contact information for the living, known family members for all the boys who were potentially buried at Dozier. Since those boys died as juveniles, they had no direct descendants.

We worked with a group of genealogists to identify possible families by constructing family trees for their siblings, aunts, uncles, and cousins. We needed the closest living family member on the maternal side of each boy to ensure we had a good mitochondrial DNA (mtDNA) sample for comparison. We may have been able to extract nuclear DNA, in which case you can test relatives from either the mom's or the dad's side of the family. However, DNA degrades over time, and nuclear DNA is the first to go. Mitochondrial DNA lasts much longer. It is how scientists have extracted DNA from Neanderthals who lived 120,000 years ago.

The genealogists started pumping names to us, but finding these family members' current contact information was a huge challenge, as that information was not usually public. However, law enforcement could track down the living and had the databases and resources needed to do it.

We also needed a law enforcement case number representing an open investigative file for each boy, so we could enter and keep track of the samples. Sheriff Gee understood the power of that number, the doors it could open. Even though the law in Jackson County wouldn't do it, Gee was able to circumvent the issue of jurisdiction through what was known as an "agency assist," when one law enforcement agency opened a case outside of their jurisdiction to help another agency.

With that case number, we could collect DNA samples from family members for the identification of unknown persons. I thought that if we could log the families into the system, that door would have to stay open, and even if we failed to excavate the remains at Boot Hill, perhaps one day they would be found and entered into the system, making identification possible for a long time to come.

The urgency came when I talked to Glen about our status. He informed me that his uncle Richard, the only living brother of Thomas Varnadoe, had been in the hospital with pneumonia. Since they were brothers who shared the same mother, they would have both inherited the same mtDNA. I told Glen we needed to secure a sample from Richard as quickly as possible, in case his health got worse and it became too late. It was a difficult conversation to have, but Glen understood and took to asking all his political and public supporters to find a way to start collecting DNA, rather than waiting for the permission to come through. Glen had even asked the nurses at the hospital when visiting Richard if they could collect a blood sample for him. Baffled and confused, they told him no, and that was when he called me.

Gee agreed to have his crime scene investigators collect DNA swabs.

We wanted to arrange an event for the families who had been speaking publicly and attending the various town hall meetings to come together and submit DNA samples. I talked to Lara Wade from USF communications about the significance of this step. It felt like a possible game changer. In every public event and speech I gave, I tried to construct a message about restorative justice. As the one who organized all

the press events, she was used to hearing me talk about restorative justice. "This is what it looks like," I told her. "This is about empowering
people to take some step toward finding a solution."

She said sharing the moment publicly would make it clearer to or-
dinary citizens how this investigation was caught between two worlds.

The problems we faced in gaining permission were by choice. An
intrinsic problem based on policies set up to guide our everyday practices in archaeology and criminal investigations. It was not a matter of
capacity, nor science, nor our ability. It was a matter of will.

Lara understood, and she suggested we do the event at USF and
invite the media. She knew that the television-viewing public loved
shows like *CSI* and would support our efforts if they could see what
we were doing. We thought, "Let's show them the lengths to which
the families are willing to go."

So we held a public event to swab DNA and invited everyone.
Major Robert Ura from the Hillsborough County Sheriff's Office
even agreed to speak, and he talked about his agency's commitment
to the meaning of restorative justice. Watching administrators from a
Florida sheriff's office talk about restorative justice—after all that had
been said and done on this project—was a proud moment.

"They get it," I thought. "They totally get what this is about."

Now, if only everyone did.

WE'D APPLIED TO the state archaeologist for a permit to conduct exhumations. We'd enlisted the help of powerful politicians like Senator
Bill Nelson, who was trying to secure for us financial assistance from
the US Department of Justice, as well as local leaders from Glen's district, like state representative Seth McKeel and state senator Kelli Stargel from Lakeland. McKeel headed the state's House Appropriations
Committee, and he and Stargel worked to allocate my university the
$190,000 in state funding that enabled our team to continue our work.

We planned to send the DNA samples to the University of North Texas Health Science Center in Fort Worth for processing, and they'd handle entering them into the National Missing and Unidentified Persons System (NamUs) database.

I told the press gathered that we aimed to provide a "small measure of justice" for the dead boys and their families, and I meant that. The project had been politicized and polarized, and there were unfathomable moments when greed and white supremacy and racial hatred had crept in, but seeing the families gathered at USF's Tampa campus reminded me to be resolute. They were why we had been working so hard.

After she gave the police a DNA sample in a moment that would be shown on the television news, Ovell Krell stayed behind to do an interview with me for National Public Radio. This was a woman who had searched so long for her brother, and not only out of love. She had vowed to her own mother and father on their deathbeds that she would find George Owen if it was in her power, that she would look for him until she drew her last breath.

When the interview began, I was surprised at how assertive this petite Southern woman was. She blamed the Florida Department of Law Enforcement and the state of Florida for not finding George Owen's body in their investigations. She was critical of the failures over the years by people who could have done more. She pulled no punches.

Afterward, when the microphones were off and we were alone, she smiled and took my hand.

"See," she said. "I can say all the things you can't."

I COULD FEEL the tension in the room as representatives from the Department of Juvenile Justice, the Florida Department of Law Enforcement, and the Florida Department of Environmental Protection slid into chairs before the Florida cabinet.

I saw lots of familiar faces. The families of the dead, representatives of the NAACP, the White House Boys, and the Black Boys of Dozier.

Their secrets had kept them apart for five decades. Some still slept with the lights on. Some felt as though they could not love or be loved. Some thought, against all reason, that if they told what happened, the men from the school might show up at their front doors to carry them away again.

If their secrets kept them apart, then their shared truth had brought them back together, on the first Tuesday of August 2013, in a government building in Florida's capital.

There sat Robert Straley, quiet and determined and reasonable, a man who had been so disturbed by the death of a Black boy at the hands of boot camp guards that he could no longer keep the monsters out of his own nightmares.

There sat Richard Huntly, who said he was worked like a slave in the reform school farm fields at age eleven, free labor for white profiteers whose paychecks came from the state of Florida.

There sat Johnny Lee Gaddy, a preacher now, who once saw, hand to God, a human hand in the pig slop he dumped in the hog trough at Dozier when he was eleven in 1957.

And there was Bryant Middleton, an old Army Ranger who would choose to return to Vietnam, where he earned two Purple Hearts, before he'd go back to the Dozier School for Boys.

Our final strategy was to have Attorney General Pam Bondi bring the issue before the cabinet for a vote. The university's lawyer worked with her office and the DEP on a land-use agreement, which laid out the scope and rules of the work. It would stand in place of an archaeological permit, exhumation order, or search warrant.

Bondi would introduce it, then call for a vote. Commissioner Adam Putnam was already showing his support, as was the state's chief financial officer, Jeff Atwater. Atwater's chief of staff had long been on speed dial, receiving regular updates about the project and providing support where possible. The state's funeral home directors fell under the CFO's authority, as did FEMORS, the Florida

Emergency Mortuary Operations Response System, an organization established by the state to respond to mass-casualty events, such as hurricanes. I asked FEMORS for their mortuary support if we were allowed to proceed. The agreement was carefully crafted to cover all possible contingencies. The only uncertainty going into the cabinet meeting was whether the governor would support it, and since there was no higher authority, it meant the decision could go either way.

"In a state as old as Florida is, we're going to have chapters in our history we're more proud of than others," I heard Agriculture Commissioner Adam Putnam say. "But there is no shame in searching for the truth."

The issue, he said, had been ignored too long by state officials.

We had found fifty possible graves using GPR and ground-truthing, but we'd never bring the peace of certainty if we couldn't unearth them to see for ourselves who they were and how they had died, and to return them to their loved ones. Some of the men believed there were even more of their brothers buried in forgotten fields. Some of them recalled their classmates disappearing, and a few even claimed to have dug boy-size holes on command.

We owed it to them to keep looking, and this government body held that permission in its hands.

After all the speeches, the cabinet finally voted, and the decision was unanimous. They approved our land-use agreement, which gave us a year to excavate the little burial ground in the hopes of finding all burials and identifying the remains. Jeff Atwater said he hoped the legislature would continue to fund our work until all the remains could be reunited with families. They had already approved spending $190,000 on the project.

The men stood and clapped. I couldn't help but smile. They ran their fingers across their eyes and hugged their wives, a band of women who had learned to live with the rage and sleepless nights.

"I'm numb," said Roger Kiser, who had been sent to Marianna after running from an abusive orphanage. He was among the original five men to revisit the campus and speak out, a ceremonial truth-telling that launched all of this. Now he couldn't find words. "I don't know what to say. I'm just glad that Florida is finally doing the right thing."

Finally.

"There's not going to be enough crime scene tape in the state of Florida to take care of this situation," Jerry Cooper told reporters.

Hyperbole, maybe, but we'd come to learn that law enforcement would be involved in unusual ways.

"We have fought so hard to get to this point," I heard Bryant Middleton say. "They're going to find out the truth."

"Marianna made slaves out of us," said Richard Huntly, who had become president of the Black Boys of Dozier in order to advocate for the African American kids who were mistreated. "They were supporting their finances on the backs of us children."

He told me before that he was sure that some of his classmates had disappeared.

"We all came back for them. We remembered," he told a reporter. "If they could hear us today. We came back for you. You boys can go home today."

It was gratifying to hear Antoinette Harrell, a genealogist and peonage researcher who had studied the school as a legalized slave plantation, a continuation of enslavement under the guise of correction, praise our work. "The ones who survived," she said, "they deserve closure."

"This is a historic day," said Robert Straley. "We finally found an administration with the guts to go back in time to help the boys who couldn't help themselves."

We planned to start as soon as we could caravan our equipment from Tampa to Marianna, possibly that very week. When the reporters turned to me, I thanked the appropriate people, even if some of them had reluctantly lent their support. I thanked the governor and cabinet, and specifically Attorney General Pam Bondi, who had worked for this behind the scenes.

"It's been a long process," I said. I had a feeling that the hard work was just beginning. "Our goal is to identify every individual. That's probably not possible, but we're going to try. Those not identified will be reinterred at the appropriate location."

I couldn't wait to tell my friend Ovell Krell. I called her as soon as I could. She told me she was thrilled that George Owen might finally come home after all these years.

Chapter 9

"OFTENTIMES, HISTORY DOESN'T INCLUDE THE GOOD PARTS"

Some townsfolk were not yet willing to come to terms with the fact that they had aided and abetted a system of cruelty. Reconciling those things—the light and the dark—came at an embarrassing cost. We tried to make ourselves at home in a place that seemed on the surface to be interested in welcoming outsiders, but we heard the whispers. They said we were in it for the money. We were in it for the publicity. We were striving for fame and media attention. We were ruining their town. We were killing tourism. We were decimating their economy. We were trying to make them look bad. We didn't understand that the abuse happened in a bygone era. We were not from there and we didn't know how things worked. The state representative from Jackson County wrote letters to the university president demanding that I stop my research. She sent the same letters to the Florida governor. Her constituents blamed us for the school closure and the loss of two hundred jobs, even though a fresh Department of Justice investigation had found deplorable conditions. They called me unethical. They accused us of trying to get African Americans riled up. They accused me of "secret communications" with reporters. They accused me of focusing on the negative examples and ignoring the thousands of boys who benefited from their stay at the school. They said the wards at Dozier had had it better than at home; at least at Dozier they got clothes and food.

All this angst festered in a place steeped in its own whitewashed version of history, a place where the church rolls had carried the same last names for two hundred years, where you could still find stately antebellum plantations lining quiet country roads like Confederate sentries. Every year they reenacted a small Civil War battle and re-vived old Rebel ghosts on graveyard tours. A tall obelisk in front of the courthouse honored the soldiers of the South—"We care not whence they came . . . their cause and country still the same—they died and wore the gray"—just a stone's throw from where Claude Neal hung in 1934.

And, of course, race was entwined in everything. On a tour of an old plantation, one county official told me that Blacks only had it bad *after* the war.

"The Civil War?" I asked, astonished.

He corrected me: "The War of Northern Aggression."

That was when it fell apart and they became impoverished, he said, without white caretakers. Before the war, they worked on the farms and had a place to live and were cared for, like one big family. He believed this. His was the same communal mentality that wanted to preserve a moral, decent image of Dozier.

THIS SENTIMENT WAS unexpected. I thought this was all behind us. Talking about racism could be difficult; it was ultimately about what people valued, and that required empathy. I felt like I had a lot of em-pathy for the feelings of the families and victims. I didn't have those conversations with the people who opposed our investigation. At first, I didn't understand the level of pushback, and I certainly didn't expect what was to come.

I had never heard the phrase *War of Northern Aggression* to describe the Civil War.

I had never met anyone who believed, in all seriousness, that enslaved Black people were better off during slavery than they were in the Reconstruction that followed, claiming they were part of the plantation family.

So when I spoke at public meetings in Marianna, meetings to which I was invited to explain what we were doing or share our results, I thought that everyone who was interested in hearing from us—white and Black—would be there. I didn't know that when it was organized by Black ministers or the NAACP, those in the white power structure wouldn't attend and in fact would actually be offended that I didn't hold a separate meeting for them. This unspoken paradigm also meant that when the whites got offended, they would then turn the conversation around to subtly portray themselves as the victims.

I was told again and again that I needed to take the community perspective into account. What wasn't explicitly said was that there were two communities.

A white Marianna farmer explained it to me: those in local government needed separate briefings for them alone. I appreciated his insight, but it didn't compel me to hold separate meetings. At the time, I felt like that would be catering to a segregationist viewpoint, or pandering to racists. "I don't play that way," I once told Senator Bill Nelson.

Could I have missed an opportunity to transform someone's ideas? Would it have made a difference? I don't know. The lack of conversations about racism within white communities, in Marianna and well beyond, had no doubt helped perpetuate the status quo.

If you peeled back the criticism from locals and examined the source, it was easy to see the power play. The town's tourism director, who claimed we were hurting the economy, was married to the lawyer who represented Troy Tidwell, the so-called One-Armed Man who was accused of beating so many boys he'd been the focus of a class-action lawsuit. The county commissioners who were opposed to our project were the ones bent on selling the Dozier land for economic development. The police chief's father was an administrator at the school for years. One local explained it like this: "He's a big man here, and his daddy was a big man. If you take down the image of his daddy, he ain't big no more."

A group of former Jackson County Chamber of Commerce Citizens of the Year gathered in front of the county courthouse one bright afternoon to let everyone know how they had been maligned.

"Here we are, citizens of the year, volunteers, people concerned about the appearance of our home county," Homer Hirt, the chamber's 2010 Citizen of the Year, said.

The 2009 Citizen of the Year, Lanet James, added: "All we ask from the state and anyone that is involved in this program: Come look, come get the good comments."

"This is a great town to live in and the people that are alive and well don't like what's been going on and it's not the truth," said 2002 Citizen of the Year Royce Reagan. "As a citizen of Jackson County, I think we need to reverse this a little bit and quit letting outsiders come in here and stir up something that is not the truth."

The entire event, which the chamber of commerce distanced itself from, had Dale Cox's fingerprints all over it. The smattering of panhandle reporters who were present didn't seem surprised when the 2012 Citizen of the Year stepped to the microphones.

"For five years we've heard the same allegations over and over and over and over with no factual basis behind them," Cox said. Cox went on to read from a tedious list of errors he thought regional television reporters had made. "You should afford the people of this community the same treatment that you give a bunch of former juvenile delinquents who come up here and make wild allegations that have been proved to be incorrect."

His frustration seemed to be boiling over.

Standing nearby, watching the white Citizens of the Year speak, was Elmore Bryant, the former head of the Jackson County NAACP.

He told a reporter for the *Jackson County Floridan* that he had a different take.

"I know Jackson County. I know Marianna," he said. "Oftentimes, we Black people feel the same way, when our history and things we have accomplished have been ignored."

"Oftentimes," Bryant said, "history doesn't include the good parts."

Chapter 10

"THANK YOU ALL FOR YOUR GOOD WORK"

To make a square, you have to calculate the hypotenuse and adjust two sides until each diagonal of the square is equal in length. To figure out the lengths, you need to apply the Pythagorean theorem. This square is called a unit, and it is proof that your math teacher was right: you do use geometry after middle school.

The unit has to be squared. It also has to be exactly on top of the grave. If you place it a little to the left or a little to the right, you are off-center, and once you dig it out, some portion of the skeletal remains will be under the sidewall. You do not want skeletal remains under a sidewall. When that happens, you have to start again in that direction, from the top. Bringing down the sidewall of dirt into your unit makes a mess. Success rests on choosing the exact right place to put your unit.

It sounds so simple until you really think about it. Imagine walking into a field and placing a tent stake into the ground. The trick is that you must place it on the right spot, which is the precise southwest corner of a perfect square that will also be squared over a grave, which is buried a meter deep. Did I mention nothing is marked on the ground surface? A reminder that real life is three-dimensional, so finding that exact, precise starting point is make-or-break.

We wanted to excavate two graves on that Labor Day weekend

in 2013. That meant finding the southwest corners of two different unmarked burials. We decided to excavate two square units on the north end of Boot Hill, those closest to the large oak tree, based on the ground-penetrating radar results and the test trenches that showed us that those locations had graves. I knew what the soil looked like, and I knew the relative depth. I also wanted to avoid uprooting the metal crosses from the 1990s that stood erect in commemoration. I wanted to avoid that area for as long as possible just to prove a point to those who denied that the anomalies we found were human burials. Christian took one grave; I started on the other. We didn't want to dance around the issue any longer.

So we staked the corners and measured the area where we wanted to dig, marking a perfect square. Then we made another square a few meters away over the second GPR anomaly. And at sunup on Saturday, in a clearing surrounded by kudzu-heavy woods, we carefully began digging square holes with flat shovels, hoping the red soil would give up its secrets.

To start, we created the first unit, a one-meter square. A grave was longer than a meter, though, and usually required two units side by side, thereby making a grid. For this excavation, we made the grids two-by-two units in size; basically a big square divided into four equal parts, two-by-two meters.

We chose Labor Day weekend for the excavation since it was the first available time we could all organize ourselves enough to drive up to Marianna and spend a few days doing fieldwork, following the cabinet approval. With the university semester starting and everyone going back to school, including my own two sons, it was our best option for working over a long weekend.

IT WAS HOT. So hot. Florida-at-the-end-of-August hot. The temperature climbed to ninety-one degrees with humidity near 100 percent. Steam rose from the soil. Camera lenses fogged over each time one of us tried to take a picture. It felt like it never stopped raining. We took cover again and again, waiting for lightning storms to pass over the little clearing in the woods.

We set up trailers, trucks, and tents for a command post, but the ground was so wet that the trucks were getting stuck in the mud. We dug trenches around the burial units so rainwater would run off, away from the graves. The water table in Jackson County was high to begin with, so water rose up from the bottom of the grave at the same time it was raining down from the sky, pouring into the grave. Fighting water was a losing battle.

Everything was wet and muddy. Me. My clothes. My hair. My paper bags for evidence, my trowels, my shovels, my shoes. Under the topsoil, Marianna was all red clay—red, slippery, wet, muddy, sticky clay. It also encased the remains we were trying to uncover. The tents and tarps we set up over the square units mitigated the rain only enough to allow the work to continue. A slight breeze, as welcoming as it may have been, pushed the rain sideways under the tarp.

I lost my favorite Ray-Ban sunglasses in the backfill, I think. The sun there was too bright to work without them. That wasn't the first time I'd lost sunglasses on a dig. I did remember to keep my phone near the command tent, but only after filling the charging port with Jackson County mud.

When the rain stopped, the mosquitoes and flies rolled in, as thick as carpet. We wanted to work as late into the evening as possible to ensure we would finish in time, and that meant long days sitting in mud and wet jeans, constantly wiping the rain and bug spray from our eyes.

Reporters traveled from around Florida and crowded into the parking lot across the street. A few grumbled that we made them give up a holiday weekend, but this was something nobody wanted to miss. The communications team from USF decided to stage the press across the street. We couldn't have reporters and camera crews trampling unchecked around what might become a crime scene. Only a small crew—CNN had come down from Atlanta, and a reporter and photographer for the *Tampa Bay Times,* formerly the *St. Petersburg*

Times, came up from Tampa—was allowed at the site, and they were responsible for providing pool photos and video to the media teams across the street. CNN was broadcasting live intermittently. The enormous satellite antenna on the CNN truck made the tiny clearing in the woods seem even smaller.

All of it felt surreal, like everyone had forgotten that archaeology tended to be an incredibly slow, deliberate, and tedious process. The day might have started with big machines or even shovels, but excavating skeletal remains required several days of work using dental picks and toothbrushes. The careful process was not very entertaining or interesting, not something you wanted to stand by and watch. It would have been like tuning into a baking show on television where you watched the oven during the fifty-five minutes it took to bake a cake, instead of watching the hostess pop the batter into one oven as she pulled out a perfectly finished cake from the next oven. The finished cake, the one that had been done ahead of time and was meant for you to see, was already waiting.

How did we arrive at this point? I mean, really, what happened? I wanted to open the oven and show everyone a perfect cake. This was live, though, not prepped ahead of time, and so whatever we would find was yet to be seen.

Under normal circumstances, a stormy weekend would have compelled us to postpone the dig. Or we would have wrapped up early and come back in a week. These were not options this time, with the eyes of the world upon us.

In truth, I work better under pressure. Extreme pressure. Somehow I tune out everything around me and focus on what is right in front of me. If I have a plan, I can execute it, ignoring pain or discomfort, mosquitoes or thunderstorms, and adapt when it goes off the rails. I had a religious studies professor in college describe finding that type of peace in chaos as a transcendental moment. Walt Whitman once wrote, "I like the scientific spirit—the holding off, the being sure but not too sure, the willingness to surrender ideas when the evidence is against them: this is ultimately fine—it always keeps the way beyond open . . ."

Robert Straley and I always shared our favorite poets with each other and would search for the right sentiment to send. His favorite was Dickinson, but he would have loved the Whitman quote.

Throughout the weekend, my phone chimed constantly with texted words of wisdom from friends back home in Tampa and Minnesota and around the country, who were keeping up with our progress through news briefings. Most of them were anthropologists or cops—my crew.

"It looks wet."

"Must be hot, you're melting."

"Why tf are you excavating in the rain?"

These served as reminders that I wasn't alone, even if it felt that way sometimes as I made my way to the bottom of a burial pit.

My favorite was a photo a television producer texted me. He snapped a picture of me sitting on the side of the burial, reading a book. All around me, the rain was pouring down, trenches were filling with water being diverted away from the grave shaft, people were working everywhere—and I was reading a book: *Standards for Data Collection from Human Skeletal Remains.* The photo made me laugh. A perfect moment.

THE ROUTINE THAT weekend was the same, day in and day out. Morning news briefings were generally okay. The day was fresh, and it was anyone's guess what we would find. After all, the whole mission was a process of discovery.

As the day wore on, the questions from reporters began to feel more existential.

"Can you tell us what is going on here today?"

"Can you describe what is happening?"

As the rain poured down, it was not vanity. Nobody would want cameras in her face, having recently crawled out of a grave.

"Don't be a smart-ass," I told myself. "Stick to the message," the voice in my head shouted. So I would smile and describe our process, and the progress we'd made. I took great pains to remind everyone, as the hours wore on, as reporters peeled away for the comfort of their hotel rooms, that this kind of science was a slow process. I thanked them, over and over, for their patience and support.

A friend who worked in the criminal intelligence division of one of our partnering agencies texted that he was enjoying my interviews. He noted that my face made a specific expression before answering a question I didn't like—a tell that only a good police detective or poker player would notice. He added that he would watch for it from then on.

Just great, I thought. Everyone was so helpful.

The routine changed very little from day to day. The excavation site had to be set up each morning around sunrise and taken down each day, well after dusk—like the daily rise and fall of a small, muddy civilization. Following that came a debriefing with the crew to hash out the next day's plan. Then we headed across the street to offer a summary for the gaggle of media and communications folks. Next came one-on-one interviews for the national news outlets, the Associated Press and National Public Radio.

Before anyone else, I called my sons to find out about their days and hear their little voices. It was unimaginable to me, the fear and sorrow my boys would have felt if they were ripped from their homes and institutionalized. I wanted to hear their laughter and bask in knowing they were safe.

Then came calls to the family members who fought so hard for this to happen and were waiting eagerly to know if we were successful. Following those calls were more calls to the supporters and allies who kept the political storms at bay, and then to our security team, and then to local law enforcement authorities, and then to staff from each of the political offices, and then to the Department of Environmental Protection, the Department of Juvenile Justice, our friends at the NAACP, and the ministers praying for us.

Finally, after all that, we loaded into trucks and SUVs, and the caravan of anthropology and archaeology students and faculty and the reporters and the communications team would caterpillar its way back to the chain hotel at the next Interstate 10 off-ramp. There were days we set up lamps, powered by generators, to illuminate the graves and work past dark. Squatting and kneeling on the hard ground for eight hours was one thing; doing it day after day was another. We needed our volunteer crew to keep coming back. That meant making sure they were well taken care of. We bought a dozen yoga mats for people to kneel or sit on—a purchase that received a lot of scrutiny from the university business office, as it didn't sound like typical lab supplies or field equipment to them.

After we cleaned up and washed all the mud away, we shared a meal. I typically voted to eat dinner at the restaurant that was the shortest walk from our hotel, though it was slim pickings. Marianna at the interstate exit was Anytown, USA. We held an off-the-record social hour back at the hotel, where we drank wine and vodka, though not together. Marianna was in a dry county, a hangover from the old blue laws, and that meant no liquor was sold in restaurants, and there were no bars. This was a bizarre and baffling way of life for me, having grown up in Minnesota, where I worked as a cocktail waitress at fifteen. There was one drive-thru liquor store across the street from the hotel, where one of my colleagues introduced us to Fireball.

The way we excavated the first two graves, in the square units, was the traditional method used in archaeology. It was not the only method, but it held up best under the scrutiny of the television cameras and was the best choice with only a long weekend to finish the work.

I waited until my long ride home at the end of the weekend to call Robert Straley in Clearwater. The road from Tallahassee to Tampa was long. Even if you took the back way, there were only two options, and both had known dead zones where there was no cell phone service. Robert answered after the first ring. He'd been waiting to hear how it went. He had watched every news program and read every article. He even read every comment that piled up at the bottom of the news articles online. He wanted to know what people thought about what we were doing. He wanted to come to our defense, if need be, in the dark and hateful corners of the Internet. He wrote editorials and sent them to state newspapers, and if they were rejected, he took another shot elsewhere.

The anticipation in his voice gave me a slight feeling of guilt for not calling him before the weekend ended. His call wasn't a quick debriefing. We sometimes talked for hours, our conversations lasting most of my drive home to Tampa. This drive was no different. The next morning he sent me a poem he wrote, a truly treasured note and a fitting ending to our first field mission.

An Ode to Archaeology
BY ROBERT STRALEY

Excavating remains of the dead,
Is not as adventurous as it would seem,
When you're in a field of tangled brush,
Prickly weeds and centipedes,
Plagued by the press and thoughts of rain,
"Tell us what you found!" they scream,
With microphones that look like trees
"Show us, explain it, how did you fare?"
Covered with clay and lipstick smeared,
"The bugs were as big as birds," She said,
And left them all in tears. . . . . . .

WHAT DID WE find?

A few hours after noon on the first day, with thunderstorms rolling in, we found the first signs of a burial at the bottom of our first shallow hole about thirty meters north of those rows of crooked pipe crosses. Faculty and graduate students from the University of South Florida and crime scene technicians from the Hillsborough County

Sheriff's Office and mortuary directors from around the panhandle—about twenty people altogether—gathered around the hole to examine a casket handle I unearthed near the remains.

I worked in Kosovo, Bosnia, and Croatia after the bombing stopped in Kosovo in 1999, as part of a large international team out of the office of the prosecutor. We were there to collect evidence that would be used at trial for war crimes and genocide. The size of the team varied, but field and morgue crews numbered over forty people most of the time, with anthropologists, archaeologists, medical examiners, crime scene officers, lab technicians, and military personnel from all over the globe. So, Marianna wasn't the biggest forensic team I had been part of, but it reminded me of that work and what could be accomplished in a multidisciplinary structure.

Lara from communications was managing the media gathered across the street. Students from our graduate program, many of whom had worked on-site over the prior year to help ground-truth the locations of each suspected burial, unloaded tools. Students like Liotta Noche-Dowdy, who had relentless patience and could provide instruction on what to do and how to excavate step-by-step to those on the team who were doing this for the first time. John Powell, a new master's student in our program, had spent hours photographing the admission ledgers from state archives. He had figured out that the photograph Dale Cox claimed was the burial ground was in fact incorrectly geo-referenced and came from the "white side" of campus, adding to the confusion about the presence of multiple burial areas. I had asked him to research hotels and rental properties for us to use, knowing the fieldwork would be extensive and long-term. He found a bed-and-breakfast he thought might work, if no one minded it was decorated as Christmas all year long. Everyone in the lab wondered what that would look like and whether it was a deal-breaker for cheap rooms. The owner turned out to be the editor at the local paper who was vocally opposed to our work up there, and that turned our contemplation into a hard no.

Rich Weltz was another new master's student who had just finished a twenty-eight-year career as a lieutenant commander and explosive ordnance disposal expert in the US Navy. He knew how to run re-connaissance—it was too good to be true! He trekked through kudzu-covered woods, swamps, pastures, and a trash dump that extended acres along the back of the property. Even the US military, following World War II, used the dump for airplane refuse. Rich would geo-track his pedestrian surveys of the landscape as he went, and John would overlay the geographic information system (GIS) data with photographs he took of anything significant so that everything was geo-referenced into Google Earth Pro. This meant that when we were on-site and searching deep into the woods, we could access all the historic information—maps, pictures, and the current data from our fieldwork over the past year—layered before us. Searching for graves meant reconstructing the way the land was once used. Finding the old roads, fence lines, and buildings—to know how the space was used—was how we started to find unmarked burial grounds.

Many of the folks on my team came from different agencies but were close, personal friends. People with whom I had worked in the past and shared a passion for this type of work. Dr. Greg Berg, whom I knew from graduate school. He got along well with Tim Hayes, our heavy-equipment operator. As if they were old friends, hand signals and a nod or two between them kept things running smooth and efficient.

Mike Hurley joined us on just about every trip we took to Mari-anna. I first met him when he was the homicide sergeant at the Hills-borough County Sheriff's Office, after the medical examiner called me to help excavate skeletal remains at a construction site for a new gas station. Their excavator had uncovered what turned out to be a ten-year-old missing person's case. A woman had been shot and buried by her husband, but her body had never been found. It was the first case I worked on for the local sheriff, back in 2007.

Other detectives and crime scene personnel from other agencies accompanied us on our many missions, but those transitions were surprisingly easy. We were used to working together in some capacity already. Brendan Fitzgerald was a homicide corporal who texted me pictures of bones at all times of the day and night as his detectives worked cases, asking, "Is this one human?"

Moises García was a veteran homicide detective who once found a skull in a cauldron.

I didn't have to go to the scene for that one; a few questions over the phone resolved the case.

"Are there sticks? A metal ladder? Other iron or metal objects with it?" I asked him back then.

"Yes, how did you know?"

"It is a case of Palo Mayombe," I told him. I'd seen this before, where skeletal remains were ceremoniously placed in a ritualistic cauldron, or *ngangas*, stemming from the Afro-Cuban religion. It was believed that the practitioner could control the dead person's spirit and gain their power or strength. This time, the call was not a homicide. He was happy.

Dr. José Pablo Baraybar, my former boss from prior United Nations missions, was not able to come, but he sent Franco Mora and Valeska Martinez Lemus from his Peruvian Forensic Anthropology Team based in Lima to assist. Lee Manning and Henry Schmidt were retired law enforcement from Massachusetts and Wyoming, respectively. They were on their second careers, working long-term missing-child abduction cases. They flew around the country helping law enforcement agencies and families of the missing, setting up search missions to look for clandestine burials. That was how I met them, when I assisted their effort in the search for Morgan Nick, a little girl who went missing from a baseball field in 1995 in Alma, Arkansas. Brought together by tragedy, we searched on our hands and knees for a week and became lifelong friends. From that point on, we put together other search strategies for missing-child cases in California, Minnesota, and Pennsylvania. They even drove down to Tampa while working a case out of Gainesville to help me on a search of a trailer's crawl space. We were looking for a woman who went missing there twenty-three years earlier. Now they were ready to dig at Dozier, to excavate burials and help coordinate human-detection dog teams from South Florida, there to search the most remote parts the fourteen-hundred-acre property.

The people who joined this team were good at their jobs, which meant we could create a great work product. More importantly, they were friends. That was comforting. It helped me feel at home in a place that otherwise was very unwelcoming and cold.

"The hardware puts it in the 1940s or later," I told them when I found the casket handle. "We'll learn more as we go."

Hours slid by. The sun burned hot, and the last rain rose in steam off the kudzu leaves.

We uncovered the first skeletal remains near the base of the big oak tree, and the teeth looked to me like they belonged to a child who was about thirteen or fourteen years old. I'd done this for a long while, so sometimes I could just tell. I wanted to be certain, since everyone was sure to ask, so I pulled out a book with dental charts. The age was right.

I thought about Ovell Krell. Her brother George Owen had been fourteen. I thought about all the people who said we would find nothing. At the bottom of the very first grave, it appeared that we had found a boy. To predict finding "nothing" was a huge commitment. Within the first day of excavation, we found human remains, excavated within a unit perfectly square over the top of the unmarked grave. It worked exactly as planned. This was why I loved science.

On my knees in the grave, I identified bones by their bumps and grooves. Some pieces were easily recognizable. Their anatomy was marked by creases, rugose markings, and foramina—the promontories and holes to which muscles attach and through which blood vessels and nerves run. Those were unique for all the bones in the body. This was how bone fragments could be reconstructed for identification, even when shattered into a hundred pieces, smaller than the palm of my hand. Pieces of skull, vertebrae, and the shafts of an arm and leg hinted that this was once a young man. He could not be removed piece by piece. He was too fragile. Instead, we had to bring him up in thick layers of earth, like big, flat bricks. As the sky grew darker by the minute, I carved away at the edges until it looked like I'd formed a square brick in the bottom of the grave. Then I slid a thin, sturdy piece of fiberglass underneath the block and carefully lifted it out of the hole. The morticians helped wrap it in tinfoil and placed it gently on a gurney, then wheeled it past the photographers.

We all stopped and watched them roll the bones away as the power of the moment washed over us.

BY SUNDOWN THAT first day, we had opened two large holes. We sifted all the dirt we removed for coffin nails, burial hardware, and other artifacts that might add context.

Tananarive Due, whose great-uncle was Robert Stephens, who died at the school in 1937, came out to the site with her family.

"Thank you all for your good work," she told us.

"Thank you for keeping the story alive," her father said.

For all the controversy, we felt fairly welcome. The Marianna police chief, Hayes Baggett, drove out to see if we needed anything. A woman approached us one night at a Mexican restaurant. "Are you the folks doing the exhumations?" she whispered. "I hope you find the truth." A local woman named Jan Poller drove out on Saturday morning. "I know you got a lot of negative responses, but this is something that needs to be resolved," she said.

OVER THE NEXT few months, we used weekends and semester breaks to focus on the rest of Boot Hill. We started on the southeast side and worked our way west over the course of five more field missions.

For the rest of the site, I decided to use a different approach. I didn't want to excavate in defined units as we had initially started. Mostly, the process was too slow and labor-intensive. Also, I wanted to open up more of the site to be able to see the burial patterns and arrangement, the shape and size of each individual grave as it was originally constructed. So we needed a different strategy.

An alternative method to what we did the first week was called *excavating the feature.*

To accomplish this, we brought in heavy equipment and removed the top layer of soil, much as we had when we dug test trenches on prior trips. Instead of narrow test trenches, we opened up whole sections of the site, exposing multiple graves at a time while being careful to remove only topsoil and stay above the actual burial, casket, or human remains.

This required a very specific type of equipment, called a gradall excavator. This was a large machine made to build roads. The arm extended out well past the top of a potential burial or point of interest and then, using a flat blade, the soil was pulled back toward the machine, without the wheels ever running over the scraped surface. The dirt was then scooped up and moved out of the way. The machine didn't drive over the scraped area like a front-end loader or backhoe, so any stained area caused by a feature was exposed. It was the perfect tool.

Using this method allowed us to remove a couple of inches of soil at a time.

It required a skilled and experienced eye to watch on the other side of the bucket and signal to the operator how deep to go, to the left or right. When to stop and pull back.

For this next operation, there was one person I trusted to serve as crew chief. Greg Berg was a good friend and skilled archaeologist. He'd been working for the US government's Defense POW/MIA Accounting Agency in Hawaii, running missions in places like Vietnam, Cambodia, and North Korea to find and retrieve the bodies of US soldiers who were prisoners of war or missing in action. Greg had accompanied me to Asaba, Nigeria, to map mass graves when I was six months pregnant. "A-Aron," he loved to yell across the site to summon me. Always with an extra-large coffee in his hand and wearing a leather field hat, the brim hanging low over face, he knew how to excavate and how to manage people. I could also trust Greg to make a precise map, to scale, of our burials. Of course, we used an electronic measurement tool called a total station and collected GIS points, but I am old-school in that way. Sketches, field books full of detailed notes, and hand-drawn maps on engineered graph paper were how we documented where we were and what we had done.

Greg knew how to excavate large-scale operations, run a crew, and manage water under the most inhospitable conditions. I needed someone with talent and a good sense of humor—it was going to be a long road.

ONCE THE TOPSOIL was removed, the dark-stained burial fill seemed to pop out from the red clay. Greg used orange spray paint to outline the burials as we moved down each section, marking grave after grave.

The burials, though still hidden under the soil, were covered with tarps until small crews could move in and excavate each feature—the stain in the soil. From that point on, soil was removed with trowels, spoons, and dental picks. It took three or four days per burial to carefully expose the remains, digging only within the original burial pit.

More than sixty-five people volunteered on-site. Students, faculty, crime scene investigators, and homicide detectives from the University of South Florida; the Hillsborough County Sheriff's Office; Hamline University, my alma mater; the Florida Emergency Mortuary Operations Response System (FEMORS); the Defense POW/MIA Accounting Agency; the Peruvian Forensic Anthropology Team, with whom I had worked in the Balkans and Peru; and fifteen other agencies. They all sent help. Even the former state archaeologist of Iowa joined our crew. Those who had experience teamed up with those who were new and were there to learn by doing.

The color and density of the soil made it obvious through touch what was backfill and what was original, undisturbed, sterile ground. The result was a roughly rectangular burial with jagged sidewalls. We could see that the marks and cuts in those walls were tool marks from the shovels and pickaxes used by gravediggers nearly a century earlier—those who dug the original grave.

This was where the real geek in me came out. Finding and documenting those original tool marks was so gratifying. Stepping back to look at the organization and patterns of the site gave us a glimpse into how the burial was dug, information that would have been lost if we cut away the walls of the burials following grid lines. Breaking down this large acreage into discrete units that reflected time and human behavior was to make sense of history in a different way. When we started, these vague questions about who was buried there, where they were buried, and why loomed large and seemed intangible. The families, the White House Boys, and the public wanted it to make sense, but so far more than a hundred years of state investigations had fallen flat. The only way to fill in the pieces and see the whole picture was to go back to the beginning and reconstruct every aspect of it. Now, here in the soil, we saw tool mark patterns showing us how they dug the burials. Each new grave revealed an unexpected pattern. It was the physical evidence needed to corroborate the historical record, and it meant we were getting closer.

As the soil was pulled back with a trowel, pieces of coffin wood and nails emerged. Handles and hardware that sealed the lid on a coffin stood out in hard contrast to the soft burial fill. The dark mottled soil was softer and easier to cut through than the virgin clay surrounding it.

Leather fragments from belts, buttons, and buckles hinted at clothing in some of the graves. Bones and teeth in anatomical order showed boys buried in a supine position, with their arms crossed over their chests, or folded over their abdomens, or lying along their sides.

The ends of long bones near joints like the knee and elbow showed lines where the bones were not yet fused together. That hinted at the age of the child buried in each grave.

Along the way, everything was photographed and measured. Each grave was sketched to scale, and the whole site was recorded onto a master site map. A total station offered an accurate way to capture 3D digital location data using GIS to create accurate site maps. It was a tool we used. We also measured everything by hand and created burial and site maps to scale.

Nothing replaced the original hand-drawn map on engineered graph paper designed for the metric system. Ten lines on the paper was a centimeter. Not all graph paper was equal. What was the one thing cops and anthropologists fought about at a crime scene? The metric system. It was the language of science. It was also intuitive and easier to calculate in your head. Everything was a unit of ten. Crime scene investigators were adamant about inches and feet.

Other than the unit of measurement, we defaulted to crime scene standards on fieldwork with the police or in historic cemeteries, cognizant of the legal implications to follow and adhering to the rules of search warrants, chain of custody, and practices that would have to be defended in court. We stuck to the same protocol.

We, too, employed the ABCs of homicide investigations: Assume nothing. Believe nothing. Check everything.

"A little more," the crew chief said as he directed the backhoe operator. "Bring it back. Slowly."

The flat blade of the backhoe's bucket drew back the topsoil, revealing dark-stained dirt amid virgin red soil. The stained dirt pointed us to burials—the remains of children who had been placed in shallow and sometimes hastily dug graves a few feet below the ground's surface. The operator surgically maneuvered his bucket with as much finesse as possible. I had to watch closely, though. Pieces of wood had begun to emerge from beneath the soil. The backhoe revealed the top of a burial container. Flakes of blue paint looked familiar to me, but I couldn't place where I'd seen this color at the school. I watched the heavy-equipment operator move on to the next grave, and I directed crews of graduate students to move in with trowels, dental picks, and brushes to excavate the fragile remains by hand.

In the soil, the crew could make out the burned fragments of bone, some white from the fire and others charred black, among the red clay and sand. They called me over to take a look. Seeing the commingled bones like that unsettled me. They were not aligned, not in anatomical order. The head should have been at one end of a grave and the feet at the other. Here, though, small fragments from the skull, thorax, and limbs were mixed together. The pieces of skull, vertebrae, and the shafts of an arm and a leg—the thickest parts of the bone that survived a fire and then a century below ground—hinted at what was once a very young child. The next grave over was similar to the one before it. Fragments of bone were broken, burned, and out of order. The second burial revealed more of the story as the soil was scraped away with trowels, and the tiny elements emerged. I saw that two right temporal bones, the thick knobby areas behind the ear, were found in the cache of small bones, indicating two boys were buried together in this grave.

Rusty, hand-forged nails secured one of the outer adult-size containers in the grave—white sand filled in around the small baby casket pressed inside. The baby coffin, unlike the outer container, appeared manufactured, in contrast to the homemade pine boxes constructed in the school's carpentry shop, the boxes in which the majority of children were buried.

As the grad students opened more of the grave, they mapped the items and took photographs of them in place. When the rain came, as it did every afternoon during this time of year, the work stopped and we hustled tarps over the top to protect items from the water. Small piles of dirt lined the edges of the tarps to keep the water out. We sloshed around in wet boots and slid in the muck.

It was a tedious job, not intended for the impatient. I remembered sometimes that even the worst day in the field beat a good day in the office.

Large sections of the burial had to be removed en bloc so we could finish the excavation in the lab, which is far easier on the knees. We wrapped the precious cargo in tinfoil and tucked the pieces into paper bags and stacked the bags inside banker boxes, then loaded them carefully into the backs of vans to drive them to the lab in Tampa. That was where the meticulous work and analysis for identification took place.

The questions were simple: Who was this boy? What was his story?

I knew that unraveling the answers to these questions—the long process of discovery—could take months or even years.

The FDLE said thirty-one graves at the most—though probably fewer.

As we extended the excavation outside the boundaries of our estimated plot map—past the possible grave sites we estimated from ground-penetrating radar data—we wanted to make sure there were no other burials.

Along the northwest perimeter, we found the irregular outlines of what appeared to be disturbed burials. Could this have been where the prisoners had accidentally dug into the burials in the 1990s—the incident that compelled school authorities to plant the metal crosses?

Had there been graves in this area? That could explain why school officials thought there were two burial areas when they drove Glen around the site on his impromptu visit to see his uncle's grave.

Where were the remains they unearthed? There were no other burials suggesting the disturbed graves were reinterred on-site. And no secondary burials, no graves that they unearthed and then reburied.

What happened to the remains they unearthed was still a mystery.

WE OPENED THE rest of the burials slowly over the next three months. We found coffin nails and handles, zippers and buttons and belt buckles. We found the 1914 fire victims. We found boys buried unceremoniously and at varying depths, the shallowest about two feet deep. We found a boy's remains bunched up near the top of a casket, with an arm over his head, lying not on his back, like most. The team and I stopped working one day and stood around a grave to look at a perfect white and burgundy stone marble we found in what would have been the pocket of a little boy's pants.

We labeled and loaded them individually for transport back to my lab at USF.

I was struck by how small the skeletons were. They were little guys.

We finished at the site in December 2013. We filled in all the holes and checked out of the hotel and headed back to Tampa to start the lab work.

We had underestimated. Our conservative analysis of the data gave us that number: fifty burials. We looked under a tree and under a fence and in the woods, and we found fifty-five graves.

Chapter 11

RECONSTRUCTION

A block of soil, hard as a baked brick, sat next to me in tinfoil on my laboratory table in the basement of the anthropology building at the University of South Florida. The dirt contained burned and fragmented bits of bone belonging to one or more of the children who lived in an overcrowded dormitory at the state-run reform school in Marianna, locked away in chains and isolated.

In the field, the crew unearthed shallow, unmarked graves and wrapped the blocks of soil for transport so the skeletal extraction could take place away from the heat, rain, and public view.

The laboratory was equipped for this type of work. The field crew exchanged work boots for lab coats and began a whole new process. The tables were typically covered in cases from medical examiners and the police, which often represented homicides or individuals who died alone for one reason or another and needed to be identified so that their families could be contacted and their remains returned to them.

The lab crew, comprised of graduate students, worked together like a well-orchestrated set of professionals, dividing tasks and passing assignments as each item was checked off the list. Bones were carefully laid out on tables, washed, and cleaned. To estimate sex, stature, geographic ancestry, health, or the presence of diseases, trauma, or injuries, each bone and tooth was analyzed. To aid in this process they were also radiographed, measured, 3D-laser-scanned, and photographed.

Fractured pieces of bone were glued back together and scanned to create a 3D model that could be rotated and viewed from all sides on the computer. Small samples of bone and teeth were collected for DNA testing and chemical isotope testing—the latest forensic tool to help establish where someone came from and whether they migrated into the region shortly before they died.

Facial reconstructions were drawn digitally over the 3D model of the skull, carefully outlining the bony anatomy, taking into account the little asymmetries, rotation of teeth, healed nasal fractures, contours of the cheeks—all the biological characteristics that make a face unique. Added into the final image was any contextual information about the victim, like their hair length and color, clothing, and age. This victimology made the face realistic and far more accurate. Would anyone recognize them? There was a chance. Mainly, it reminded us all of their humanity.

The reform school remains were all juveniles, besides the two staffers. Their ages could have been essential in helping assess their identity, since we had an idea of who we were looking for and knew their ages at death. A six-year-old. A lot of boys between twelve and fourteen. One who was twenty-one and died while paroled to a farm, presumably to work for his bus fare home.

To find the age of a child, we looked at their tooth development and noted which teeth had erupted and how complete the roots formed under the gum line. The union and fusion of bones to one another also hinted at a person's age. As children grow the bone centers form, develop, and fuse. Infants are born with about three hundred bones and epiphyseal centers—cartilage, the precursor of bone—which ultimately fuse together in such a way that adults are left with 206 bones. The age at which bones fuse together is fairly predictable and so can hint at someone's age. We also used their height, though less reliably. Stature became stunted in times of nutritional deficiencies, infectious diseases, or other health problems, thereby causing children to appear biologically younger than they really were. This was especially the case for children with a history of neglect, abuse, or poverty.

Since many of the skulls were excavated en bloc, thereby preserving the soil around the bones, we X-rayed the whole block before excavating the bones and teeth in the lab. This way we could assess tooth eruption and root growth before disturbing the remains.

The lab was large, with six long tables on which remains could be spread. There were separate smaller rooms for cleaning and recording the associated artifacts—all of the more than one thousand belt buckles, buttons, nails, and coffin hardware preserved in the small graves.

Computers with large screens for visualization of the images and data analysis dotted the lab. Along the walls, bookshelves overflowed with manuscripts, binders of raw data, and reference books with titles like *Skeletal Trauma*, *Identification of Skeletal Pathology*, and *Cremation Analysis*.

The walls in my lab were covered with images of my students and me doing fieldwork, portraits of families of the missing, and documents detailing our success stories, remains we'd positively identified and returned to families. In one corner of the room was a stack of yellowed newspapers chronicling our work at the reform school: the latest findings, columns, and editorials urging state officials to do the right thing—to join the effort that grew into a movement for the families of the missing. The historical records, maps, interview transcripts, photographs, reports, and research materials were so voluminous, they were designated their own bookshelf. We secured the remains in three evidence rooms.

For the soil block sitting on the table, my tool of choice was a dental pick, but the clay-rich soil caused the pick to catch and stick over and over again until I was able to chip away earth from the delicate remains. Sometimes using water helped melt the amalgamation. Pieces of brown, black, and white colors emerged amid the contrasting red soil. Sorted piece by piece, the fragments of bone were separated from clay, melted glass, and wood, then stacked on brightly colored cafeteria trays. Melted glass, charred wood, and burned bone—this burial was from one of the fire victims.

Picking away at more of the compact soil, the charred, delicate black bone stood out in the fluorescent light overhead. In contrast, bluish-colored fragments remained intact and hard. They had burned longer and hotter. Since there was so much variation in one block of soil, I was always asking questions of the material: Would the patterns of color tell us something about the fire or the location of its victims? Or maybe even where they were in the building that burned? I was excited to lay out the bones so I could start to answer some of those questions, but I also knew I couldn't rush the process.

Chalky white flakes crumbled under my touch and fell from fragments that now heaped in little piles and hinted at shallow burials with a high water table. We knew about the high water table; we'd fought the water coming up from the bottom of the graves as we excavated. Here was physical evidence of that experience. Evidence of a watery grave in the form of how the bone was preserved.

Bumps and grooves in the texture of bone told us the source. Some pieces were easily recognizable, their anatomy marked by creases, rugose markings, and foramina.

I laid out the pieces on the table in anatomical order: a tooth, the outer ear canal, an aspect of the knee. From the charred mass, the remains of a small child started to emerge, piece by piece, and I could see that the surfaces of bones that typically fused together as a person grew had not yet been joined. This boy, I could plainly see at that moment, had been younger than ten years old when he died.

Some fragments in the block of dirt repeated. I found two left ear canals and knew I was dealing with the remains of two humans whose fragmented bodies were buried together in the same casket.

We laid the bones on the tables covered in brown paper. Those that were repeated or differed by age were placed next to each other and we used a marker to draw a line across the paper, separating individuals from one another.

Once the bones were separated for each burial, the individual bones identified and sorted by duplicity and age at death, we took a sample from each individual for DNA testing. Among the fire victims, we had three individuals spread out in seven caskets. The remains included bones from an adult, a teenager, and a child under the age of ten.

I couldn't do this work without thinking about the stories attached to the names of the known dead. It helped to imagine their faces. Perhaps one of these belonged to Charles Evans's uncle or cousin? Looking at the bones, I started to see a profile of who that person was on a basic, biological level. Their sex, their age, their health, how they died. The tip of a rib showed a partial fusion among the joint surfaces, indicating it belonged to a boy who was older than the first body we constructed—between fifteen and eighteen years old.

I noticed that small facets on the spine had been preserved, calcined white and bluish in some places and cracked from burning, but nonetheless revealing an irregular margin and lipping on the joint surface, which indicated osteoarthritis, a more mature bone of someone who was more than thirty years old at death. That was the clue I needed. It had to be one of Charles's relatives—they were the only adults who were reportedly victims of the fire.

Increasingly, the bones flaked as they dried out in the lab. We used tweezers to extract the bones from the soil. We wore cotton gloves to help, but the charred bones stuck to the cotton fibers. Piece by piece we plucked fragments from the earthen mass and sorted them on lab tables lined with brown paper so that the name of each bone could be written in black marker on the paper next to it.

Each table represented a grave, and so far each grave contained more than one victim.

At the burial site, we found a coffin with a glass viewing window and a white engraved plaque that read, "At Rest." A child's intact spinal column was stuck to the glass, so we wrapped them together with cotton cheesecloth and newspapers. Now, in the lab, we unwrapped the glass with its spinal column attached, like a delicate present.

From the same grave, the ends of the long bones near the elbow revealed a faint thin line, a junction where two portions of growing bones came together. The visible line told me that the bone had still been in the process of fusing when death occurred. It was from the arm of a child between the ages of fourteen and eighteen. Most of the fragments we had gathered from this coffin were too incomplete and small to estimate age.

I took a close look at the vertebrae, which had many facets—round surfaces where the bones articulated to one another through the spinal column and to the ribs. Amid the pile of fragments on my tray, a thoracic vertebra from the center spine was present alongside the fragments of a child's arm and spine. The vertebra's facets were irregularly shaped and lipped along the margins of the bone. This was not what I expected. The vertebra was not from a child, but from a middle-aged adult with significant osteoarthritis, probably someone with complaints of a sore back. There was now enough evidence that the remains of multiple people were buried in the same coffin as before, so I began the detailed process of separating the bones by age.

Across the lab, thousands of burned bone fragments covered the tables. The blocks from seven graves, containing burned bone, were excavated together among the fifty-five burials we uncovered at the school. We analyzed those graves that contained burned bone in the lab together, thinking that maybe we could piece the broken fragments back together.

Seven out of fifty-five burials contained burned bone from the 1914 fire. They consisted of coffins containing the commingled and incomplete remains of at least three people spread out among the caskets. Some melted debris from the building, materials burned in the fire, was among the bone fragments. Melted glass. Metal fragments. Bedding, perhaps?

Although there was evidence of three victims buried from the fire, the amount of bone was very small. They easily fit into an infant-size casket—and were. The small parcels were then placed into larger, adult-size boxes for burial.

The question I kept asking myself, like the big elephant in the room, was: Why would the remains of the people be spread out in seven coffins? Did the men who buried these remains think there were seven fire victims? If so, what happened to the remains of the others?

"They didn't bury seven bodies in these coffins," I told the students who were diligently working at different tables. "We don't have everyone."

Some of them paused and looked up, while others kept working, deep in thought.

The amount of remains we had could have fit into one adult-size coffin. Though there were three people represented among the remains, the way in which they were fragmented and buried suggested that at the time of the burial, no one burying the remains could separate the remains.

"Let's make an inventory for each individual," I said. "List the duplicated elements and their ages. We'll need to select the best samples from each for genetic testing to see if we can even get a DNA sample from bone so badly burned."

Testing would destroy the samples, so it was possible we would be afforded only one chance at finding out the identities of the bones we had unearthed. Even as I gave testing instructions, I knew our chances for getting DNA results from such badly burned remains were slim. Unlikely, really. We had DNA reference samples for several families of those who perished in the fire, like Charles Evans, Earl Morris, and Joseph Weatherbee, so we had to try.

Liotta walked over to me carrying a red tray. "What about all these tiny pieces that can't be separated or identified? What do you want me to do?"

I sighed, surveying the hundreds of bits of bone before her. They looked like crumbs.

"Put them in a plastic bag and weigh it."

This answer felt so inconclusive, like so much of this work.

"Write a description of what is there and take a photo," I added.

One question was answered, but two more were raised. One step forward, two steps back. That was the evolving wheel of research, of science—the constant drumbeat of inquiry, proof, and interpretation. In the pursuit of consistency, there was little certainty except that it would lead to more questions.

What was clear? If we could find the exact location of the dorm that burned on the school grounds back in Marianna and excavate that site, perhaps we could find more answers about what happened. Maybe we could even find the rest of the fire's victims. Though our initial fieldwork was done, it was now apparent that we were missing a big part of the story and a lot of bone. To complicate matters, the dorm that burned was on the side of the property that would soon be released for sale and possible development. What would that mean for the families whose remains we didn't find?

"And one more thing," I added, interrupting the students again. "We have to go back to the field."

ON THE SOUTHEASTERN side of the Dozier complex, near the administration building, north of the old barbershop complex, in an area that had been used as an orchard in recent years, stood an open field bordered by roads on the north and west.

A small gazebo and associated concrete pad were in the northwest portion of the project area, as well as several mature fruit trees. Several manholes leading to tunnels containing steam and water pipes were located below.

Our strategy was to place deep trenches throughout the length of the project area, approximately three meters apart, to determine if there was evidence of a prior burned building in that location in order to recover human skeletal material. Prior testing of the area using a core sampling technique indicated that burned debris and other cultural materials were buried beneath the surface. We were likely in the right place.

If evidence of the building was found, a sample of the sediment from within the trenches could be screened to determine if there were human remains present. The screening system was designed by my colleague and crew chief, Greg Berg, who used similar water screening stations in the mountains of Vietnam while searching for the remains of American pilots who crashed in the Vietnam War. The use of high water pressure let us sift through a large amount of soil quickly.

The screening stations consisted of two oversize, mesh, high-pressure wet screens that allowed us to sift more than 220,000 pounds of soil right there at the site over the course of a week. Two layers of screens with quarter-inch and one-eighth-inch mesh caught important artifacts and any remains. We were running out of time on the property. Any longer and the Department of Juvenile Justice was going to make us sublease the land from them.

We had to harness two high-pressure fire hoses to feed lots of water to each system.

Like everything else, dealing with local officials was complicated. We had to hassle with commissioners in Marianna to convince them to turn on the water for us. It took some negotiations.

A crew of four to six individuals was employed per screen to process the sediments. All artifacts and possible bone fragments were kept for additional analysis.

Brick fragments were separated from the materials and photographed at the end of the project for inventory and size estimates. Water and sediment runoff was accomplished by using a slit trench leading to a holding pond to trap the sediment while allowing the water to run off into a natural drainage pond. The sediment trap was cleaned out on an as-needed basis.

Mechanical trenching began with heavy equipment, this time a backhoe to excavate until completely sterile sediments were encountered. Five more trenches up to forty meters long and two meters deep were placed on the site area, parallel to the first one and across the northernmost street, in between the sidewalk and the existing building.

The burned layer appeared to be mostly within the basal layers of four of the trenches, near the center of the project area. Each trench was excavated until the top of the burned layer was present.

Only those sediments in the burned layer were screened from this test unit. A total station was employed to map in all the site excavation boundaries, trench-mapping datum, trenches, the test unit, and all pertinent landscape features. All drawn trench profiles were similarly captured. We took aerial photographs from multiple directions and then backfilled the site.

We screened and sifted 220,000 pounds of dirt, looking for the tiniest evidence of human remains.

Artifacts were initially sorted by raw material type into categories for ceramics, glass, ferrous and cupric metals, clothing, building materials, and miscellaneous items, such as buttons, buckles, a jack, and other burned items. We found two bullet fragments and a shotgun shell. We found a lot of burned debris, melted glass, and marbles scattered throughout.

A majority of temporally diagnostic materials dated to the late nineteenth and early twentieth centuries, which generally corresponded to the dormitory's span of use, ending with its burning in 1914. However, some artifacts, specifically a metal label for "Florida Industrial School" and "hobbleskirt" Coca-Cola bottles, dated to 1915 at the earliest, postdating the dormitory. The presence of some later materials was not surprising given the continued use of the area and may in fact have reflected the sporadic use of the burned dormitory site as a trash dump. In later years, a sewage pipe and drainage field were also placed through this area.

And then we finally found what we were looking for: fragments of bone from an upper thigh, broken into two pieces, about five feet below the ground surface. The bone's size indicated it likely belonged to an adolescent.

Other bones found in the trenches were significantly burned and charred black. To separate bone fragments from other burned fire debris like melted materials and charred wood, they would have to be analyzed using magnified visualization and digital radiography. These remains would have to be compared radiographically to known bone fragments from the Boot Hill burials.

We'd have to do that back at the lab.

■ ■ ■

AT THE TIME I started fieldwork at Dozier, I had two boys, ages three and eight years old. Sean was a little gentleman, reflective and deliberate, while Reid was born ready to conquer the world. I never went a whole week without seeing them. Though the project required months and months of fieldwork over several years, I drove home to see them on the weekends or to bring them up to the reform school campus with me. That meant carefully planning schedules so that I could drive home on weekends when the crew and volunteers rotated out, or coordinating rides so the boys could ride up with family members or Kaniqua Robinson, a graduate student who planned to do her dissertation research on the reform school. She was bringing an important perspective to the project as a Black feminist anthropologist writing about her experiences in Marianna and the role of religion in the development of the school. The boys adored her, so Kaniqua took care of them when I was away. She remains an important person in their lives and is the only person I know who can make a single game of Uno last two hours. Part of me didn't want them to know what this place was, as though I could protect them from knowing tragedy somehow by distracting them with card games. Kids are too smart for that.

Sean liked to take photographs as he walked around the reform school grounds. They were treasured pieces of the research, as they provided a child's perspective and were quite literally often the foundations of buildings or what was eye level to him. He took pictures of buildings with barred windows and signage about rules and work. He took pictures of overturned bunk beds and rusted-out farm equipment and remnants of a working farm, like milking stations, stables, and a slaughterhouse. He shared the pictures back at school. A new generation was hearing about the reform school, but in a very different way than the generations who were threatened with being sent there, as many Floridians recalled.

There was one building—the sweat box, as it was referred to in historical records, where Earl Wilson died, maybe the smallest building on campus—that I didn't want him to see or even know existed.

A few months into his stay in 1944, Earl Wilson was confronted by school authorities about two boys who had been caught smoking. When questioned about whether he saw them smoking, he answered yes. All three of the boys were taken to the White House for beatings, then to confinement. When the three boys arrived there were six others already in confinement.

On the "colored side," confinement was inside the sweat box, a small, sweltering concrete structure containing one set of bunk beds, an open bucket for a toilet, a second bucket for drinking water, and a single lightbulb that was never switched off.

When I stepped into the sweat box for the first time, it was hard to imagine how nine boys could fit into that space. If you spread your arms out, you could almost touch both walls. It was brutally hot. The thick mold made it hard to breathe.

Of course they fought. Can you imagine? Nine boys in a closet for two weeks. I stopped wondering how one died and started wondering how anyone had survived.

The youngest was twelve. The four arrested for Earl's death pointed to the other boys, who testified against them as the true culprits. As eyewitnesses, they reported to the court a cause of death that was different from what the physician testified. Today it would be hard to win a conviction in a case where the eyewitnesses and medical examiner provided conflicting accounts of what happened, including the nature of the injuries inflicted.

Beat with a stick. Strangulation.

Earl's family believed the guards murdered him. This account was supported by a boy they knew who was there at the same time.

The four boys charged with his murder were William Foxworth, Charles Bevels, Robert Farmer, and Floyd Alexander. The medical evidence, as described on the death certificate and in court documents, was given by the reform school's doctor at the time, Dr. Charles Whitaker, who was summoned when Earl was found dead. He reported that the death was caused by blows to the head with a blunt instrument, not choking.

One attorney was appointed to represent William Foxworth and two of the other boys, Charles Bevels and Robert Farmer. The fourth, Floyd Alexander, had privately retained counsel.

The prosecution's theory was that the four defendants had choked Earl Wilson by holding him down and pressing a stick against his throat. Witnesses also testified that earlier in the day, one of the defendants, Charles Bevels, had struck Earl Wilson repeatedly with the stick. A dissection of the decedent's neck muscles revealed no bruises.

Regardless of the inconsistencies in testimony, the boys were tried jointly and the jury convicted all four, though they recommended mercy on account of the fact that they were so young. Florida had no juvenile statute at that time, so the four faced a sentence of death in the electric chair if convicted, but the Marianna court gave their version of mercy and imposed life sentences on all four.

The story of Earl Wilson was a poignant reminder of what juvenile justice was like before civil rights or protections for children in custody.

People were outraged after Earl Wilson's death in the sweat box. The school changed its policy and stopped using sweat boxes as a form of punishment.

A BIG CHART listing each burial took up most of one wall in our lab, and we slowly added information we gleaned from the artifacts and remains. We hoped to find good matches, of course, to one day be able to say specific bones belonged to Nollie Davis or Grady Huff or Robert Stephens. Right then, it was hard to imagine that they were boys at one point, their entire futures before them.

We wanted to be sure of who they were, so we were also shipping bone fragments and teeth to the UNT Health Science Center in Fort Worth, Texas, for genetic testing.

They arrived in Fort Worth inside a big cardboard box marked "FRAGILE." Ben Montgomery from the *Tampa Bay Times* reported on their arrival. On the sixth floor, they were spread atop a table. Scientists sanded the bones to remove dirt, then cut the bones in two—one small piece for testing, one for the archives. They decontaminated the pieces with bleach and water and ethanol, and then ground them to a fine powder to ready them for the DNA extraction. To reach the unique genetic material inside the cells, scientists added a solution to decalcify the bone powder and a detergent to pop open the cells. The scientists were looking for both types of DNA: nuclear and the longer-lasting mitochondrial. Nearly every cell in the human body has forty-six chromosomes in the nucleus, which hold most of the information, inherited from both your parents, about who you are. Outside the nucleus live hundreds of mitochondria, tiny, energy-producing organs, which contain only the mother's DNA. A mother has the same mitochondrial profile as her children, and if her daughter has children, theirs would be the same, too.

If the boys weren't identified by DNA, their biological profile would be entered into databases for missing and unidentified persons. Until 2007, no one really knew how many unidentified dead there were in the United States. That year, the Bureau of Justice Statistics surveyed two thousand medical examiners across the country, who said they had a total of 13,486 unidentified remains in their morgues. That was medical examiners alone, so the bureau knew there were more. The official estimate is over forty thousand.

Maybe folks would turn to the database decades from now, looking for a great-uncle who was sent to the Dozier School for Boys and never returned. Maybe it would help fill in blanks in a family tree. Maybe it would answer a question that had long dogged a family. We could only guess.

What we knew was that we found an answer for Ovell Krell.

Chapter 12

IDENTIFICATION

I drove west toward Lakeland, hoping to deliver the news in person. Major Robert Ura and a few sheriff's deputies from Hillsborough County came with me.

Ovell Krell was home.

"Are you sure?" she asked.

"Yes," I said.

She repeated her question. Several times. Yes, I kept repeating my answer.

The Texas lab had made the first identification. George Owen was coming home, after all these years.

Ovell Krell was my inspiration. She reminded me of the mothers and grandmothers in Peru and the Balkans, women who could not find rest until their questions had been answered. By coincidence, George Owen Smith's remains were the first we'd exhumed, the ones CNN viewers watched come out of a grave that was only two feet deep, as though he'd been buried in a hurry. What I couldn't tell Ovell was how her brother had died. The remains were too decomposed; he'd been buried in a pine box without embalming, in a shallow grave frequently filled with water.

The same was true for most of the others, but we diligently worked to identify them and return them to their families.

The fundamental purpose of forensic science and crime scene processing is to identify, collect, and preserve tangible physical evidence that can be used to understand the circumstances surrounding a death in order to reconstruct the event. Physical evidence is critical for corroborating the statements obtained from survivors and witnesses and can prove the truth, with varying levels of certainty.

The first positive result, the first DNA hit and identification, was George Owen Smith. This entire effort—the research, the interviews, the funding proposals, the press conferences, the movement Ovell Krell unknowingly started when she wrote to the FDLE during their 2008 investigation—was about this moment, this discovery, this opportunity to finally return George Owen to her. He finally went home. We will never know exactly how George died or why his case was handled the way it was. We do know that he is now buried under his own name, beside family members who longed for answers.

After all these years, this child—and he was still a child—was afforded dignity that is every human being's right: the right to have their existence recognized. The Danish philosopher Søren Kierkegaard said, "Life can only be understood backwards; but it must be lived forwards."

Through George Owen's story, we understood this was an era when authorities could pick and choose when to fulfill their duties and responsibilities with impunity. We saw from the remains of his shallow burial, an unclothed boy pinned in a shroud, lying on his side against the edge of his grave, that it was a hasty burial. I believed that such practices should not be endorsed by the passage of time and continued inaction on the part of those who had the knowledge and the capacity to act.

Ovell Krell taught us that it was never too late for courage and that we had everything when we had hope. It was our hope that this was the first of many identifications to come. We hoped to restore justice and find resolution for all the families still searching whom we had come to know and respect.

"SOME OF THE children died natural deaths, but the sheer number of bodies suggests that there may have been many killings, a possibility buttressed by eyewitness accounts," wrote Tim Wu for the *New Yorker*. "Yet Florida's prosecutors have yet to file a single criminal charge, or even open a criminal investigation. To pass over crimes of this magnitude without investigation seems the very definition of injustice."

There was no statute of limitations for murder. The closest we came to evidence of murder was what we found in grave #23.

The burial contained the skeletal and dental remains of a boy between thirteen and seventeen years old, most likely of mixed African American and American Indian ancestry. He was buried in clothing, evidenced by the presence of buttons and a metal belt buckle. The condition of the remains was poor due to erosion of the tissues from root damage and termites. His cause of death could not be determined due to the condition of the remains. DNA profiles were obtained, though no identification has been made. Also within the grave, along with the remains, near the left lower abdomen or upper thigh region of the body, was a small lead ball consistent with a projectile. It was submitted to the FDLE crime lab in Tampa by the Hillsborough County Sheriff's Office. FDLE ballistics experts concluded that the "lead ball cannot be definitively determined to be an ammunition component due to damage and corrosion; however, it is consistent with 000 Buck size shot pellets for various muzzle-loading balls based on weight, size, and physical appearance." We presumptively identified the boy as John Williams.

In Florida, it had long been the case that all capital cases had no statute of limitations. In fact, when these crimes were allegedly committed, forcible rape was punishable by death—especially if the victim was a woman, and especially when the perception of race entered the equation.

The federal statutes that made sex with children under twelve years old a crime, one without a statute of limitations, weren't yet created and so couldn't be applied retroactively.

There were difficult challenges to prosecuting old crimes. Even if we could say with certainty that a boy was killed, how did we figure out who was responsible for the killing? Many of the old guards had already died, as well as the school's longtime superintendent, Lennox Williams, who died in 2010. We didn't convict people posthumously.

A man named Freddie Williams accused Lennox Williams of rape. Freddie wrote to Ben Montgomery at the *St. Petersburg Times* that he was sent to the Marianna reform school from Clearwater around 1959, at thirteen, for stealing food and running from an abusive home. He hadn't been there long when two men came in the night, pulled his covers off, and took him to the White House. Like all the other boys, he was forced down onto a soiled cot and told to hold the bed rail tight. One man, Maurice Crockett, beat him with a leather strap. The other, Lennox Williams, stood in the doorway.

Through the school's 111-year history, no one was criminally charged for sexual abuse. The closest that official recognition for any sex abuse crimes came was when three male employees—a priest, a psychologist, and a cottage father—were terminated by the Florida Legislative Investigation Committee, also called the Johns Committee, in 1962 for "acts of homosexuality" with inmates.

"Mr. Williams walked in the room," Freddie's letter said. "He told Mr. Crockett that was enough and I was going to be a good boy all I need is a good talking to. Mr. Crockett left the room and Mr. Williams sat on the side of the bed next to me, he started rubbing my back, my legs and my butt telling me it was going to be alright as long as I be a good boy nobody would beat me again."

Then the longest-serving superintendent at Florida's oldest reform school raped him, he said. "He was hurting me, but it didn't hurt like the beating I had got so I just laid there."

The abuse continued for months, Freddie wrote, and he was often rewarded with homemade cakes and cookies. He was sent home to Clearwater but soon ran away again and wound up back at Marianna. "Mr. Williams had changed," he wrote. "He had other boys, little boys from Bunch Cottage . . . He was not my friend anymore."

You couldn't bring criminal charges against a dead man.

Troy Tidwell, the school employee known to the boys as the One-Armed Man, was asked about deaths at the school when he was deposed as a part of the lawsuit brought by the White House Boys.

"During the time that you were with the school," the White House Boys' lawyer asked, "were there any deaths that resulted to boys who were students at the school?"

"Yes," said Tidwell, who started working there in 1943.

"How many boys died while you were there?" the lawyer asked.

"There was a boy on the basketball team warming up and just fell dead right there. So—and then there was a boy that was drown, and a little boy that was killed by a boy by the name of Frank Murphy in a—underneath—there was a tunnel, a drain that laundry used to dump their water and sometimes clothes would pass through the—and emptying their water, you know, to—into the drain. And so Frank Murphy talked this young boy into going down there to check on the clothes that might be down there. But other things happened and I don't know the details on that. But I know Frank was responsible for his death. And let's see. That's the—that's the only ones I believe I can remember at this time."

What he didn't mention was that the boy who dropped dead in the gymnasium was running drills, and several witnesses—including Jerry Cooper, the president of the White House Boys organization, who said he was there that day—claimed Tidwell was the coach who was ordering players to run drills. When the boy, Edgar Elton, asked for a break, Jerry said, Tidwell wouldn't allow it.

Tidwell died in April 2021. He was ninety-seven. His obituary, which ran in the *Jackson County Times*, said he "went to be with our Lord."

Even in death, he did not acknowledge his misdeeds.

"While working at the Boys School, Troy taught boys how to barber, ran the canteen, worked in the finance office, was a cottage parent, and retired as Homelife Supervisor in April 1982," the obituary read. "Many boys who were residents of FSB returned over the years to visit him with their families, praising his assistance during their stay at the Boys School."

THE SECOND AND third identifications came in September 2014. One was Earl Wilson, the boy who was murdered in the sweat box.

Cherry Wilson, Earl's sister, had provided a DNA sample. She said her parents were notified about Earl's death by a letter that said Earl had been killed and was buried at the school. Over the years, several members of the Wilson family visited the school in hopes of finding Earl's grave and to better understand what happened to him. He was buried in an unmarked grave somewhere on the property, and like the others, from that day forward, no one was ever able to point to his grave. Missing, according to the family but not to authorities.

The family was not notified in order to be present when Earl Wilson was taken into custody and sentenced, same as they were not notified in time to claim his body upon his death nor to attend the trial of those accused of killing him.

Cherry said that her mother's heart broke the day she learned of her son's death. She died of a heart attack a short time later, which Cherry attributed to losing Earl. Cherry's grown sons also talked with us about the weight of growing up with their mother's grief and search for justice. It was a heavy burden to bear, and the trauma could be passed down through generations.

Earl's family heard from another boy later who said Earl died when school officials stuffed his nose with cotton as punishment for smoking. The boy also said staffers administered beatings three or four times per day.

We found Earl's grave within the area of marked crosses, though his was not specifically marked. He was buried in a simple wood casket, likely made at the school's carpentry shop, and found lying with his arms along his sides. There was no evidence of clothing or personal artifacts that remained.

The skeletal autopsy performed showed that he was suffering from a severe pathology of the left ear, known as mastoiditis, a middle ear infection that was severe enough to have affected the surrounding bony tissues. No other trauma related to the cause of death as discussed during the trial could be determined, due to the degradation of tissues over time.

As we made this identification and shared our findings with the Wilson family, our nation marked the fiftieth anniversary of the Civil Rights Act of 1964.

When then president Lyndon B. Johnson signed the bill, he said that it was a "challenge to all of us to go to work in our communities and our states, in our homes and in our hearts, to eliminate the last vestiges of injustice in our beloved country."

The Dozier school proved to be a vortex for the civil rights movement as well. When sixteen Black juveniles were arrested for sitting at a "whites only" counter in a St. Augustine Woolworth's store in 1963, they were some of the youngest civil rights activists to ever be arrested and spend time in jail.

County Judge Charles Mathis Jr. ordered seven of them to spend the night in jail, and if they agreed not to participate in further demonstrations, he would release them. Three parents agreed to the offer, and they were freed. The others—Audrey Nell Edwards, Joe-Ann Anderson, Willie Carl Singleton, and Samuel White—became known as the "St. Augustine Four" when they refused the order and were remanded to stay in custody. The girls were sent to the Lowell Correctional Facility for Girls and the boys were sent to the reform school in Marianna. At the time, the conditions were reported as harsh, and the attorney general, James Kynes, asked the judge to release them, but he refused. The case received national attention and was described as humiliating for Florida on a grand scale. Baseball legend Jackie Robinson stepped in to help get the children released. His support, along with threats of national demonstrations at Florida's booth at the New York World's Fair, forced the Florida governor and cabinet to release them in 1964.

The plight of children like Earl Wilson, though, reflected a segregated time when neither children nor Black people were considered citizens. Finding Earl's grave and repatriating him so that his sister and their family could bury him beside his parents demonstrated a change in attitude. Our capacity to go back and apply modern science to historical injustices was about righting a wrong by empowering families to exercise their rights in order to find resolution and peace.

Biological markers of poverty were present throughout the skeletal remains we recovered. There was substantial evidence of nutritional deficiencies and delayed dental and skeletal development. There were signs of slowed or delayed growth, given the boys' ages. We found acute ear infections resulting in abnormal changes to the surrounding bony tissues among more than half the boys. There was almost no dental care. The vast majority of boys had extensive cavities, abscesses, and dental disease. Forty boys had untreated dental cavities. Only one boy had dental amalgams showing dental work. In nineteen cases, dental hypoplasias were present, which shows nutritional stress during the time the enamel was forming.

The next boy we identified was one of the last to come out of the ground back in December. To identify him after eighty years was statistically improbable but not impossible.

His name was Thomas Varnadoe.

THE SHORT OBITUARY ran in the newspaper eighty years after his death.

VARNADOE, Thomas, 13, of Brooksville, Florida, died on October 26, 1934, in Marianna, Florida. He died under suspicious circumstances after 34 days of incarceration at the now closed Florida Industrial School for Boys, aka The Arthur G. Dozier School for Boys. With aid from the University of South Florida, his family recently recovered his unmarked remains on the school grounds.

Thomas is survived by his brother, Joseph Richard Varnadoe of Salt Springs; nephews Gene Varnadoe of Faber, Virginia, Glen Varnadoe of Lakeland, Randy C. Varnadoe of Brooksville, and Rudolph A. Varnadoe, Jr. of Belleview; nieces Pam Varnadoe Reed of Telford, Tennessee, Marsha Varnadoe Patterson of Brooksville, Brenda Varnadoe Allman of Asheville, North Carolina, Jeannie Varnadoe Littleton of Jacksonville, and Becky Varnadoe Schwarz of Plant City. His parents Thomas H. Sr. and Josephine Folks Varnadoe; and siblings Hubert E. Varnadoe, Rudolf A. Varnadoe, and Ethel Varnadoe Tankserly, have since joined him in eternal rest.

A private graveside service of remembrance will be held on Monday, November 24, at Hopewell Memorial Gardens, Plant City. Thomas will be laid into eternal rest next to his brother Hubert, who was incarcerated at the school alongside Thomas, and endured the same tortuous environment of the failed school.

The Varnadoe family gathered at the cemetery in Plant City, Florida, to stage a funeral that had been a long time coming. What remained of Thomas, who died after thirty-four days at the state reform school, would now, finally, be buried in the family plot, near his brother.

I don't go to many funerals. My job is bringing the bones out of the ground. Someone else puts them back in.

On a clear Monday morning in November, I drove past strawberry farms and orange groves east of Tampa and pulled off State Road 39 at Hopewell Memorial Gardens. As I walked toward a tent where family members shook hands and hugged, a man wearing a short tie walked toward me.

"Gene Varnadoe," he said, extending his hand.

"I'm Erin—"

He cut me off. "I know who you are," he said, locking eyes. "Thank you for everything. Forever."

Gene, seventy-one, drove down from Virginia to be with his brother, Glen, and his uncle Richard, eighty-five, who sat in the front row. This was an important day for Gene and the rest of the family. This was an amendment to a history of which they'd been robbed. This was reparation.

Richard was five when the law came to drag his brothers away to some foreign place in the panhandle. Eighty years later, he could still hear his poor parents pleading with the county sheriff.

Richard saw me and gave me a hug.

"Because of you," he said.

I brought a small white box for the family that contained the artifacts we found with Thomas's remains. There were some rusty hand-cut nails, some eye screws, some corrugated fasteners, and a few small pieces of pine that made up his coffin. The building materials suggested to Glen that they'd made the box in ten minutes, quickly and carelessly.

Thomas's bones were in a stone box now, atop a card table up front. Below the ground was his brother Hubert—Glen's father and Richard's brother.

I took a seat. The graduate students, who had worked so hard for this, stood in the back.

Then the family held a funeral. If you drove by on State Road 39, you would never know that this family was burying a boy who had died eighty years before.

When Glen spoke, he talked about how long and hard they'd fought for this day, about the journalists who wouldn't let the issue die, about our work to find and exhume Thomas. Gene spoke next, and he told of how the unanswered questions had haunted them all, a canker on the family tree.

"We can only imagine the horror," Gene said. "Some of the Old South slave mindset died hard in Florida."

Glen invited Richard up front. It was the old man's turn. He faced the small crowd, but he could barely talk. A small gasp escaped his lips, and then the words tumbled out.

"I feel like we plucked my brother out of the depths of hell," he finally said.

There were still questions about Florida's oldest reform school, about who the rest of the remains belonged to and how those boys died. This chapter felt closed. A family had answers, and they had a box containing the bones of a boy who belonged with his family, forever.

As I walked toward the car with my students, I felt an overwhelming range of emotions about the day. So grateful to be welcomed into the lives of this family, honored that we could help them and share this precious moment, blessed to be included, relieved the search was over, but also angry. Angry that they had to go through this. Angry at the thought of one boy burying his brother in an unmarked grave and having to stay at that school, then dealing with the trauma of his experience for the rest of his life. Angry that the state took children and put them at risk. Angry that the state had made it so hard for them to find the truth.

That anger kept me motivated to help others in the same situation.

A small burial crew moved in. They lifted a piece of plywood to reveal a hole in the ground. They lowered the stone box inside and fetched dirt from the back of a John Deere tractor. A little boy, maybe five or six, watched his father shovel earth on top of the box engraved:

THOMAS VARNADOE
March 13, 1921–October 26, 1934
Brothers Together Again

Chapter 13

"IT'S NOT EVEN PAST"

Billey Jackson used to pull his sister, Mattie, around Daytona Beach in a little red wagon. He was sweet to her, and they were two peas in a pod. He was everything she had.

So when men came for thirteen-year-old Billey for skipping school three times in 1952, Mattie Jackson felt robbed of her brother and her best friend. They shipped him to Marianna—323 miles from home—and put him to work.

His death certificate said that the teenager died of pyelonephritis. A man named Johnnie Walthour of Jacksonville told me that he remembered helping bury Billey's body in October 1952. Johnnie remembered that Billey got in trouble and got dragged to the White House for a beating, and when he returned to the cottage, Billey's stomach was bloated and bruised. Mattie Jackson's mother told her that Billey was beaten to death. Pyelonephritis can occur from natural causes, but in children it mostly results from trauma to the abdomen. His death certificate left off the proximate cause.

Mattie Jackson locked the memory of her brother away in a quiet place in her mind and didn't speak of Billey again until 2009, when her own grandson was sent to Dozier.

Guards broke the boy's arm, and Mattie couldn't take it anymore. Not another generation. She called her niece and said, "Don't let them do what they did to my brother."

The new information sent that niece, Ida Cummings of Washington, D.C., on a mission for truth. She found out about our work and quickly found Billey's name among the Dozier school dead. She got in touch.

I'd thought a lot about Billey's death. Two witnesses—men with no connection after they left the Dozier school—both told me the same story. Billey had run away a few times, got a beating at the White House. Then he was in the hospital, they were told. Then, a few weeks later, both boys were recruited to help dig a grave at Boot Hill.

They remembered Billey because he was a small boy who was often picked on.

In 2012, I met one of those men at Boot Hill. Woodrow Williams was frail and needed a walker to move around. The terrain around the burial ground was bumpy and the grass was overgrown. So after climbing out of his car, I put my arm around Woodrow's waist and then under his arm, to help steady him as we walked.

As soon as I slipped my arm under his, he spoke up.

"When I was here, they would have beat me for looking at a white girl," he told me. "Just for looking at her."

He was leaning on me, holding my hand for support. At first, I didn't know what to say. So I asked him, "What about holding her hand?" He laughed and squeezed my hand.

We'd come a long way.

In moments like this, I understood what William Faulkner meant when he wrote, "The past is never dead. It's not even past." We all live with our experiences. They are part of us. Not history. The idea that you can let sleeping dogs lie is senseless.

The White House Boys drove to Daytona Beach on a Saturday morning in 2016 to help bury Billey Jackson. They didn't call it a funeral. They called it a "rescue."

The mayor of Daytona Beach was there. He put into words what everyone was feeling.

"There was a time or two that I cut class," said Mayor Derrick Henry. "The only right that we can make of this is to atone."

Mattie, seventy-three years old by this point, sat nearby in a wheel-chair.

"It was just the two of us," she told a reporter. "He was everything I had until they took him away."

Her brother was back now, sixty-four years later.

"I don't know what to say," she said at the funeral, her voice first breaking. "Why would they beat him? How could you do these boys this way? Not only Billey. Look at the rest of the boys. How? How could they let it go on like that and say it wasn't true?"

"Somebody needs to pay," Mattie said. "Who's going to pay?"

Billey Jackson, surrounded by men who loved him and a sister who did, too, was laid to rest in a blue casket at Mount Ararat Cemetery in his hometown.

ROBERT STRALEY AND I stayed in touch after our work at the Dozier school was over. We would chat and continue to swap favorite po-ems. He wrote poetry and painted and never gave up working on the White House Boys website. Even during his treatment for cancer, he took calls from men who were still coming forward to share their sto-ries or answered a reporter's questions. He dropped off light-up toys from his carnival days for my boys and we exchanged Christmas gifts. He was a good listener and gave great advice infused with dry humor. He also supported our other projects and was always an advocate for our cold-case work.

I am not sure when he told me about his cancer, but they found it in his pancreas, and I knew what that meant. They caught it early, he said, a rare thing for that type of cancer, and so he held out hope. I checked in regularly with him after that. He was treated for almost nine months, and he lost weight and color in that time. I brought him ridiculously big balloon bouquets, one in the shape of a dolphin, to liven up his hospital room. I brought him a chocolate raspberry Bundt cake when he finally got to go home. He'd lost so much weight and hardly ate, but he loved cake and it seemed to be the only calories he could keep down.

I also met with him at the hospital when they wanted to discuss hospice. He asked me to be there and help him understand it. He was alone in the world. His closest friend and neighbor didn't even know about Dozier—he kept it out of his personal life. The neighbor was the one person with whom Robert could be himself, not a victim.

I met with him and the hospice administrator and asked all the tough questions, trying to be his advocate for the final time. I fought back tears, I didn't want to cry in front of him, a very difficult thing to do. He wanted to die at home, so he politely declined the offer for hospice care.

I went to see him before leaving for a road trip I'd planned with my boys, from Minneapolis to Mount Rushmore. I showed Robert pictures of the Black Hills and the wide-open ranges of South Dakota. He'd traveled all over the country selling novelties at festivals, but he said that was the one place he had never been, and he always regretted it. He was excited for the kids to take a road trip and see the majestic Black Hills. I told him I would come see him as soon as we returned. I hated to say goodbye, so we agreed to see each other in a few weeks. He looked so frail and was in constant pain. A few days later his neighbor called. Robert wanted to say goodbye. He knew he was slipping away. I was already in Minnesota and regretted not being there with him. Thinking about our final words to each other still breaks my heart.

Robert did not belong to a church, and he wasn't ever religious. Facing the end made him question whether there was something more. He decided to leave the possibility open. I called the Rev. Dr. Russell Meyer, a Lutheran pastor and friend who had become an advocate, representing the Florida Council of Churches. He supported our efforts tirelessly throughout the Dozier investigation. Reverend Meyer attended all our events and often met with us and other church leaders to strategize ideas about the reburials and memorials that would ultimately follow. I asked Reverend Meyer to visit Robert that day, to be there with him at the end, and he agreed. He later told me when Robert passed away and offered to hold a memorial service at his church.

"In the name of Martin Talbert and Martin Anderson and every other kid abused by adults who get their paychecks from the state of Florida, he decided that enough was enough and he put together a massive media campaign, launched a dozen protests, prompted a handful of state investigations and a slew of newspaper headlines, organized a legal campaign, and his efforts ultimately brought about the closing of a brutal 111-year-old reform school and the exhumation of a mass grave, and the reunification of families with the lost bones of their ancestral kin," someone said at the service. "What Robert did that cannot be measured—not now, not by us—is to position himself over the shoulder of every prison guard and every juvenile detention employee in every dark corner of the justice system and whisper, over and over: 'I'm watching you. I'm watching you now.'"

A handful of friends who loved Robert carried his ashes up to a mountain in eastern Tennessee and spread them on the wind.

Several months before he died, Robert wrote a letter to the editor of the local newspaper. He'd been working to make sure the Dozier boys would be properly memorialized.

"I don't know how many administrations have passed since 1900, when the Florida Reform School opened, with its many additional names, but I felt the legislators in those passing decades must have had hearts of stone, knowing full well that boys were being abused far and beyond the guidelines for corporal punishment of juveniles," Robert wrote. "I hope with all my heart that they will be remembered for changing history. They will write words in stone on two monuments—one in Tallahassee, one in Marianna—and the White House will stand as a reminder.

"While hearts of stone did nothing, this administration will leave a message in words written in stone. I do not know what they will be, but I'm pretty sure they will stand as a reminder of what happened and a warning to the future, that if you harm, abuse or kill one of Florida's children, the State of Florida will pursue you, regardless of the passage of time and you will be found and face judgment."

Chapter 14

"WHERE IS HE?"

One death puzzled me more than most.

A boy named Thomas Curry had served twenty-nine days in 1925 for delinquency, records showed, then tried to run away.

Thomas's body was found by some railroad tracks near Chattahoochee. The historical record showed that Thomas's remains were first brought to the Florida State Hospital, near where they were discovered, thirty-six miles from the reform school he'd fled. The doctors there issued a death certificate and served as the undertaker. This hospital had its own casket factory and a close relationship with the reform school. The coroner couldn't tell what killed him. "[C]ame to his death from a wound to the forehead, skull crushed from unknown cause" was written on death certificate.

Someone shipped Thomas home by train to his grandmother. Services were held, and a casket was buried. I thought he would have likely been embalmed if he was shipped all that way. Maybe we could determine his cause of death, so elusive in the other cases.

I contacted the boy's family in Philadelphia to ask if they had more information about what had happened to Thomas, and I sought the help of Pennsylvania State Police cold-case detective Corporal Thomas McAndrew.

I had met McAndrew a few years earlier, when he asked for assistance on a Jane Doe cold case. A pregnant teenager, near full-term, was murdered, mutilated, dismembered, and stuffed into a suitcase. He was trying to identify the victim.

McAndrew, with a thick Pennsylvania accent, questioned me for a good twenty minutes about the testing we would do—its scientific validity, the limitations and potential. He wanted to understand it. He wanted it to lead him to the victim's identity. So, when I told him about Thomas, he immediately reached out to Thomas's family, the church that buried him, and to Philadelphia assistant district attorney Brendan O'Malley about supporting our efforts. O'Malley's response to our seeking a court order reflected the sensibility I tried to bring to Marianna:

Need an exhumation order to know what caused injuries to a kid who died in custody?

Sure thing, we can talk to the judge.

Would that be a problem?

No, not at all. The excavation should be done.

The exhumation order came through in August 2014.

I hoped skeletal trauma and fracture-pattern analysis would yield vital clues about what crushed the boy's skull and whether it was an accident or inflicted injury. In Philadelphia, we visited the church that held his funeral and nearby funeral homes, and ultimately searched cemetery records where he was buried. The church records said he was hit by a train. I didn't expect that. The death certificate said the source of blunt trauma to the forehead was unknown. I had seen cases of individuals hit by trains; there was no doubt what caused the massive trauma to the whole body in such cases. Why weren't the church and the boy's family told that the circumstances surrounding the cause of injuries were unknown?

So I caught a flight to Philadelphia—United flight 1925, coincidentally, the year Thomas was born—to exhume his body from the Cathedral Cemetery and try to learn his cause of death. I'd been studying the thousands of names in the bound Dozier ledgers and wondering about the boys who died while trying to escape—boys like Lee

Goolsby, who died in 1918 of an unknown cause after an escape, and Robert Hewett, who at sixteen died from a gunshot wound after he escaped. Robert's family told us that authorities said he shot himself with a 12-gauge shotgun, found nearby, but the family thinks he was killed by somebody looking for him. His death certificate states he was shot "by person or persons unknown." Why would a boy successfully escape only to kill himself? And with a shotgun to the chest?

His sister told us that her family always believed for a fact that the men who came looking for Robert shot him dead. She was afraid to speak out about it. She had to live in that community. The fear of the law was ever present. Buried in a nearby cemetery, Robert's epitaph read: "God alone understands."

And then there was Thomas Curry.

In early October 2014, the sky over Cathedral Cemetery in Phila-delphia was gray and cloudy. I'd received permission in the form of a court order from a judge obtained by O'Malley.

Leaves blew across the graveyard. Pennsylvania State Police troopers, who were helping with the dig, had stretched crime scene tape around the area. A backhoe provided by the cemetery opened the deep grave, and then I went to work inside with a hand trowel. Liotta helped me. The cops watched from above. Soon, I found something—the top of a shipping box, maybe. I started passing pieces of wood out of the hole.

"You're handing me some bad mojo, aren't you?" one of the cops said. "My bare hands, too."

The contradictions among the records were troublesome.

If Thomas was hit by a train, why would the death certificate say the cause of death was unknown? Having been issued by the physician who examined the body, injuries to a pedestrian hit by a train would not leave uncertainty.

Thomas was one of ten boys who died at the school after running away between 1906 and 1952. The other boys who ran away died from blunt trauma, shotgun injuries, and inclement weather. One was run over by a vehicle—in 1932, in a county with very few cars. The others died of unknown causes, according to historical documents and death certificates.

The coffin was stacked on top of two prior interments, according to cemetery records. The graves beneath Thomas's were his great-grandparents'.

As I dug deeper, I could see that the burial consisted of two wood boxes that had collapsed as a result of ground pressure. At a depth of twelve feet below the ground surface, it looked like the external wooden crate may have been the shipping container that housed the coffin. Shipping boxes were used to protect coffins during transport, and in many cases they doubled as a vault for burial. Shipping boxes used as vaults were often placed into the grave, then the casket was lowered into the box and closed in, and the grave filled.

It was standard practice at the time, and still today, to not open a coffin prior to burial. In other words, the coffin may have been removed from the shipping container for the funeral, but no one would have opened the coffin to look at the body.

We started to find remnants of coffin hardware consisting of a single-lug handle, stamped ferrous metal, and gray paint. There were also two white metal thumbscrews cast in a two-dimensional urn motif, a whole cap lifter—both the top and base—made of white metal, and an unidentified decorative item cast of white metal in the shape of a crown.

We also found a cross constructed of white metal or copper alloy and remnants of a black cloth bow. Between the layers of wood was an unidentified fibrous material and straw-like grass matting.

It appeared that the bow and cross were likely part of a wreath and rosary placed on the casket at the time of the funeral in Philadelphia, prior to burial.

The type of handle recovered could be traced to three burial furniture catalogs dating from 1912 into the 1950s. The handle was included in the 1912 Cincinnati Coffin Company catalog but absent from the company's 1906 catalog, therefore dating it after 1906.

Less helpful were the decorative thumbscrew tops recovered from the casket. They were widely used in the late nineteenth century, and although they declined in popularity during the early twentieth century, they continued to be sold into the 1950s and '60s as outer box fasteners, similar to fasteners we found at Boot Hill.

"I guess we should just get all this wood out and be careful, in case anything is in there," I told the troopers standing above me. "I don't think there is."

We extracted more and more wood until we got to a second coffin. The nameplate belonged to Thomas's great-grandmother.

"I need to climb out of this grave," I said. No surprise, but I had a fear of being buried alive and this hole was too deep for my comfort, especially in light of the realization forming before me.

"Where is he?" asked McAndrew. "That's the bottom, right?"

"Yeah," I said. "If he was in here, his teeth should be here, even if nothing else is. We have wood."

Confused and with a look of surprise, the man who ran the backhoe spoke up, asking what all the stunned cops wanted to ask: "Where are the bones?"

Silence.

I climbed out of the deep grave and walked away from the burial, away from the state police and volunteers and cemetery managers. I needed to think. I ran through all the possibilities in my mind, several times. Why wasn't the body here? Did we excavate the wrong grave? Had Thomas completely decomposed? Was the body never shipped? What had just happened?

Eventually I made my way back to the open grave. It was nearly the end of the day, and O'Malley had come to see the progress. He was waiting and had been told no remains were present. "Where the fuck is he?" he asked in his thick Philly accent, his trench coat blowing in the wind.

It appeared somebody shipped home a coffin in a box. Thomas Curry wasn't there. If he wasn't there, where was he?

I didn't believe his remains decomposed beyond recognition. We found wood and straw, which were also organic and should have decomposed long before bones and teeth.

We may never know what happened to the remains of Thomas Curry or how he died. In my opinion, either reform school officials or the administrators at the state hospital who took custody of his body and examined it to issue the death certificate buried Thomas somewhere in Florida, then later shipped an empty coffin home by train to appease a mourning grandmother, trusting that no one would ever open the lid.

The state hospital had a large cemetery and their own casket factory. Every morning their undertaker dug several graves in anticipation of the deaths to follow. The reform school's superintendent had been the director at the state hospital for more than a decade before Thomas was there, but left under questionable circumstances and was hired to run Dozier. It was also standard practice for school officials to bury the dead the same day of death or discovery of a body. They would notify the families afterward.

In the school's ledgers, it appeared Thomas was an orphan with his next of kin living out of state. There was a delay between the time of death and when the coffin was shipped. There were also several cases in which remains exhumed from Boot Hill had not yet yielded a viable DNA sample. So while no matches had been made to the Thomas Curry reference samples, the possibility still existed that Thomas was buried at the Boot Hill burial ground or even at the cemetery located at the state hospital.

Thomas's nephew contacted us after seeing his name in a newspaper article.

He told us that Thomas's brother, his own father, had always been very tight-lipped about his childhood. Thomas was killed in a railroad accident—that was all anyone knew. His own father had shot and killed his mother, Alma, then died by suicide. That was why Thomas lived with his grandmother in West Philadelphia before taking off for Florida.

The family asked to give a DNA sample and for the opportunity to give Thomas Curry a final resting place, if his remains were found. They, too, wanted to know what happened, and they wanted to reconnect with distant family members who had become separated as a result of their tragedies, the family members we had already been in touch with the help of the Pennsylvania State Police.

Chapter 15

"THE UNIMAGINABLE HAPPENED AT DOZIER"

In 2015, Dr. Antoinette Jackson and I called a meeting to discuss memorialization, and we invited a range of stakeholders to Tallahassee. Jackson was a cultural anthropologist whose research focused on gender, race, and heritage resource management. She was a critical part of the team, oversaw Kaniqua Robinson's research, and had been interviewing people about how to best memorialize Dozier.

We explained that, on one hand, we had one very practical problem with a variety of different threads. How and where should we bury human remains?

What type of burial container or casket should we use? How should they be arranged? Would they require vaults? Should we use the funeral home that has been volunteering all their time for us through this project? On each trip for excavation, funeral home director Pat Brewster was there. Or do we have to bid it out? And most importantly, on whose credit card should we charge it?

On the other hand, burials should be about more than putting a body somewhere. They should have meaning. What does this project mean to us? What does it mean to the families of the children we will need to rebury? What does it mean to Floridians and to our greater communities?

And most importantly, how should we capture and communicate that meaning for future generations?

There had been a few efforts to commemorate in the past. The white crosses placed in that small clearing in the 1990s were an effort to acknowledge the burial ground and, in doing so, the children buried there. The plaque placed outside the door of the White House in 2008, the one that called for an end to cruelty and for vigilance against it, was also an attempt to acknowledge abuse that happened in that building and what it represented.

We knew it had great meaning to the men who were part of it, like Robert Straley. We also knew that brick and mortar didn't always last. If someone didn't like a plaque or a monument, they took it down. If people didn't feel invested in a place, they let kudzu grow and diminish it.

For physical spaces to have meaning they have to be transformed.

The plaque on the White House isn't there anymore. Nor is there access to the White House for those for whom it has meaning. Families have asked us for access, and it wasn't until it was opened for us, with Senator Bill Nelson's powerful help, that the world was let in.

So for a place—a burial ground, a cemetery, any space—to have meaning, it has to have elements of what it once was, or what it meant at some time, and it must be transformed into what we want it to represent. Often, that means a transformation from a point of conflict into a place of understanding, acknowledgment, and peace.

Our goal in organizing this meeting was to propose that all the reburial and memorialization planning and discussion be done in a public way, so that what has been recovered, learned, and experienced could shed light on the past, bring justice to victims, and educate current and future generations about the systems that created and sustained an institution that considered some lives to be throwaways.

For a model, we proposed the work done by the International Coalition of Sites of Conscience, a worldwide network of historic sites, museums, and memory initiatives that activate the power of places of memory. The idea is that space is used to create a deeper understanding of the past and to protect human rights.

Reverend Meyer wrote to the group and state leaders: "We know that designing the memorial for the school's victims will involve a wide conversation, including surviving family and residents of the school, academic and civic leaders, and all interested parties. We hope such conversations are conducted in ways that welcome healing and new awareness on all sides. It is an important conversation we must take up. The German martyr Dietrich Bonhoeffer said, 'The ultimate test of a moral society is the kind of world that it leaves to its children.' Even if we failed the children of Dozier, a proper memorial for the Dozier boys may help us succeed with generations to come."

Following the meeting, Masterson & Hoag, the St. Petersburg law firm that represented the White House Boys, pointed out that the memorial should also "serve as a reminder that hundreds of children were physically, emotionally and sexually abused at the Boys Schools in Marianna . . . We feel it is important that those who are living and were subjected to abuse are not overlooked or forgotten. The abuse that these men were subjected to as children has impacted most of their lives in a significant way."

The lawyers also predicted that the protests would come from familiar quarters.

"We do not feel that the people of Marianna would welcome such a memorial," they wrote. "Many deny that the abuse and unthinkable acts ever happened. Most of the people who have expressed their views seem to feel that the exposure of the facts is a stigma to their community. In addition, if the objective is to have the memorial serve as a reminder of the obligation of society to protect children, it will receive a very low profile in the Marianna area. We are fearful that a memorial erected in Marianna will be quickly forgotten, as was the case with the White House plaque that was placed several years ago."

Their most salient point came next: "We also question whether the children and families of children who lost their lives in Marianna would want the bodies to remain in the facility for eternity under the circumstances that exist. For the bodies to be interred in the location where many lost their lives under suspect circumstances and hundreds of children were abused physically and sexually, seems inappropriate to us."

State lawmakers passed two consecutive bills.

First, they allocated $500,000 for the reburial of remains removed from Boot Hill. For those identified, families could be reimbursed for reburial. The bill also established a committee to decide how to create a memorial at the reform school.

Only three legislators, all Republicans, voted against the proposal: Matt Gaetz from Fort Walton Beach, John Tobia from Melbourne Beach, and John Wood from Winter Haven.

The Florida House voted 114–3 for the bill, which was sponsored by two Democrats from Tampa, Senator Arthenia Joyner and Representative Ed Narain. The bill also passed the Senate and was later signed by Governor Rick Scott.

"More than a tragedy happened at Dozier," Narain said. "In the eyes of any human being with a heart and a soul, the unimaginable happened at Dozier."

Narain said that the boys who were put in the hands of the state deserved better than unmarked graves.

"This is a start toward that closure for the families who lost someone," Narain said on the House floor during debate.

The following year, lawmakers set aside an additional $1.2 million for burials and two memorials.

Reverend Meyer wrote us a note.

"Today the Florida Senate, as the House did earlier, officially apologized to the Boys of Dozier," he wrote. "This day has been made possible by your tireless labors after the truth and diligence in pursuing justice for the known victims of Dozier. On behalf of the Interfaith Commission on Florida's Children and Youth, I express our profound gratitude for your efforts in forensic anthropology and oral history. It has been a highlight of my ministry to follow your work in seeking to expose the darkness of abuse to the light of society."

The Dozier Memorial & Monument Review Committee was tasked with selecting artists to design, create, and install two pieces to serve as memorials to boys who died at the reform school.

The location of the reburials remains controversial.

"The issue of figuring out where to put the bodies has been a contentious one. Former attendees of the school disputed assertions that the bodies should be buried at Dozier, since some believed it would tarnish their memories," the Sunshine State News reported.

The White House Boys said that burying the remains of those boys back at Boot Hill would be adding insult to injury.

The families who gave DNA samples but for whom we could make only presumptive identifications didn't want any of the burials back in Marianna, including the three other families whose relatives' bones were commingled with Charles Evans's, the school employee killed with the boys in the 1914 fire.

The NAACP worried that the whole thing would be forgotten with the sale of the land. They suggested the land be treated as sacred and preserved as a memorial site.

Even locals from Marianna didn't want the boys brought back. The county commissioners said a memorial outside of the rural panhandle country would receive better exposure.

The one exception was a distant relative of Charles Evans's. She fought, despite the wishes of all other families for whom we had not been able to make a positive identification, to have the remains of the fire victims returned to Boot Hill. The woman, Rhonda Dykes, wasn't Evans's legal next of kin, which was why we never met her nor asked her for a DNA sample. Charles's cousin and namesake provided that. She wasn't even a resident of Marianna. She let it be known she did not approve of the excavation or what we had done: she wrote a letter to the *Jackson County Floridan* saying ". . . the fire victims never should have been exhumed from where they had lain for 99 years, as their causes of deaths were already known and they were not part of any alleged abuse or murder allegations."

Ultimately, the state legislature agreed to move some of the bodies to Marianna and set up two burial grounds—one in Tallahassee and one in Marianna.

Land enough for forty-seven caskets was donated by Art Kimbrough, who, I was interested to read, was a former president of the Jackson County Chamber of Commerce and the longtime owner of cemeteries in both Tallahassee and Marianna.

"I am doing this simply because I care about our community and I have the capacity and the space to provide an appropriate place to address the issue of reinterment and memorialization," he told a reporter. "My wish in making this offer is to provide a solution that will bring lasting resolution to a problem of historic proportions for Marianna and the state of Florida, and in the process help bring healing to our community and all individuals and groups involved."

At the time of this writing, there are no memorials on-site nor permanent grave markers for those who were reburied by the state. Not in Tallahassee. Not at Boot Hill.

Chapter 16

"YOU HAVE THE TRUTH
ON YOUR SIDE"

In January 2016, we presented a final report to the Florida cabinet. It felt very different than the last time we were there, nearly four years prior, to plead for their support. The chamber was packed with families of the boys who fought for their rights to know the truth, the White House Boys and the Black Boys of Dozier, the media, USF students and faculty, and representatives from the Hillsborough County Sheriff's Office and other state agencies who assisted us, such as Florida Department of Law Enforcement, the Department of Juvenile Justice, and the Department of Environmental Protection.

Before the first cabinet meeting, waiting in the cafeteria of the capital, I spoke with Sheriff David Gee on the phone. I was nervous about how this would play out. He told me not to worry.

"You have the truth on your side," he said. "All you have to do is tell it."

His involvement made the difference in winning the fight to secure the land-use agreement, as it had in opening the door to collecting and comparing DNA samples. From the start, this process would have been routine had law enforcement opened an investigation. It was anything but routine. When Gee saw the need, he stepped in. He took on a responsibility that wasn't his to bear. To me, that represented what a good sheriff was supposed to be and stood in such contrast to the 111-year legacy of failure after failure in the juvenile justice system. There are sixty-seven elected constitutional sheriffs in Florida, and each one is the top law enforcement officer in his or her county. Hillsborough County was the eleventh-largest sheriff's office in the nation. When he got involved, people took notice. When I wasn't nearly getting myself arrested or having to navigate state politics, Gee and I talked about scientific tools and technologies related to crime science investigations. He was a scientist at heart. A helicopter pilot. I think that was our connection. We had used ground-penetrating radar to find Abraham Shakespeare, the multimillion-dollar lottery winner who was brutally murdered by a "friend" who conned him into assigning her power of attorney. He was buried more than nine feet deep, and the excavation in Sheriff Gee's jurisdiction in the eastern part of Hillsborough County was a textbook example of how to use remote sensing and stratigraphy to find and excavate a burial. He's retired now, but you can find him flying a helicopter out west, putting out forest fires.

This time meeting at the capital, with all the interested parties and families attending and the hard work behind us, it felt like a homecoming.

We were supposed to summarize our findings and make recommendations for burial and memorialization. As I prepared my comments, I thought hard about what to say. How much detail should I provide? Should I include quotes by Søren Kierkegaard or Dick Gregory, as I had in the past? Mark Ober, the Hillsborough state attorney, read my draft. He smiled and approved. He and Sheriff Gee were the two men who led the second investigation into Martin Lee Anderson's death. The pressure was on them. "You kill a dog, you go to jail," Benjamin Crump, the family's attorney, said after the first investigation resulted in no charges. "You kill a little black boy, nothing happens." With an honest investigation, they brought charges against the seven guards and one nurse who suffocated the teen.

Gee and Ober were with us through this effort. Maybe this was what the justice process was supposed to look like. Access for everyone.

The presentation of facts and context to understand and acknowledge what happened. A system robust against the trite wrangling for power by a few men.

Ridiculously idealistic, I know. I know. But in these moments it does happen. It was happening in this cabinet hearing. So how can we ever accept less?

When we were done, really done, we all breathed in relief. We were successful in meeting the tasks we had set out to do. It was finally over.

Cabinet members apologized for the past abuses, made speeches, and took photographs with the White House Boys and the Black Boys of Dozier. No one officially mentioned the pending bill for reparations for them.

Adam Putnam, the Florida agriculture commissioner, said what happened at the school was unconscionable and stressed that it should never be forgotten. "I'm very sorry for what these men and generations of boys endured while wards of the state," he said.

And for the first time, Governor Rick Scott publicly commented on the issue.

"For everybody that spoke today, all the individuals that have been in Dozier, thanks for how you handled yourself," he said. "Wish it never happened . . . I can't imagine it. None of us can, and we hope it never happens again to anybody in our society. You can see the people in this room want to do the right things. So, it's a very good day for our state, because you can see things are heading in the right direction."

The remains of those identified were returned to families and buried next to their parents and siblings.

Each family buried the fragile, small bones in caskets in the locations of their choosing. Earl Wilson's family, including his sister Cherry, released a dozen white balloons into the air. Robert Stephens's family's minister delivered a sermon next to the grave, and afterward his family presented us with a beautiful glass sculpture engraved with their names and mine. Mattie, Billey Jackson's sister, held a ceremony, livestreamed on Facebook, so everyone could be part of it. We returned to her the marble we'd found with Billey's remains, the worn burgundy-and-white-colored stone marble that was found in the area of the front left pocket of his pants. That marble remained the only symbol of childhood I ever found during excavation. It was a symbol for the White House Boys, and many of the men now carried a marble with them at all times.

The ceremonies were all different from one another, but they shared one thing: they brought people together.

Families and friends came together, shared pictures, and told stories about their childhoods. Many connected with or even met distant family members they had never met before. They shared memories about those they lost and talked about their parents, now deceased, and the promises they made to them long ago to never give up searching. They talked about the state and why it was so hard to find answers.

They welcomed us into their homes. We ate with them. We compared politics to geology. Like the formation of mountains, only pressure and time swayed most politicians to take action. We all agreed on that point.

Mostly we marveled at what a challenge it had been.

We were invited to and attended many of these gatherings. We were shown so much gratitude and praise. I felt like the lucky one, so privileged to be able to share this with these families, grateful they included us in such intimate, meaningful gatherings.

It felt like tragedy and joy, all bundled into the same ceremony. It was so difficult to work through, and that was probably why it was done surrounded by the people who meant the most to them. To be invited into that private, personal world by families who suffered decades was very special. For me, it was all about those moments. That was why we did this work. When we shared answers and started to understand what happened—why it happened, and how, and to acknowledge it—hopefully that was what put them on a path to find acceptance. Maybe even peace.

Richard Varnadoe, Thomas's brother, brought Glen and me to the grave several months after his reburial ceremony. The marker they ordered had finally arrived, and he wanted to show it to me. As we walked to the grave site, he held my hand and told me that finding

Thomas was the best thing that ever happened to him in his whole life. I couldn't hold back the tears that time, and to this day, I don't know what to feel exactly. It's both rewarding and tragic. I am honored that I could help him in this way. I'm also saddened that for his whole life, for eighty-five years, this was what he sought and couldn't find.

It should have never happened. Thomas should not have been sent to that school for trespassing. He shouldn't have died there. He shouldn't have been buried by his own brother in an unmarked grave. The location and details surrounding his death shouldn't have remained elusive to the family for nearly a century. Richard shouldn't have lived with a shadow of trauma over his entire life to bring us to this point.

The name of a boy now returned to his families was carved in stone. A marker had been placed at the burial site to memorize the life lost.

The burned remains of those who died in the 1914 fire were brought back to Marianna and buried at Boot Hill. They were laid in eight adult-size coffins, in a row, commingled and spread out the same way they had been unearthed in 2014. All the other unknown boys were buried in a similar fashion, but in Tallahassee.

AT THE SAME time we were presenting our final report to the cabinet, *Miami Herald* investigative reporter Carol Marbin Miller, who broke the initial White House Boys story, was publishing a series with Audra D. S. Burch titled "Fight Club," about ten years of youth maltreatment in the state system, including beatings, cover-ups, sexual exploitation, and medical neglect.

It was the very same decade that followed the death of Martin Lee Anderson, the shuttering of the state's boot camp–style juvenile justice centers, the closing ceremony of the White House, whose plaque had pledged to protect children, and the closure of Dozier. The Pulitzer website called the series "a sweeping investigation of Florida's juvenile justice system, prompted by the tragic death of a foster child and told in heartbreaking detail, that spurred legislative reform intended to better protect that state's young charges" when it was listed as a finalist for the 2018 investigative reporting prize. The cleansing light of journalism had again sparked change.

The death the Pulitzer committee referenced was Elord Revolte's, another Black boy killed while locked up in 2015. Even though the boot camps were closed following Anderson's death, all other juvenile centers in Florida remained privately owned, though they were overseen by the state. Revolte was killed by fellow inmates at the urging of the guards, who paid boys vending machine treats to beat up certain other boys, a common practice known as "honey-bunning." During the ten-year period that Miller and Burch investigated, they found fourteen hundred complaints of guard misconduct, an average of three per week. They wrote that the guards threatened to extend boys' release dates if they wouldn't participate in the barbarism, even when compliance meant committing a crime and beating up other boys.

The guards could claim they never touched anyone.

IN APRIL 2018, before a gallery filled with former wards of the Dozier school, the Florida legislature passed a resolution acknowledging the state's responsibility for the pain and suffering of so many.

WHEREAS, the Florida State Reform School, also called the Florida Industrial School for Boys and later known as the Arthur G. Dozier School for Boys, referred to in this resolution as "Dozier School," was opened by the State of Florida in 1900 in Marianna to house children who had committed minor criminal offenses, such as incorrigibility, truancy, and smoking, as well as more serious offenses such as theft and murder, and

WHEREAS, many of the children who were sent to Dozier School were sentenced without legal representation before the court, often without a known basis for being sent to the school or a specific duration of confinement, and

WHEREAS, within the first 13 years of Dozier School's operation, six state-led investigations were conducted in response to reports of children being chained to walls in irons, severely beaten, and used for child labor, and

WHEREAS, throughout Dozier School's history, reports of abuse, suspicious deaths, and threats of closure plagued the school, and

WHEREAS, many former students of Dozier School have sworn under oath that they were beaten at a facility located on the school grounds known as the "White House," and

WHEREAS, a psychologist employed at Dozier School testified under oath at a 1958 United States Senate Judiciary Committee hearing that boys at the school were beaten by an administrator, that the blows were severe and dealt with a great deal of force with a full arm swing over the head and down, that a leather strap approximately 10 inches long was used, and that the beatings were "brutality," and

WHEREAS, a former Dozier School employee stated in interviews with law enforcement that, in 1962, several employees of the school were removed from the facility based upon allegations that they made sexual advances toward boys at the facility, and

WHEREAS, a forensic investigation funded by the Florida Legislature and conducted from 2013 to 2016 by the University of South Florida found incomplete records regarding deaths and burials that occurred at Dozier School between 1900 and 1960, and that families were often notified after the child was buried or denied access to their remains at the time of burial, and

WHEREAS, the excavations conducted as part of the forensic investigation yielded 55 burial sites, 24 more sites than reported in official records, and

WHEREAS, given the lack of documentation and contradictions in the historical record, questions persist regarding the identity of persons buried at Dozier School and the circumstances surrounding their deaths, and

WHEREAS, in 1955, the State of Florida opened a new reform school in Okeechobee, called the Florida School for Boys at Okeechobee, referred to in this resolution as "the Okeechobee School," to address overcrowding at Dozier School, and staff of Dozier School were transferred to the Okeechobee School where similar practices were implemented, and

WHEREAS, many former students of the Okeechobee School have sworn under oath that they were beaten at a facility on school grounds known as the "Adjustment Unit," and

WHEREAS, former Governor Claude Kirk toured Dozier School in 1968 and stated, "If one of your kids were kept in such circumstances, you'd be up there with rifles," and

WHEREAS, Dozier School was closed in 2011 after investigations by the Florida Department of Law Enforcement and the Civil Rights Division of the United States Department of Justice, and

WHEREAS, more than 500 former students of Dozier School and the Okeechobee School have come forward with reports of physical, mental, and sexual abuse by school staff during the 1940s, 1950s, and 1960s, and resulting trauma that has endured throughout their adult lives,

NOW, THEREFORE, Be It Resolved by the State of Florida: That the state regrets that the treatment of boys who were sent to the Arthur G. Dozier School for Boys and the Okeechobee School was cruel, unjust, and a violation of human decency, and acknowledges this shameful part of the State of Florida's history.

BE IT FURTHER RESOLVED that the state apologizes to the boys who were confined to Arthur G. Dozier School for Boys and the Okeechobee School and their family members for the wrongs committed against them by employees of the State of Florida.

BE IT FURTHER RESOLVED that the state expresses its commitment to ensuring that children who have been placed in the State of Florida's care are protected from abuse and violations of fundamental human decency.

The apology wasn't salve for some; it rang hollow. For others, the men who had been fighting so long, there was reward in the simple acknowledgment that their suffering diminished their potential.

"This might be my legacy," said Robert Straley, who was seventy years old then. "I think it's the only good thing that I've ever done that's not for myself."

IN EARLY 2019, a cultural resource management firm hired by a company to excavate buried diesel tanks on the northwestern edge of the old reform school's former farm sent a letter to Florida governor Ron DeSantis. The firm told the governor that they had found twenty-seven anomalies while running ground-penetrating radar over the parcel. They interpreted these anomalies as possible burials. Their report was unlike other similar reports from companies contracted to conduct archaeological surveys before construction on state land. This report discussed the history of the former reform school and tried to make a case for interpreting their ground-penetrating radar data as clandestine graves, given that the data didn't really fit what they would expect in a historic burial ground.

They had done GPR on about two acres of property.

They never ground-truthed it.

Even so, when word got out, the news splashed across the country.

"27 More Graves May Have Been Found at a Notorious Florida Boys School," read a headline in the *New York Times*.

"Florida Governor Says 27 Possible Graves Have Been Found Near a Controversial Boys Reform School," said one on CNN.com.

The *Washington Post*, *Time* magazine, *The Guardian*. The story was big, and it sparked a strange new hope in some of the folks who were sure we'd find two separate burial grounds. On one hand, it would've been strong evidence of nefarious burials. On the other, more dead boys.

Governor DeSantis asked Jackson County officials to work with state leaders to develop a plan for investigating this new claim. David Clark, formerly of the Department of Environmental Protection, was the governor's assistant chief of staff, and he called me to see what we could do.

The crew got back together. Greg Berg flew in from the Pacific. Christian Wells came up from USF. Many of our USF graduate students, including some who had been at the original excavations and some who were new, joined us on-site.

And this time around, my son Sean was not a little guy running around taking pictures, or climbing the mountains of dirt created by the gradall excavator, or playing in the Walmart pool set up by John Forty, a local farmer who lent us the use of his vintage fire truck for the burned-dorm excavation. Sean was part of the crew now, officially interning for the summer with our Institute for Forensic Anthropology and Applied Science, learning a range of new skills.

I put him to work under Wells's direction and, like the rest of us, he navigated his way through the heat, rain, hotel bedbugs, and thick swarms of mosquitoes.

We had lunch one day in one of the old farm buildings. It was cool and out of the sun. The floor of the old building was littered with dead roaches. Sean sat on a folding chair, holding his lunch in his lap. I remember telling him he would have quite a story in the fall if he had to write the classic *What I did last summer* essay, though I hoped it wouldn't bring social services to our door. He laughed.

Like before, I wrote a scope of work that outlined our strategy to investigate the possibility of twenty-seven additional burials at the reform school and set about studying the report from the firm that found the anomalies, hoping to better understand how they came to their conclusions.

I broke the project into three phases. It was a challenge since rather than doing the GPR in this area ourselves, we were relying on the data obtained from the private firm. We analyzed their data, geo-referenced their GIS data, and went to work analyzing historic photographs and maps of this corner of the property.

Long ago, the school had a gas pump for the farm vehicles, which was why they buried diesel tanks. That was what had prompted the survey in the first place, since officials were trying to develop the land. The state had given the former Dozier grounds to the City of

Marianna. The city wanted to dig up the tanks for a new construction project but didn't want to do it without checking for more burials, given its proximity to Boot Hill.

Behind the gas pump was an open field, evident in aerial photographs from the 1930s and '40s. Across the road were the barns for livestock. This was a large, productive farm in its day, complete with a cattle-dipping vat used by folks throughout the county. Jackson County farmers brought cattle to walk through the arsenic bath to kill fleas and other bugs. The toxic solution was dumped regularly into the farm pond. We had thought maybe this was the source of the high concentrations of lead that we found in the soil throughout Boot Hill. Now I wondered if the buried tanks of diesel, leaking for the past twenty years, were the more likely source.

It was hard to estimate how much time we would need in Marianna. It depended on what we found. I wasn't convinced we would find anything.

A clandestine burial was an intentionally hidden grave, typically associated with homicides.

Twenty-seven burials made a burial ground.

There was no mention in records or interviews of another burial ground across the road from the barns, a road in regular use for some seventy years. Yes, we had suspected a second cemetery at one point, before we excavated Boot Hill. That was before finding the boys were buried together, Black and white. We still had five more bodies than we had names for.

The mission I planned went like this: We would mark the anomalies the survey firm found, then ground-truth to see if they were burials. We would run lidar—flying drones that created an accurate 3D scan of the earth's surface. If we found human remains, we would excavate and bring them back to the lab for analysis.

My most important equipment request was for a gradall.

The survey firm recommended in their report that the two acres be excavated by hand. With trowels. Delicately.

That recommendation was made without even confirming through ground-truthing if there were in fact burials. We didn't have a lifetime to dedicate to these two acres, so I was very specific. We would use the same method and process we had in the past. Open the area by removing the topsoil, and search for graves. We would mechanically excavate to the bottom of every feature the survey firm identified, so as not to miss anything. We would also open more of the surrounding area, at least as much as we could, to ensure we didn't miss anything.

Unlike last time, when we had to report directly to the Florida cabinet, this time we were contracting the work through the state's Division of Historical Resources. They reported to a new secretary of state, and she was from Tampa.

The Division of Historical Resources hired a local company for the mechanical excavation equipment we needed, and the man in charge assured DHR that they had the exact equipment I requested. Sadly, they showed up on-site with a backhoe and a front-end loader. Not what I requested. Also, their bucket blades had ground-destroying teeth, and they wouldn't be able to swap the blades for flat ones, the other thing I had requested. Looking at the machinery that arrived, I told them this would not work. The heavy-equipment operators on-site were insistent that it would.

"This is what you need," they said, as many men do.

DHR didn't know where else to turn. The state deferred to the heavy-equipment company, and those men wanted us to . . . just . . . give it a try.

I can't count the number of times I have been mansplained on-site about heavy equipment. Lead the fieldwork, write a scope of work, list what is needed—experience guides the plan. We trust the plan. Then some ol' boy shows up and tells me I need to do something different, when I know perfectly well his plan won't work. Then I am forced to wait patiently in the heat for him to fail, like I know he will, and to listen to him hem and haw.

I had a crew on-site, ready to work. What I didn't have was time to waste.

I asked David Clark. He found exactly what we needed and had it on-site within a few hours.

Greg Berg worked with the heavy-equipment operator who, as it turned out, had little experience using a gradall and was nervous. A couple of days of practice and he started to get the hang of it.

For most of my career, I have been the only woman in the room. Homicide detectives, their command staff, medical examiners, university administrators, heavy-equipment operators, politicians—especially in Jackson County—were mostly all men. Mostly all men in the decision-making seats. So as a woman, I had to work harder, prepare for all the contingencies when things went off the rails, and then patiently wait for them to accept that I knew what I was doing.

An Associated Press reporter named Tamara Lush once wrote that patience was my superpower. I always thought that came from the painstaking and sometimes frustrating work in cold cases, but perhaps it was from many years of negotiations in a male-dominated career. The lawyer Bob Bolt, when trying to secure the injunction for Glen Varnadoe, said that I was his best secret weapon because I was constantly being underestimated. "They don't see you coming," he said.

Having the right equipment, we set to work. We dug around each of the anomalies. We dug into them. We dug past them and well below them. What we found were fence post holes, buried water lines, and tree roots. All twenty-seven. There were no graves. The field in the middle of the farm, behind the gas pump, was not a second burial ground. Given all the research we had done and knowing how that space had been used, I was not surprised.

I RETURNED TO Boot Hill in 2020. The burial ground had changed. There was a new road leading past the county jail and up the hill, a gravel road now, through thick woods. Hurricane Michael had destroyed much of the surrounding forest two years before and killed the large oak tree that had towered over the north end of the burial ground for more than a hundred years.

Some of the cedar trees lining the original boundary remained, but a new iron fence with a gate was placed around the burials, and benches were added as a place for reflection.

The mulberry tree that once stood directly on top of one of the burials had been such a point of contention during the Boot Hill excavation but was now thriving and lush. Part of our original land-use agreement stated we could not cut down any tree more than four inches in diameter, but as we excavated it became apparent that the mulberry tree was growing atop one of the burials. The excavation was fully underway when we realized that one hard rain could wash the remains, now exposed, out of the sidewall of the grave. I was told to write a memo explaining why I needed to remove the tree and my request would be taken into consideration, winding its way back through the bureaucratic chain. When could I expect an answer? A couple of weeks. Probably.

David Clark, a former paratrooper, knew how to make things happen. He fixed all our problems, from locked buildings to closed access roads to curt security guards to police officers with trail cameras to loss of power to lack of running water. It wasn't hard to plead my case to him. The solution was obvious to most of us. Still, it was one more favor.

"Please, help," I said. "If we can't get approval today, we will have to come back. That means filling in the soil around the grave, coming back, excavating it out again. It will add weeks and a lot more money."

I think that was the ammunition he needed. State and county officials wanted this done so they could sell the land as quickly as possible.

Later that day David called with good news. We were granted permission to cut down the tree.

Only, we didn't cut it down. We dug it up and set it aside. Then, after carefully excavating the remains of the child buried beneath it, we replanted the tree where it had been. Whenever I spoke about Dozier, I made a point to let folks know, the mulberry tree was still thriving.

For me, it was a symbol of the struggle and triumph of this effort.

You wouldn't know the Boot Hill cemetery exists from the main road that cuts through the campus. Nothing on the site explains what it is, its history, or who is buried there. The graves are evident by their sunken depressions, in a neat row beneath the mulberry tree. Sunken earth is the hallmark of any burial ground. Eerily, that's the same description given by Ovell Krell as she remembered searching for her brother there in 1941.

There are no names of anyone who is buried there. There's nothing that explains or even acknowledges the abuse victims or the school's legacy of institutional racism. The only identifiable traits are our forensic lab numbers printed on paper markers at the head of each grave. They are crumbling and tattered.

I wonder how long they will last.

Chapter 17

WHAT REMAINS

Difficult boys are easy to forget. We remember.

We remember that twenty of the boys died within the first three months of being remanded to the school. Half of those within the first thirty days.

We remember that seven boys died while trying to run away.

We remember that three of the boys had attempted to run away and were returned to the school and faced punishment in the White House and were then isolated, all immediately preceding their deaths.

We remember that isolation took place in "dark cells" located in different parts of the grounds. They were segregated. African American boys were placed in sweat boxes, such as the one in which Earl Wilson was found dead in 1944. Also, there were different patterns based on perceptions of race.

We remember that throughout its history, the majority of the boys at the institution were Black. More Black boys died, and among those, they tended to be younger in age.

We remember that the burial location was unspecified as Boot Hill or "shipped home" for nearly three times more Black than white boys.

We remember that in 1917, the state of Florida began requiring that death certificates be issued when a death occurred. However, between 1920 and 1941, at least twelve student deaths occurred for which no death certificates were issued.

We remember that among those whose burial locations were unspecified, only three were issued death certificates in 1932. The three boys for whom there was an issued death certificate all died of influenza and these deaths were certified by Dr. N. Baltzell, the school physician. The causes of death for the remaining boys are undocumented.

We remember that the general trends as to why boys were committed to the school appear the same for white and "colored" boys: delinquency, larceny, and breaking and entering, which were the highest categories. The cases of incorrigibility and running away—non-criminal charges—were more frequently assigned to Black boys, consistent with the Jim Crow practices of the time.

We remember that there were at least twenty-two student deaths in the records for which no burial location and no cause of death are documented. This absence of records is again suggestive of intent to cloud the causes of the students' deaths and the location of their burials. While other state-run institutions—such as the Florida State Hospital in Chattahoochee—kept meticulous records of burials made on their property, the school was notable for the fact that it did not keep any records showing the location of specific graves, nor did the school even mark the graves. This lack of record keeping and absence of grave markers suggest intent to obfuscate the true number of burials located at the school and to hinder later potential investigations into the true causes of specific individuals' deaths.

We remember that throughout its history, the school consistently underreported the number of deaths that occurred in their biennial reports to the state. References to a death may appear in state investigative reports or newspaper accounts, but they differ from the school's own records. The school's superintendent and other staff wrote reports for the board of managers, who created biennial reports for the governor. For example, references to the deaths of at least fourteen different "colored" boys were made, but no names or specific information about the deaths were provided, including burial locations.

The lack of documentation and conflicting information in the records makes the identification process more challenging. Other examples include the following boys who died at the school or following escape from the school but were not reported to the state: William McKinley, a Black boy who died from unknown causes in 1915; Thomas Curry, a fifteen-year-old white boy who died of blunt trauma in 1925 after running away; and Robert Hewett, a sixteen-year-old white boy who died of gunshot wounds in 1960 after running away.

We remember that the possibility of undocumented deaths at the school is an important piece in the effort to identify the children buried at the school. In the end, we exhumed fifty-five burials but had only forty-six names for possible identification, and this was based on the assumption that, among all those who died but were not documented, none were sent home for burial. A really big assumption. We were able to positively or presumptively identify twenty-four boys.

We know that the forty-six names represent the missing person's pool. Among those names, twelve were white and thirty-four were documented as "colored" or African American and are 74 percent of the group. Also within this group, only nineteen (41 percent) were issued death certificates, twenty-two (48 percent) were recorded as buried at the school, and twenty-seven (56 percent) have a listed cause of death in the records.

We remember the youngest, a six-year-old Black boy named George Grissam, who had been paroled for labor as a house boy and was brought back to the school unconscious in 1918. His older brother was eight-year-old Ernest Grissam, and he also disappeared from the records in 1919, when he was listed in the school ledger as "not here." Efforts to find out what happened to him and the relatives of their mother—Peg Grissam from Caryville, Florida—have been unsuccessful.

We remember that we found one boy buried in his knee brace, a reminder of the many disabled children sent to the school.

We remember Sam Morgan, who was positively identified. He had also been paroled out for labor from the school. He entered the school at the age of eighteen. The ledger entry states he was first received on

September 23, 1915, paroled on January 18, 1918, then brought back again on February 10, 1918, only twenty-three days later. The ledger further states under the column "how released" that he was "indentured," which is why we believe he died in the custody of the businessman or farmer who had acquired him. He was buried at the Boot Hill burial ground on the school's property. However, his burial location had been unknown, as the school's own records do not list him as deceased and provide no information about him, his death, or his burial. The 2009 FDLE report lists his date of death as 1921 with no other information. The Morgan example highlights why the identification process is so difficult. In this case, the school's own records don't state that he died. In many cases there is no entry about how a boy was released. Therefore, the fact that we have more remains than possible names is not unexpected.

More of us remember. Great numbers of people have learned the history of the Dozier School for Boys. By May 2013, updates about our findings and the request for exhumation were regularly appearing in the national news, carried by outlets like the Associated Press, the United Press International, the *Wall Street Journal*, the *New York Times*, the *Los Angeles Times*, and National Public Radio. The story spread across the US borders and was covered by *Der Spiegel* in Germany, *La Paz* in Spain, and the BBC. A single press conference in August 2014, to announce our most recent findings, generated more than eight hundred stories worldwide. The university estimated that it reached approximately 1.18 billion people through print, online, and broadcast media around the world.

We remember that the Dozier school is but one institution within a system structured to define people by color and class, a system designed to accept that some people are just "throwaways."

We remember that the door was closed to us in the search for historic justice by many who had the power to open it, citing a lack of jurisdiction, a statute of limitations, the antiquity of the graves, the sanctity of burial, the lack of documentation. Yet despite all the objections and reasons provided that we would fail, we did not fail.

ACKNOWLEDGMENTS

More than a hundred people from at least twenty agencies volunteered their time, skills, and expertise to help with the investigation that ultimately led to this book, providing technical assistance, knowledge, and friendship along the way. I want to thank everyone who contributed their time and offered support.

I am especially grateful to Ben Montgomery for bringing this story to my attention, his incredible investigative work into the school for over a decade, his enduring friendship and encouragement throughout the process, and for his help writing this book. It was a long time in the making and because of him it finally came together.

I want to offer my deepest gratitude to the following people for their help, friendship, and guidance, from the investigation to the writing of this book: Vickie Chachere, Lorraine Monteagut, Moises García, Katy Hennig, Antoinette Jackson, Christian Wells, Eric Eisenberg, Ralph Wilcox, Gerard Solis, Kevin Yelvington, Lara Wade, Kelsee Hentschel-Fey, Liotta Noche-Dowdy, Gennifer Goad, Kaniqua Robinson, Chris Turner, Melissa Pope, John Powell, Richard Weltz, Lee Manning, Henry Schmidt, Ivett Kovari, Susan Myster, Lori Collins, Travis Doering, Robert Ura, Mike Hurley, Greg Thomas, Mark Ober, Brendan Fitzgerald,

Glen Varnadoe, Ovell Krell, John and Tananarive Due, Johnny Lee Gaddy, John Bonner, Richard Huntly, Elmore Bryant, Adora Obi Nweze, Dale Landry, Rev. Dr. Russell Meyer, Tom McAndrew, Brendan O'Malley, and Rick Richter.

I am extremely grateful to Greg Berg for his friendship, willingness to make the long treks from Hawaii, and helping to lead this crew and effort. His experience, knowledge and humor made it possible. I thank Senator Bill Nelson (ret.) for his lasting commitment throughout this endeavor and his unwavering support. I want to thank Sheriff David Gee (ret.) for his wisdom and everything he did to support and encourage me. I am grateful to David Clark for always being available and his ability to get things done.

The administration at the University of South Florida never wavered in their support for academic freedom, and for that I am very grateful. I also want to acknowledge and thank all of those who reported on this story, shedding light on a dark corner that would have remained in the shadows if not for their tenacity and commitment to investigative journalism: Carol Marbin Miller, Brendan Farrington, Ed Lavandera, Rich Phillips, Greg Allen, and Megan Towey.

Most of all, I want to thank my own family for their love and encouragement: my parents, Marcia and Craig, for supporting a career in anthropology when no one else thought it wise; my sister, Angie, for her humor and friendship; and my aunt Gloria for her love and encouragement. Finally, the two guys who inspire me every day, I thank my own children, Sean and Reid, for their support, love, and always inspiring me to approach the world through imagination.

The following forty-six names are a list of the men and boys positively and presumptively identified from the Boot Hill burial ground. Positive identifications based on DNA are indicated in bold. Presumptive identifications are listed on the site diagram on the last page of this book's photo insert. DC stands for Death Certificate. The burial number corresponds to the grave number excavated. The site diagram in the photo insert also shows the burial layout and has the corresponding numbers.

DATE OF DEATH	NAME	AGE	ANCESTRY	DC	CIRCUMSTANCES	BURIAL NUMBER
11/18/1914	Bennett Evans	Adult	White	No	Fire	25, 50, 51, & 52
11/18/1914	Charles Evans	Adult	White	No	Fire	25, 50, 51, & 52
11/18/1914	Harry Wells	-	White	No	Fire	11, 12, 25, 50, 51, 52, & 55
2/28/1916	Sim Williams	18	Colored	No	Unknown	30 or 40
5/25/1916	Tillman Mohind	17	Colored	No	Unknown	30 or 40
1916	James Joshua	-	Colored	No	Unknown	30 or 40
4/16/1918	Thomas Adkins	12	Colored	No	Unknown	45
10/6/1918	Lee Goolsby	13	White	No	Escape/ Unknown	43
10/23/1918	George Grissam	6	Colored	No	Paroled Labor/ Unconscious	19
10/25/1918	Willie Adkins	13	Colored	No	Unknown	20
11/4/1918	**Loyd Dutton**	**14**	**White**	**No**	**Unknown**	**42**
11/6/1918	Ralph Whiddon	16	White	No	Unknown	41, 44, or 45
11/6/1918	Hilton Finley	16	White	No	Unknown	41, 44, or 45
11/8/1918	Puner Warner	16	White	No	Unknown	41, 44, or 45
ca. 1918	Wilber Smith	10	Colored	No	"Reported Flu"	47
2/12/1919	Joe Anderson	17	Colored	No	Unknown	
5/9/1919	Leonard Simmons	13	Colored	No	Unknown	
12/12/1920	Nathaniel Sawyer	12	Colored	No	Unknown	

DATE OF DEATH	NAME	AGE	ANCESTRY	DC	CIRCUMSTANCES	BURIAL NUMBER
2/26/1921	Arthur Williams	12	Colored	No	Unknown	
1921	Sam Morgan	21	White	No	Paroled/ Unknown	26
7/9/1921	John H. Williams	15	Colored	No	". . . Accident"	33
4/15/1922	Schley Hunter	16	White	Yes	Pneumonia/ Influenza	2
12/31/1922	Calvin Williams	15	Colored	No	Unknown	
8/19/1924	Charlie Overstreet	15	Colored	Yes	Tonsillectomy	
12/4/1924	Clifford Miller	15	Colored	No	Unknown	
5/16/1925	Edward Fonders	18	Colored	Yes	Drowning	
12/18/1925	Walter Askew	12	Colored	No	Unknown	
1/30/1926	Nollie Davis	15	Colored	Yes	Lobar Pneumonia	
4/8/1929	Robert Rhoden	15	Colored	Yes	Pneumonia	
10/15/1929	Samuel Bethel	16	Colored	Yes	Tuberculosis	
1/5/1932	Lee Smith	17	Colored	Yes	Rupture of Lung	
4/10/1932	James Brinson	12	Colored	Yes	Pneumonia/ Influenza	
4/21/1932	Lee Underwood	16	Colored	Yes	Pneumonia/ Influenza	
4/22/1932	Fred Sams	15	Colored	Yes	Pneumonia/ Influenza	
4/22/1932	Archie J. Shaw Jr.	12	Colored	No	Influenza	
5/9/1932	Joe Stephens	15	Colored	Yes	Influenza	
10/26/1934	Thomas Varnadoe	13	White	Yes	Lobar Pneumonia	53
2/23/1935	Richard Nelson	12	Colored	Yes	Pneumonia/ Influenza	3
2/24/1935	Robert Cato	12	Colored	Yes	Pneumonia/ Influenza	5
3/4/1935	Grady Huff	17	White	Yes	Nephritis/ Hernia	54
3/16/1935	Joshua Backey	14	Colored	No	Blood Poison	6
4/30/1936	James Hammond	14	Colored	Yes	Pulmonary Tuberculosis	7
7/15/1937	Robert Stephens	15	Colored	Yes	Knife Wounds	10
1/24/1941	George Owen Smith	14	White	No	Escaped/ Unknown	1
8/31/1944	Earl Wilson	12	Colored	Yes	Blunt Trauma	4
10/7/1952	Billey Jackson	13	Colored	Yes	Escaped/ Pyelonephritis	24

ACLU	American Civil Liberties Union
CFO	Chief Financial Officer
COD	Cause and/or Circumstances of Death
DC	Death Certificate
DEP	Department of Environmental Protection
DHR	Division of Historical Resources
DJJ	Department of Juvenile Justice
DNA	Deoxyribonucleic Acid
FDLE	Florida Department of Law Enforcement
FEMORS	Florida Emergency Mortuary Operations Response System
FIS	Florida Industrial School for Boys
FSB	Florida School for Boys
GIS	Geographic Information System
GPR	Ground-Penetrating Radar
HCSO	Hillsborough County Sheriff's Office
ID	Identification
IFAAS	Institute for Forensic Anthropology and Applied Sciences
JJOC	Jackson Juvenile Offender Center
KKK	Ku Klux Klan
mtDNA	Mitochondrial Deoxyribonucleic Acid
NAACP	National Association for the Advancement of Colored People
NAFTA	North American Free Trade Agreement
NamUs	National Missing and Unidentified Persons System
NATO	North Atlantic Treaty Organization
PRIDE	Prison Rehabilitative Industries and Diversified Enterprises Inc.
UID	Unidentified Persons
UNT	University of North Texas
USF	University of South Florida

"A Thief as a Reformer." *Holmes County Advertiser* (Bonifay, FL), November 28, 1914.

"Acts and Resolutions Adopted by the Legislature of Florida." Florida Legislature, 1905.

Allen, Greg. "Florida's Dozier School for Boys: A True Horror Story." National Public Radio (NPR), October 15, 2012.

Alvarez, Lizette. "At Boys' Home, Seeking Graves, and the Reason." *New York Times*, February 9, 2013.

"Appendix to the House Journal." Florida Legislature, House, 1907.

Associated Press. "Bondi Seeks Court Order to Exhume Bodies at Dozier Boys School." WFSU Public Media, March 12, 2013.

Baltzell, N. A. "Appendix to the Biennial Report of the Board of Managers of the Florida State Reform School." Florida Legislature, House: House Journal, 1913.

"Belated Report of the Marianna Board of Managers." Florida Legislature, House: House Journal, 1907.

Belch, S. "Report of Superintendent to the Reform School Board of Commissioners." Florida Legislature, House: House Journal, 1909.

"Biennial Report of the Florida Department of Education for the Two Years Ending 30 June 1920." Tallahassee: Florida Department of Education, 1920.

"Biennial Report of the Florida State Reform School." Florida Legislature, House: House Journal, 1913.

"Biennial Report of the State Superintendent of Public Instruction." Vol 3. Tallahassee: Florida State Department of Education, 1865–1869.

"Biennial Report of the State Superintendent of Public Instruction." Tallahassee: Florida State Department of Education, 1900–1902.

Blackmon, Douglas A. *Slavery by Another Name: The Re-Enslavement of Black Americans from the Civil War to World War II.* New York: Anchor, 2009.

Boyle, Kevin. *Arc of Justice: A Saga of Race, Civil Rights, and Murder in the Jazz Age.* New York: Henry Holt and Company, 2004.

Brown, Canter, Jr. *Ossian Bingley Hart: Florida's Loyalist Reconstruction Governor.* Baton Rouge: Louisiana State University Press, 1997.

Buchli, Victor, and Gavin Lucas, eds. *Archaeologies of the Contemporary Past.* London: Routledge, 2001.

Buckhalter, Deborah. "Plan Set for Re-Burial of Dozier's Dead." *Dothan Eagle*, August 21, 2018.

Carper, Noel Gordon. "The Convict-Lease System in Florida, 1866–1923." PhD diss., Florida State University, 1964.

CNN. "School Graves Could Hide 'Evil' Past." CNN video, 5:38. October 12, 2012. https://www.cnn.com/videos/topvideos/2012/10/12/pkg -lavendera-marianna-boys-reform-school-graves.cnn.

Collins, Patricia Hill. *Black Feminist Thought: Knowledge, Consciousness, and the Politics of Empowerment.* New York: Routledge, 1991.

Cook, Angie. "Citizens Speak Out Against Dozier Coverage." *Dothan Eagle*, March 13, 2014.

"Concurrent Resolution No. 5." Florida Legislature, House: House Journal, 1907.

"Confidential Files at the Marianna and Okeechobee School for Boys." Form letter and letters gleaned from general correspondence.

Conyers, Lawrence B., and Dean Goodman. *Ground-Penetrating Radar: An Introduction for Archaeologists.* Lanham, MD: AltaMira Press, 1997.

Cordner, Sascha. "While Split Over Dozier Memorial, Task Force Agrees to Help Fire Victims' Descendant." WFSU Public Media, August 5, 2016.

Cox, Billy. "150 Years Later, Civil War Still A Raw Nerve." *Herald Tribune*, February 23, 2014.

Davidson, Millard. "Biennial Report of the Florida Industrial School for Boys." Florida Industrial School for Boys, Marianna, FL: Class in Printing, 1928–1930.

Davis, John W. "Legislature, Joint Legislative Committee Report of the Joint Legislative Committee Appointed to Visit the Florida Industrial School for Boys: Report on the Fire." Florida Legislature, House: House Journal, 1915.

Dozier, Arthur G. "Annual Financial and Statistical Report, 1964–1965." Division of Child Training Schools, Marianna, FL: Class in Printing, 1965.

Edwards, Cortland. Training Manual. Florida School for Boys, 1969.

"Eleventh Biennial Report of the Florida Commissioner of Agriculture." Florida Department of Agriculture, 1909–1910.

Fairfax, J. Correspondence with Leroy Clark, legal counsel for the Singleton case. Jacksonville, FL: Johnson and Marshall, legal files, July 19, 1966.

Farrington, Brendan. "Digging into Reform School's Past." Boston.com, December 10, 2008. http://archive.boston.com/news/nation/articles/2008/12/10/digging_into_reform_schools_past.

Fisher, Robin G., M. O'McCarthy, and R. Straley. *The Boys of the Dark: A Story of Betrayal and Redemption in the Deep South.* New York: St. Martin's Press, 2010.

Florida Department of Law Enforcement (FDLE). "FDLE Releases Response Regarding Dozier School." Florida Department of Law Enforcement News, December 19, 2012. https://www.fdle.state.fl.us/News/2012/December/FDLE-releases-response-regarding-Dozier-School.

Florida Department of Law Enforcement, Office of Executive Investigations. "Arthur G. Dozier School for Boys, Marianna, FL: Investigative Summary." Case No. EI-73-8455. May 14, 2009.

———. "Arthur G. Dozier School for Boys Abuse Investigation: Investigative Summary." Case No. EI-04-0005. January 29, 2010.

Florida Board of Commissioners of State Institutions. Minutes.

Book E: 27 November 1914; 5 January 1915; 18 December 1916; 18 October 1918; 4 November, 14 November, 16 November, and 28 November 1918; 16 January 1919; 6 February 1919.

Book F: 8 November 1919; 30 September 1920; 16 August and 22 October 1921.

Book G: 30 July 1923.

Book I: 24 September 1926.

Book J: 31 July 1928.

Book K: 15 January 1931.

Florida Industrial School for Boys, Marianna. The Light, Marianna, FL: Class in Printing, March 1, 1922.

Florida School for Boys. *Learning to Live at the Florida School for Boys at Marianna.* Marianna, FL: Division of Child Training Schools, 1958.

Florida Senate. Victims of Reform School Abuse. CS/SB 288. Introduced in January 26, 2021. https://www.flsenate.gov/Session/Bill/2021/288/BillText/Filed/HTML.

Florida State Archives. Florida School for Boys, administrative records, 1923–2010, 000630/.S 2247.

———. Florida School for Boys, newspaper clippings, 1956–1958, 000630/.S 2248.

———. Florida School for Boys, payroll ledgers, 1923–1961, 000630/.S 2246.

———. Florida School for Boys, photographs, ca. 1920s–2010, 000630/.S 2241.

———. Florida School for Boys, student ledgers, 1915–2011 (vol. 1–8, 18–22, 31), 000630/.S 2256.

Florida Statutes. 1957. 380-965. Laws of Florida. 1897 Chapter 4565; 1905 Chapter 5388; 1907 Chapter 5721; 1913 Chapter 6529; 1925 Chapter 10203; 1927 Chapter 11808; 1957 Chapter 57-317; 1963 Chapter 63-368; 1967 Chapter 67-295; 1968 Chapter 68-22; 1973 Chapter 39.

Foucault, Michel. *Power/Knowledge: Selected Interviews and Other Writings, 1972–1977*. Edited by Colin Gordon. New York: Pantheon, 1980.

"Governor Broward's Message to the Legislature." Florida House Journal, 1905.

"Governor Broward's Message to the Legislature." Florida House Journal Appendix, 1907.

"Governor Jennings' Message to the Legislature." Florida House Journal, 1901.

Harvell, J. H. "Special Committee Inspecting the School, Report." Florida Legislature, House: House Journal, 1923.

Jackson, Antoinette T. "Shattering Slave Life Portrayals: Uncovering Subjugated Knowledge in U.S. Plantation Sites in South Carolina and Florida." *American Anthropologist* 113, no. 3 (2011): 448–62.

"Joint Committee Report on Marianna Reform School." Joint Committee on Marianna: House Journal, 1905.

Keller, Oliver J., Jr. "First Annual Report to the Legislature." Tallahassee: Department of Health and Rehabilitation Services, Division of Youth Services, August 31, 1968.

———. "Second Annual Report to the Legislature." Tallahassee: Department of Health and Rehabilitation Services, Division of Youth Services, 1969.

Kent v. United States, 383 U.S. 541 (1966).

Kimmerle, Erin H. "Forensic Anthropology in Long-Term Investigations: 100 Cold Years." *Annals of Anthropological Practice* 38, no. 1 (2014): 7–21.

———. "Practicing Forensic Anthropology: A Human Rights Approach to the Global Problem of Missing and Unidentified Persons," *Annals of Anthropological Practice* 38, no. 1 (2014): 1–6.

———, and John Obafunwa. "Trauma Patterns in Cases of Extrajudicial Executions." *Annals of Anthropological Practice* 38, no. 1 (2014): 89–100.

———, E. Christian Wells, and L. Collins. "Phase II: Report on LIDAR and GIS Fieldwork for Continued Investigation into Possible Burials Identified by New South Associates, Inc. at the Former Arthur G. Dozier School for Boys, Marianna, Florida." Submitted to the Division of Historical Resources, Florida Department of State, 2019.

———, E. Christian Wells, and A. Jackson. "Summary Findings on the Deaths and Burials at the Former Arthur G. Dozier School for Boys, Marianna, Florida." University of South Florida, January 18, 2016.

———, et al. "Final Report on LIDAR and GIS Fieldwork for Continued Investigation into Possible Burials Identified by New South Associates, Inc. at the Former Arthur G. Dozier School for Boys, Marianna, Florida." Submitted to the Division of Historical Resources, Florida Department of State, 2020.

———, et al. "Interim Report for the Investigations in the Boot Hill Cemetery, Located at the Former Arthur G. Dozier School for Boys, Marianna, Florida." University of South Florida, December 10, 2012.

Kiser, Roger Dean. *The White House Boys: An American Tragedy.* Deerfield Beach, FL: Health Communications, Inc., 2009.

Knight, M. S. "Biennial Report of the Florida Industrial School for Boys." Florida Industrial School for Boys, Marianna, FL: Class in Printing, 1923–1925.

Knott, W. V. "State Comptroller's Message to the Legislature." Florida Legislature, Senate: House Journal, 1901.

Litwack, Leon F. *Trouble in Mind: Black Southerners in the Age of Jim Crow.* New York: Random House, 1998.

Lundrigan, Nathaniel George. "Development of the Florida Schools for Male Youthful Offenders, 1889–1969." PhD diss., Florida State University, 1975.

Mancini, Matthew J. *One Dies, Get Another: Convict Leasing in the American South, 1866–1928.* Columbia, SC: University of South Carolina Press, 1996.

"Message from House of Representatives." Florida Legislature: Extraordinary Session, House Journal, 1918.

"Message of Governor Sidney J. Catts on Conditions at the Marianna Industrial School." Florida Legislature: Extraordinary Session, House Journal, 1918.

Montgomery, Ben. "A Lingering Pain." *St. Petersburg Times,* September 13, 2009.

———. "Dig for Truth, or Bury Past." *Tampa Bay Times,* April 14, 2013.

———. "First Remains Unearthed at Dozier Site." *Tampa Bay Times,* September 3, 2013.

———. "Ground Truth: In Dozier's Neglected Cemetery, a Search for Lost Boys and the Reasons Why They Died." *Tampa Bay Times*, April 11, 2015.

———. "Raped as a Boy at Dozier, He Seeks Pardon for Crimes as a Man." *Tampa Bay Times*, May 25, 2016.

Montgomery, Ben, and W. Moore. "Answering for Nightmares." *St. Petersburg Times*, May 22, 2009.

———. "Brutal Reform School Closing." *St. Petersburg Times*, May 27, 2011.

———. "Details Buried with Dozier's Dead." *Tampa Bay Times*, December 20, 2009.

———. "For Their Own Good." *St. Petersburg Times*, April 19, 2009.

———. "Questions Linger as Inquiry Ends." *St. Petersburg Times*, May 16, 2009.

———. "Researchers Find More Graves at Dozier Than State Said Existed." *Tampa Bay Times*, December 12, 2014.

Orser, Charles E., Jr. "The Challenge of Race to American Historical Archaeology." *American Anthropologist* 100, no. 3 (1998): 661–668.

———. *Race and Practice in Archaeological Interpretation*. Philadelphia: University of Pennsylvania Press, 2004.

———. *The Archaeology of Race and Racialization in Historic America*. Gainesville: University Press of Florida, 2007.

Petition Denied. Exhumation of Unidentified Human Remains Buried at the Dozier School for Boys. (13-239 CA). Circuit Court of the Fourteenth Judicial Circuit in Jackson County, Florida. May 24, 2013. https://myfloridalegal.com/webfiles.nsf/WF/JMEE-97ZSCN/$file/Dozier May24.pdf.

Petition for the Exhumation of Unidentified Human Remains Buried at the Dozier School for Boys. (13-239 CA). Circuit Court of the Fourteenth Judicial Circuit in Jackson County, Florida. https://miamiherald.typepad .com/files/dozier-petition.pdf.

Phillips, Rich. "The Original Forensic Investigation at the Dozier School (2012–2016)." CNN, July 17, 2019.

———. "Florida to Exhume Bodies Buried at Former Boys School." CNN, September 2, 2013.

———. "New Investigation of Additional Graves at Florida's Dozier's School for Boys." CNN, July 17, 2017.

Powell, J. C. *The American Siberia*. Chicago: J. J. Smith and Co., 1891.

Pratt, O. F. "The Development of the Florida Prison System." Master's thesis, Florida State University, 1949.

Pulitzer Prizes. "Finalist: Carol Marbin Miller and Audra D. S. Burch of Miami Herald." The Pulitzer Prizes, 2018. https://www.pulitzer.org/finalists/carol-marbin-miller-and-audra-ds-burch-miami-herald.

Rawls, Walter. "First Biennial Report of the Florida State Reform School." Florida Documents Tallahassee: Tallahassee Book and Job Print, 1901.

———. "Superintendent Report of Florida State Reform School 1901." Florida Legislature, Senate: Senate Journal, 1901.

"Report of Committee of Physicians and Conditions at Industrial School for Boys." Florida Legislature: Extraordinary Session, Senate Journal, 1918.

"Report of First Special Investigating Committee of Marianna Reform School." Florida House Journal: Legislature House, 1903.

"Report of Joint Investigating Committee." Florida Legislature, House: House Journal, 1911.

"Report of Joint Legislative Committee Appointed to Visit the Florida Industrial School for Boys, 1915." Florida Legislature, House: House Journal, 1915 and 1919.

"Report of Special Investigative Committee on the Marianna School, 1913." Florida Legislature: Senate Journal, 1913.

"Report on Joint Investigative Committee Under House Concurrent Resolution No. 5, Relative to the State Reformatory at Marianna, Florida 1911." Florida Legislative, Joint Committee: Senate Journal, 1911.

"Report on Reform School." Florida Legislature, Joint Legislative Investigating Committee: Senate Journal, 1909.

Riley, Sid. In Defense of Dozier (blog). *Jackson County Times*, January 29, 2009. http://jctimesnews.blogspot.com/2009/01/in-defense-of-dozier-12909.html.

Rhyne, Janie Smith. *Our Yesterdays*. Marianna, FL: Floridian Press, 1968.

Robin, F. E. "Reform School: A Study in Institutional Sociology." PhD diss., Columbia University, 1950.

Sheats, W. N. "State Superintendent of Public Instruction Report." Tallahassee: State Department of Public Instruction, 1901.

Trammell, Park. "Message to Florida Legislature." Florida House Journal, 1913.

"Twelfth Biennial Report of the Florida Commissioner of Agriculture." Florida Department of Agriculture, 1911–1912.

United Press International. "Florida State Hospital Cemetery: Efficient, Anonymous." *St. Petersburg Times*, August 16, 1976.

U.S. Department of the Interior, National Park Service. "John Milton." National Park Service, updated June 17, 2015. https://www.nps.gov/people

/john-milton.htm#:~:text=He%20is%20best%20remembered%20for
,a%20gunshot%20to%20tht%20head.

U.S. v. William H. Bell. 1912. 5209 Rev. Statutes of U.S., "B" Criminal Final Records Book. Pensacola, FL: U.S. District Court, Northern District of Florida, 192–97.

Vananlandingham, W. L. "Biennial Report of the Florida Industrial School." Florida Industrial School for Boys, Marianna, FL: Class in Printing, 1925–1927.

Wallace, Jeremy. "Victims of Shuttered Dozier School Get Some Closure Before Florida Cabinet." *Tampa Bay Times*, January 21, 2016.

Wasserman, Adam. *A People's History of Florida 1513–1876: How Africans, Seminoles, Women, and Lower Class Whites Shaped the Sunshine State*. Adam Wasserman, 2009.

Wilkerson, Isabel. *The Warmth of Other Suns: The Epic Story of America's Great Migration*. New York: Random House, 2010.

Wilkie, Laurie. *Creating Freedom: Material Culture and African American Identity at Oakley Plantation, Louisiana, 1840–1950*. Baton Rouge: Louisiana State University Press, 2000.

———. "Black Sharecroppers and White Frat Boys: Living Communities and the Appropriation of Their Archaeological Pasts." In *Archaeologies of the Contemporary Past*, edited by Victor Buchili and Gavin Lucas, 108–18. London: Routledge, 2001.

Williamson, Joel. *The Crucible of Race: Black-White Relations in the American South since Emancipation*. New York: Oxford University Press, 1984.

Willie Carl Singleton, a Minor by Neva Singleton, His Mother and Next Friend, et al., Appellants, v. Board of Commissioners of State Institutions, et al. Appellees, 356 F.2d 771 (5th Cir. 1966).

Wiseman, Brent. Personal communication, cola bottle dating, 2012.

Woodward, C. Vann. *Origins of the New South, 1877–1913*. Baton Rouge: Louisiana State University Press, 1951.

Wu, Tim. "Fifty-Five Bodies, and Zero Trials, at the Florida School for Boys." *The New Yorker*, January 30, 2014.

Youngblood, Joshua. "'Haven't Quite Shaken the Horror': Howard Kester, the Lynching of Claude Neal, and Social Activism in the South During the 1930s." *The Florida Historical Quarterly* 86, no. 1 (2007): 3–38. http://www.jstor.org/stable/30150098.

Zarrella, John, and S. Candiotti. "Autopsy: Boot Camp Guards Killed Teen." CNN, published May 5, 2006. http://www.cnn.com/2006/US/05/05/bootcamp.death/index.html#:~:text=%22Martin%20Anderson's%20death%20was%20caused,blockage%20of%20the%20upper%20airway.%22.

ERIN KIMMERLE, PhD, is a forensic anthropologist, author, and artist in Tampa, where she lives with her two sons. She is the director of the Florida Institute for Forensic Anthropology and Applied Science and an associate professor in the Department of Anthropology at the University of South Florida. Erin's research in forensic anthropology is on long-term missing and unidentified persons, cold-case investigations, forensic art, and skeletal trauma. She led the investigation into deaths and burials at the former Arthur G. Dozier School for Boys in Marianna, Florida, for which she received the AAAS Scientific Freedom and Responsibility Award in 2020 and the Hillsborough County Bar Association's Liberty Bell Award in 2017.